University of Texas Press,

THE INVENTION
OF THE
JEWISH GAUCHO

Villa Clara and the Construction of Argentine Identity

JUDITH NOEMÍ FREIDENBERG

FOREWORD BY JUNE NASH

The Jewish History, Life, and Culture Series is supported
by Milton T. Smith and the Moshana Foundation, and the
Tocker Foundation.

Copyright © 2009 by the University of Texas Press
All rights reserved
Printed in the United States of America
First edition, 2009

Requests for permission to reproduce material from this work should be sent to:
Permissions
University of Texas Press
P.O. Box 7819
Austin, TX 78713-7819
www.utexas.edu/utpress/about/bpermission.html

♾ The paper used in this book meets the minimum requirements of
ANSI/NISO Z39.48-1992 (R1997) (Permanence of Paper).

LIBRARY OF CONGRESS CATALOGING-IN-PUBLICATION DATA
Freidenberg, Judith.
The invention of the Jewish gaucho : Villa Clara and the construction of Argentine identity /
Judith Noemí Freidenberg ; foreword by June Nash.
p.   cm. — (Jewish history, life, and culture)
Includes bibliographical references and index.
ISBN 978-0-292-72569-0
1. Jews—Argentina—Clara—History.
2. Gauchos—Argentina—Clara—History.   3. Oral history—Argentina—Clara.
4. Jews—Argentina—Clara—Ethnic identity.   5. National characteristics, Argentine—History.
6. Europe, Eastern—Emigration and immigration—History.
7. Argentina—Emigration and immigration—History.
8. Entre Ríos (Argentina)—Emigration and immigration—History.
9. Clara (Argentina)—Ethnic relations.   10. Clara (Argentina)—Social conditions.   I. Title.
F3011.C57F739 2009
307.76'208992408221—dc22
2009004627

To the memory of Sebastian, who left us on June 20, 2002

*To Gabriela and Julian, who lovingly encouraged me
to complete the project and live on*

To the people of Villa Clara

CONTENTS

Foreword by June Nash ix

Preface: The Story behind the Story xiii

Acknowledgments xix

CHAPTER 1
Social Memory as Part of Villa Clara's History
1

CHAPTER 2
Entre Ríos, Mi País: Immigrants Becoming Argentine in a Province
13

CHAPTER 3
Colonia Clara and the Emergence of the "Jewish Gauchos" (1892–1902)
41

CHAPTER 4
From Jewish Gauchos to Gaucho Jews: Regional Economic Development
and Intercultural Relations at the End of the Nineteenth Century
65

CHAPTER 5
The Rise and Demise of Jewish Villa Clara (1902–1930s)
81

CHAPTER 6
Rural Depopulation and the Emergence of a Multiethnic and
Socially Stratified Landscape in Villa Clara (1940s–1990s)
103

CHAPTER 7
The Present as Politicized Past: Legitimizing Social Structure
through Heritage (1990s–2000s)
123

Epilogue: The Jewish Gaucho Revisited 143

Appendix I: Methodological Notes 151

Appendix II: Chronology of Relevant Events in Villa Clara 159

Notes 161

Glossary of Terms 171

Bibliography 173

Index 179

FOREWORD

In the last quarter of the nineteenth century, Latin American countries began to open their borders to European immigrants. The national goals were often expressed in racist terms of "civilizing the nation," with the covert—and sometimes overt—aim of settling the immigrants in national territories still occupied by indigenous people. Argentina was late in extending the institutional organization of the pampas, which were occupied by indigenous people and Creoles until the mid-nineteenth century. As immigrants began to settle in the expansive pampas to the north of Buenos Aires, a new vibrant culture emerged as they interacted with the poor Creoles and indigenous peoples.

Judith Freidenberg introduces us to this heritage with a description of a tour she and her mother took to Villa Clara in the province of Entre Ríos, where her parents grew up in the early decades of the twentieth century. In a journey through time and space, Freidenberg seeks an understanding of how immigrants—Jewish, French, Spanish, Belgian, German, Russian, and Swiss—made an impact on the formation of the Argentine nation as they learned to live together. The Jews were the most cohesive immigrant group seeking a new life in the country, primarily because they had fled the pogroms of the old country. Because they depended on the Jewish Colonization Association, which controlled the land where they lived and worked, they were tied to the community by bureaucratic as well as communal relations. Yet, their survival depended on their remarkable adaptation to a lifestyle developed by the gauchos, often poor Creoles, who preceded them in taming a harsh environment.

Throughout our tour into this often romanticized past, the author admonishes us to listen to the many distinct voices of people who claim this history as theirs. Using archival material, some formalized in written deeds and published local histories, along with specific memories of descendants, the author encourages us to develop our own understanding of how immigrants from many distinct backgrounds constructed new lives and new economies in an utterly foreign environment. The Jews adapted elements of the gauchos' nomadic horse-riding society to create their own settled crop cultivation, administrative, and commercial systems. Construction of a railroad promoted urban growth of the village, with the "iron horse"—a term used by North American Indians for trains—bringing in new settlers and taking out crops to be sold in regional, national, and global markets.

This process of adaptation to an often unfriendly natural environment is illuminated by a rich array of sources—oral narratives of the settlers, cultural material in the local museum, and archival sources unearthed in the course of research—that Freidenberg uses to tell a story of the unfolding constructions of a multilayered cultural heritage. What is gained, and what is invented in this unfolding production, reveals the transformation of people who invented a nation as they learned to live together. Villa Clara has now transformed from a producer of goods and services to a producer of heritage. Freidenberg meticulously examines this process as she explores and observes the panoramic displays of a changing society in the periodic commemorations of the settlement's founding. As the social memory of the immigrants is constructed, individual memories combine with, and sometimes contradict, collective memories to create a vibrant whole.

The formation of a multicultural country out of the binary opposition of indigenous people and Spanish conquerors was not peaceful. The resolution of this conflict occurred in the pampas, with the symbolic figure of the gaucho as often admired—particularly by the children of the settlers—as reviled by the Spaniards in their early ventures into the pampas. Gaucho society was a male culture in both imagery and action; the Jewish gaucho was formed in this matrix, which has inspired many colorful histories noted in Freidenberg's text. Women were bearers but not recorded actors of the Creole and immigrant cultures that met, reproduced, and ensured survival in the formative years of the nation.

Jews, as Freidenberg tells us, draw their strength from relatives. This includes not only genetically related kin, but also people who are ritually accepted as relatives by the group who carries out the commandments. The religious quorum required to carry out the laws is composed of at least ten men, and though descent is through women, these male leaders define the religious entity that constitutes community. I would not have realized the force of this core element if I had not heard of my deceased husband's grandfather, who immigrated to Argentina but was in a settlement that failed to gain a quorum of ten men. He returned to Roumania only to be killed in a pogrom. The son he left behind in Roumania succeeded in immigrating to the United States, however, where he was granted citizenship after enlisting in the U.S. Army, and the son he fathered lived to tell the tale. Yet, despite the exclusivity of those who fulfill the commandments, the gaucho culture provided a context in which the children of these immigrants could engage with the new environment and preexisting social groups. Thus, while family solidarity helped all immigrants retain their culture in the melting pot, the survival of the Jewish culture was probably reinforced by the religious definition of community.

Sorting out the trilingual correspondence with relatives in Europe, Freidenberg illustrates how the settlements that first arrived in 1892 progressed. The monthly reports required by the Jewish Colonization Association aided her efforts, even as they disclosed the rebellion of young settlers against that organization. The largess of the German Jewish benefactor Baron Maurice de Hirsch did not come without strings: the lands were sold to the settlers and paid fully and on time with interest rates. The administrators of Argentine headquarters in Buenos Aires were German and Sephardic Jews who had little understanding of the multitude of plagues and droughts that afflicted the newcomers as they desperately tried to pay the loans. Inequalities increased as some prospered and others were forced to sell their lands and work as laborers. Communities rose and fell as the railroad arrived then left behind the stations and commerce generated by their presence, mirroring the kind of boom and bust captured by Bertolt Brecht in *Rise and Decline of the City of Mahogany*. The meticulous scholarship that Freidenberg brings to her task in recording the settlements' failures, however, does not diminish the reader's sense of their enormous success. The socialist origins of some migrants, along with the religious commitment of community, led to the rapid development of schools, libraries, hospitals, and cultural centers. The producer and distributive cooperatives they established often sidestepped the control of administrative centers of the Jewish Colonization Association.

Freidenberg also discusses the inequities in the national laws of land entitlement, which did not consider the rights of gauchos. A multifaceted model of the Jewish gaucho emerges to overshadow the stereotypes of folk hero like Martín Fierro, opposer of landlords; of patriot fighting in Argentina; and of model of assimilation.

The current interest in multicultural globalization will be enhanced by this study, which combines the cultural forces generated in the encounter in the pampas with the global political economy of change. We learn of the global forces that went into the formation of settlements and the ephemeral commercial impetus provoked by the railroads and their withdrawal. The transformation of the countryside with highly capitalized technology in the second half of the twentieth century led to further inequalities among those who stayed and those who migrated to urban centers. Changes stimulated by such foreign investment as the British Railroads and Perón's nationalization of enterprises, as well as the current return to privatization, are closely related to these cultural trends.

Periodic commemorations mark the cultural transformations that occurred during this panoramic change. The 1910 Centennial included the inauguration of the Jewish burial ground, at which guests were served with an *asado con cuero* (grilled beef with the hide), and the elders ate it, hair and all. The 1994 commemoration inaugurated a museum that focused attention on the immigrants, leaving out most of the material on gauchos, indigenous people, and poor Creoles. Collective memory then caught up with the planners of the centennial by the turn of the millennium, when the Municipality of Villa Clara, part of the Circuito Histórico de las Colonias Judías, organized an eight-day celebration with photo exhibits; horseback riding; gauchos; and food, drink, and crafts of all the immigrant groups. This restructuring of the legacy reflected multicultural heritage by showing each group's contribution to the nation.

Judith Freidenberg has proven her case that the transmission of identity is promoted by collective, as well as kinship or genetic, inheritance in this historically concerned ethnographic account connecting global, regional, and local memory. It will serve us and future generations with a memorial of what was accomplished and what was denied as we revisit the past in order to understand our future.

JUNE NASH
Distinguished Professor Emerita
City University of New York, Graduate Center and City College

Preface: The Story behind the Story

My Villa Clara experience started in 2001, when my mother and I embarked on a tour, the Circuito Histórico de las Colonias Judías del Centro de Entre Ríos,[1] a recent addition to Argentine cultural tourism. The tour would take us to northeastern Argentina, a six-hour journey by bus from the capital city of Buenos Aires, where my mother resided and I was born. We would be displacing ourselves geographically, of course; but even more important, we would also travel back in time, toward our shared past: the immigration of my mother's and my father's parents from Eastern Europe to the province of Entre Ríos. My grandparents had settled in the region at the end of the nineteenth century, making my parents the first generation born in rural Argentina and part of the memorialized "Jewish gauchos" of the *colonias* (rural settlements of immigrants). We had been warned that the tour might take longer than anticipated, and it did: there were sites that we could not reach due to heavy rainfall just before our arrival and others that we could only get to after taking long detours.

Although I was prepared for those traveling contingencies, I only now realize that I was totally unprepared for the emotional impact of the tour on my mother. Though we were both conscious of the passage of time, my mother remained incredulous that so little remained there of so much that she remembered. As we neared her grandparents' house in San Gregorio, my mother became very talkative, reminiscing about the chestnuts surrounding the property that, she assured us, would help us identify it easily. As we drew near, we saw no chestnuts or other distinguishing signals that would lead us to believe that anybody had ever lived there. The same scene repeated itself as we drove past the home of her parents-in-law. A neighbor who had stayed in the area pointed to a huge tree under which my paternal grandparents' house, he thought, had probably stood. Only memories remained of the experience of the Jewish Colonization Association, the organization that had helped these immigrants flee the Europe of their birth: there seemed to be few material traces of the homes they had first inhabited. Here is what my mother wrote about our trip:

> I enjoyed visiting the places in San Gregorio where my father, my uncles, and my grandparents lived. My heart jumped often. I did not wish to say anything, but I saw all of them. I saw the beds with several mattresses piled up and the small ladder they made for us to get up there, since we were small. Grandfather with his beard that made us itch, grandmother with her clean handkerchief and her gray dress. Always so loving. They were *zeide* and *bobe*,[2] not Salomón and Ana. I remember them well. I saw them. To get to their home we had to go through about 100 meters, I figure, covered by trees—nut

The family of Sara Furrer.

trees, almond trees, olive trees, plum trees, peach trees. We were very happy spending our summers there. My uncle, their oldest son, lived very close. He was an excellent musician, he played violin, viola, mandolin, and he taught his children . . . My uncle Nissim lived in another *colonia*, Las Moscas . . . Do you notice my poor handwriting? It's because I am touched by remembering all of them. And other things, like the breakfast, and the afternoon tea with traditional Russian pastries. The *peones* [rural employees] told my grandfather: *Zeide, mir un gusien arbetein*? [Shall we go to work, grandfather?]. My father left and moved to the city, Concordia, because he wanted to *adelantar* [go forward, progress] as they would say then . . .

When we arrived in Villa Clara we heard more stories about the displacement of the Jewish gauchos from the area, but we also heard about the histories of immigration of other Europeans and regional migrations of *criollos* (children of European parents born in Argentina). Such cultural variety in the human tapestry of such a small locality made me eager to return and undertake fieldwork to unearth its rich past while sharing daily life. When my mother and I returned early the next year as Villa Clara was organizing for the celebration of its centennial, I rented space from the Alvarez family, descendants of Swiss and Spanish immigrants, and moved in during a sabbatical semester in 2002. Their kindness made me feel at home sooner than expected, and sharing the excitement of fieldwork with students kept me grounded. Later I would become so involved in the reopening of the village museum that I decided to write a book about the material, oral, and written heritage of Villa Clara through public consultation and to donate its proceeds to contribute to the museum's activities.

Memorias de Villa Clara, written in Spanish for general audiences and published in 2005, did not quell the curiosity of some Clarenses (residents of Villa Clara). Some (particularly older descendants of the initial Jewish founders, a kind of intelligentsia that kept the initial history of the village alive) kept asking about "the other book," the one I had told them about when I first made the village my temporary home. I had spoken about my interest in understanding the village as a case study of the impact of nineteenth-century European immigrations on the construction of Argentine national identity and about my plan to weave together written sources and oral memories through dialogic discourse. The present book returns to my original intention: immersing myself in the daily life of the locality to account for the historical development of the village within the larger contexts of region and nation. A case study, based on a small sample, illuminates both the history and social organization of the larger society; and, conversely, the local events are better understood within the context of larger units of analysis (region, nation, transatlantic countries of origin).

History becomes enlivened through the ethnographic present. While an official national history disseminates a written version of the immigrant past—unless or until contested—through schools, museums, historical societies, tourist plans, and commemorative events, another history is latent and spreads in the course of daily interaction in localities. The national ideology favoring European immigration to Argentina might be unknown or forgotten at the local level, but the arrival of the first immigrants in the province or their influence on the social history of the village might be vividly remembered. Because this latent history based on memory and disseminated orally is rarely written or accounted for in private documents, it is less likely to survive. The interface between the written and the oral repositories of memories and the implications of remembering and forgetting for understanding the influence of the nineteenth-century European immigrants' saga on the construction of Argentine national identity provides the context for writing the social history of Villa Clara.

The term *criollo* is extremely complex and has a multiplicity of meanings. In

Argentina, the term has three different meanings that change according to social context and historical period. The original meaning dates from the conquest of America, when the children of Spanish conquistadors born in the Virreinato del Río de la Plata, where the future Argentina would emerge, were called *criollos*. This use was prevalent during the colonial period, although there was a marked difference among the social statuses accorded individuals depending on whether both parents were born in Spain, born in America, or preceded the Spaniards (Amerindians). Eventually, this meaning was extended to anybody born in Argentina, as opposed to Europe, and social status was accorded by social class rather than by country of birth. The term gradually took a connotation of "rural dweller" and, although new terms did not appear to distinguish *criollos* by degree of ethnic mix, or *mestizaje* with indigenous populations or dislocated Africans, the term implied low socioeconomic status. When massive waves of European immigrants arrived in the Río de la Plata countries of Argentina and Uruguay at the end of the nineteenth century and early twentieth century and a sense of national identity became more pronounced, the term evolved to mean anybody who was native to the country and could claim citizenship.

Currently, *criollo* is the generalized term employed to mean anybody who is "from the country" in the Rioplatense region, often in marked contrast to "foreigner." There is an unstated understanding, however, that the social gradient that separates a wealthy from a poor *criollo* will be respected and acknowledged.

Chapter 1 traces the ideology of the new Argentine nation and its policies favoring the entry of European immigrants. As a metaphor for Argentine history, Villa Clara provides a way of reading the past as a succession of liberal and nationalist ideological periods.

Chapter 2 illustrates the implementation of immigrant policy at the provincial level. It traces the immigration of Europeans to Argentina and their settlement in Entre Ríos from 1850 (when the first cohort of Western Europeans arrived) to 1892 (when the last sizable influx, this time of Eastern Europeans, took place).

Chapter 3 focuses on the village's immediate surroundings. It narrates the saga of the Eastern Europeans' arrival and their daily life in an agricultural settlement closest to contemporary Villa Clara: Colonia Clara, founded in 1892 by the Jewish Colonization Association.

Chapter 4 begins with the opening of the railroad station in 1902 and the official founding of Villa Clara that attracted many of the new Jewish gauchos of the area. The people I talked to painted daily life vividly, alluding to sacrifices as they transported hard-won harvests to the railroad station through mud streets and as they organized themselves institutionally.

The nationalization of the British-owned railroad in 1947 spurred a halt in the economic advancement of the village, by then a regional development center, that triggered important demographic changes through regional population displacements and increasing urbanization. Chapter 5 traces the impact of such changes, as immigrants' descendants transformed into ethnic groups. The themes in the interviews depicted daily life centering at this time around internal rather than transatlantic migrations, as the rural areas became economically unsustainable. Low-income housing projects were built to accommodate the incoming *criollos*, many previously hired by immigrant farmers. As many Jewish gauchos living in the village or its hinterland moved to large cities (primarily Buenos Aires), many descendants of other immigrant cohorts (mainly from Western Europe) moved out of the rural areas and arrived in Villa Clara. For the first time in its history, Villa Clara experienced unemployment and poverty.

Chapter 6 begins with the closing of railroad passenger services in 1994. It epitomizes what people perceived as the end of an era when, as they put it, "there was work for everyone." Villa Clara became transformed from a producer of goods and services to a producer of heritage: the history of the immigrant cohorts residing in the village became reduced to their ancestors' arrival and settlement sagas, re-created in public performances that reified myths of origin. Furthermore, as ethnic diversity increased with the arrival of new populations, the voices claiming to tell the history of the village increased and clamored for attention in the space of a museum, a centennial celebration, and a project in cultural tourism. And yet the "official" version of the village's history—the one chosen for public presentation to the outside world and thus passed on through the educational system and disseminated by the writers of history—is often at odds with the versions told by people whose identities are framed by citizenship, ethnicity, and social class.

This case study advocates using the ethnographic method to elicit plural versions of local history and thus contributes to the understanding of a more inclusive and diverse social history. This approach, which can be replicated in a variety of situations, is particularly persuasive when the voice of immigrants is deemed relevant to tell national history. Immigration speaks to global connections: we should resist the provincialism of narrowing immigrant life to a particular place at a particular time. Villa Clara's case study may be used to open up research that connects immigration, memory, history, ethnography, heritage, and culture and to understand the political economy of memory and forgetfulness.

Acknowledgments

My greatest debt is to all those who shared their histories and opinions with me and to the village of Villa Clara for hosting and honoring me. I particularly thank Mario Alvarez, Juan Pablo Baldoni, the Comisión de Amigos del Museo Histórico Regional de Villa Clara (Berta Constantin de Alvarez, Lito Araceli Constantin, Zulema Danses de Fink, Bibiano Lyardet, María de las Mercedes P. De Kler, Lidia A. de Mendelevich), Marta Muchinik, the Municipalidad de Villa Clara (former mayor Julio César Den Dauw and mayor Raúl Darío Guy), Abraham Schejter, and Ida Isuz de Schulman, among many others. My ninety-six-year-old mother, Sara Furrer de Freidenberg, shared trips and memories and embodies the past I am trying to recuperate and share in this book.

I also express my gratitude to the colleagues who have taken the time to read drafts or provide insights on this manuscript: Alicia Bernasconi (Centro de Estudios Migratorios Latinoamericanos, Argentina [CEMLA]), Nancy Bonvillain (Bard College at Simon's Rock), Jim Burr (University of Texas Press), David Cantor (Office of NIH History, National Institutes of Health), Ruth Fredman Cernea (independent scholar), Erve Chambers (University of Maryland), Sandra Deutsch (University of Texas at El Paso), Ana María Dupey (Instituto Nacional de Antropología, Argentina [INA]), Ricardo Feierstein (Asociación Mutual Israelita Argentina [AMIA]), Rosana Guber (Instituto de Desarrollo Económico y Social, Argentina [IDES]), Osvaldo Quiroga (Museo de las Colonias Judías del Centro de Entre Ríos, Argentina), Marsha Rozenblit (University of Maryland), Stephen Sadow (Northeastern University), Catalina Saugy (Instituto Nacional de Antropología, Argentina), Leonardo Senkman (Hebrew University, Israel), Paul Shackel (University of Maryland), Saúl Sosnowski (University of Maryland), Mónica Szurmuk (Instituto Mora, Mexico), Bradley Tatar (Korea Advanced Institute for Science and Technology, South Korea), Naúm Wainer (independent scholar, Argentina), Ana Wainstein (Asociación Mutual Israelita Argentina), and Linda Winston (independent scholar). Roberta Cosentino (University of Maryland) and Laura Kostlin and Christine Danklmaier (Universidad de Misiones, Argentina) collaborated with fieldwork and María Eugenia Mendizábal (Instituto de Desarrollo Económico y Social, Argentina) with analysis. Katie Tracey and María Walsh (University of Maryland) graciously volunteered to translate quotations from Spanish into English. María Walsh painstakingly proofread the manuscript, and William Fennie (University of Maryland), Verónica del Valle (Universidad de Buenos Aires), and Horacio Suárez (Editorial Antropofagia) helped make the text more presentable.

I acknowledge the University of Maryland for its support of the research that led to this book. Thanks, specifically, to the Department of Jewish Studies, for awarding me a Travel Award (2001), an Equipment Award (2002), and a Samuel Iwry Fellowship (2003); to the Department of Anthropology, for granting me a sabbatical semester in the fall of 2002; and to International Programs, for dispensing Travel Grants to conduct research in the fieldwork area in 2002 and 2004. Sadly, this book was published after the passing of Ruth Fredman Cernea (March 31, 2009), a literary midwife and loving friend who will be sorely missed.

The Invention of the Jewish Sancho

Chapter One

SOCIAL MEMORY AS PART
OF VILLA CLARA'S HISTORY

Several thousand Eastern European Jews immigrated to Argentina at the close of the nineteenth century, and Jews had become one of the country's sizable minorities by the mid-twentieth century. The largest early influx of Jews arrived in the northeastern province of Entre Ríos and settled in an agricultural colony, Colonia Clara. By 1902, as the railroad meandered around the *colonia*'s outskirts, some farmers moved closer to the station. They gave birth to a more urban settlement, Villa Clara, and played a central role in its initial growth and prosperity.

By the mid-1930s over a thousand villagers could reminisce about the transatlantic trip and boast of their transformation into Jewish gauchos, a hybrid symbol of acculturation of the new immigrant to the world of the native gaucho, the landless native then despised by the elites. The 1940s, however, saw the abandonment of the Jewish families' assigned plots of land in the colony and their homes in the village. By 2002 my household survey of generational memory revealed that only a few households, mostly composed of single elders, traced their ancestry to the Jewish colonization program of the late nineteenth century. While some of Villa Clara's current residents descended from Western European immigrant waves

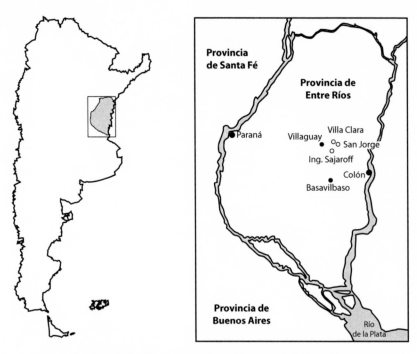

Argentina   Entre Ríos

Provincia
de Santa Fé

Provincia de
Entre Ríos

Villa Clara
Paraná   Villaguay   San Jorge
                              Ing. Sajaroff
                                   Colón
                         Basavilbaso

Provincia de
Buenos Aires   Río
                              de la Plata

Location of Villa Clara in Argentina and in Provincia de Entre Ríos.

(particularly from France, Belgium, Switzerland, Italy, Great Britain, Germany, and Spain), the majority considered themselves Creoles (*criollos*): that is, native born. How do the contemporary residents of Villa Clara remember the history of the village? What are the main themes chosen to represent the immigrant saga? Who is remembered, and who is forgotten? And why?

Answering these questions called for a reconstruction of the village's history through ethnographic fieldwork that combined the memories of its present inhabitants with historical research. My primary aim was to understand the connections between the village's past—the successive arrival of Eastern European and Western European immigrants and the contested timing of the first arrival of poor *criollos*—and its present, which memorialized a multiethnic past that was reasserted in the present social structure. While interweaving oral, material, and written versions of the past, I realized that they at times illustrated, at times contested, and at times confirmed one another. As the emerging social history of the locality acquired depth and color, the meaning of similarities and differences among alternative versions of the past became apparent, even when domains of divergence might have seemed minimal at first. What was remembered or forgotten in one but not another version of the past? Which personal memories were kept private, and which were selected to be disseminated to the public and thus entered the domain of officially accepted versions of the past? Which media were chosen to pass on the history of the past to villagers and the general public alike? And what is the political history of remembering and forgetting? Who remembers what, when, and why?

The transformation of social history (or the history of a people as told through written, oral, and material sources) into social memory occurs selectively over time and becomes manifested at the local level, where distributions of power are legitimized or contested through the discourse of ethnic, social-class, and national identities. Understanding the process of social and political construction at the local level enhances the understanding of both the past and the present, because social memory is related to individual memory and is grounded in concrete spaces.[1] Jacob Climo and Maria Cattell (2002: 4) explain:

> Collective or social memories are shaped by social, economic, and political circumstances; by beliefs and values; by opposition and resistance. They involve cultural norms and issues of authenticity, identity, and power. They are implicated in ideologies. Social memories are associated with or belong to particular categories or groups so they can be, and often are, the focus of conflict and contestation.

Several issues need to be considered when reflecting on whether, and to what extent, memory adds to understanding how and why history is created. One issue relates to whether memory is based on actual experience of historical fact, on narratives produced by others, or on written or material records. A second issue is the need to reexamine the emphasis of the literature on the social construction of memory, since memory cannot be said to be solely a social construction; memory is also a subjective selection made by an individual who chooses, consciously or unconsciously, to highlight or reject the recalled past. A third issue that affects memory is the degree of literacy of the informant; those with access to written records will have conflated personal with scholarly constructions of the past. This combination of elements in the actual conformation of a memory bank influences the resulting report that the researcher obtains and brings a fourth issue to the fore: the "purity" or the "truth" of the informants' representation of past reality. In fact, most informants tend to share idealized renditions of the past with the researcher or partial histories of what really happened. The reasons vary, including believing that the past was better than the present, holding an interest in preserving what is believed to have a measure of worth for the next generations, or marketing a proud past as heritage to the outside world. Truth is a controversial issue that touches on the ethics of research as well: as the researcher I also provide a construction of the past as I combine the informants' reports and the historians' records to construct my own interpretation.

I was conscious that I was tapping informant memory rather than the direct knowledge based on actual experiences. Memory based on what one is told by others can be imperfect if recollected inaccurately or distorted through the passage of time, the medium of transmission (household, school, church, etc.), the personal characteristics of the transmitter (age, sex, social standing, etc.), or opportunistic, motivated recollection. Memory, as recollected information, is thus related to the question of truth. I started by tapping a common recollection: the place of birth of four generations related to the informant, two ascending and one descending. An ethnographic map, drawn with data obtained through a generational survey, overlaid social class and ethnicity on geographical space. How does social memory of the past validate current social hierarchy? When I prompted residents to reminisce about the village's past as it illustrated their own life-course, I learned about political history, predicated on class and ethnic hierarchies, but also about cultural space: they were preoccupied by "what I believe I (or people like me) think about people like them."

The social history and public memorializing of an immigrant village, while important in and of itself, may also contribute to understanding the role played by immigration in the construction of the Argentine nation. At that juncture, the local village can also become a metaphor to understand the global displacement of thousands of Europeans and their relocation in Argentina and the role played by European immigration in the governing elites' imagined nation. The social construction of selfhood and otherness, however, can only be discerned at the local level, at a particular point in time, as diverse versions of history are politicized to legitimate the present individual or collective social position. In the village as an "imagined community" (Anderson 1991), some of the past is remembered and some forgotten by different social groups in the course of daily life, though that heterogeneity might be silenced to provide the generalized public with a unified version of the past.

"Official" History versus History "of the People" and the Construction of National Identity

The story I tell here combines history (written, archival, material) and the social memory of current residents of Villa Clara. Though they are intimately related, there are major differences between the two: written history, in particular, provides a chronological ordering of all sources compiled by a scholar, while conversation with contemporary people elicits just the remembered past, drawing on either personal or narrated experience. The inherent selectivity of life history research often results in a significantly more diverse and conflictive rendition of the past than the historian's. By focusing on everyday life—work, family, and other domains of private life—the personal stories situate the personal within the conflictive larger social context, whereas the written and material history legitimizes consensus on a unified view and often romanticizes the past. But there are also similarities between written and life histories: both are selective and confer authority on their sources. Thus, whether we are referring to a scholarly author or an anthropological informant, the storyteller's voice masquerades as a collective voice, making a case for the future preservation of a presumably truer cultural portrayal of the past.

Understanding Villa Clara as a Metaphor for Argentine History

Villa Clara is both locality and metaphor. A municipality of the Department of Villaguay in the province of Entre Ríos in northeastern Argentina, it was home to 2,748 inhabitants in 2001 (*Censo de Entre Ríos* 2001).[2] The economy of the village, set in a traditionally agricultural and cattle-raising and, more recently, rice-producing region, has been negatively affected by economic recessions and the 1994 closing of the General Urquiza Railway system that connected it to Buenos Aires. Now, as in the past, national and international events mold life in this small village. Its railroad station, currently unused for transportation, now houses the local museum, the Museo Histórico Regional de Villa Clara. Conscious of its role in epitomizing the nation's history, Villa Clara still zealously preserves the past through exhibits, anniversary celebrations, and cultural tourism programs. What is the relevance of this history to understanding the nation's role in the world system of capital expansion?

During its nation-building process in the nineteenth century, Argentina was one of a few countries in the Americas that favored the entry of large numbers of European immigrants. The province of Entre Ríos was noteworthy in its promotion and implementation of the nation's liberal project. The social history of Villa Clara is told here to enliven the official history of European immigration to Argentina, including that of the Jewish founders of Villa Clara, interweaving records of the past with memories elicited from current residents of the village.

There are several important omissions in the officially accepted written history of Jewish immigration to the province of Entre Ríos. First, this history overemphasizes the repressive regimes in the homelands of the immigrants, to the detriment of the numerous constraints encountered in the new land. Depicted in a written history and literature more copious than for the other immigrant waves to the province, the story of Jewish immigrants focuses on their success. The Jewish gauchos became a metaphor for the successful acculturation of newcomers to the world of native inhabitants of the new land, and the frequent failures that led to a short-lived, nonsustainable agricultural project were obscured or minimized.

Second, the official history of the Jewish immigration is isolationist. In general, the Jewish farmers were not portrayed as part of a province where other European immigrants had settled in agricultural colonies or in relation to the ideology of the new nation that equated the arrival of European immigrants with progress. Overall, non-Jewish populations are relatively absent from the officially accepted history, unless they are members of Jewish networks such as the indigenous *criollos* and the over-idealized gauchos. Within the context of daily interaction, especially during the initial settlement, the gauchos are lauded as disinterested teachers or as hired hands; mostly they are depicted as friends, though, exceptionally, they could become murderous intruders. In illustrating this official history, the Museo Histórico Regional de Villa Clara uses artifacts, rather than oral histories, to glorify Jewish life during the first few decades of village history. A small niche, the Rincón Gauchesco (Gaucho Corner), and dispersed artifacts on Western European immigrants account for non-Jewish life in the village, as if their histories were separate from that of the Jews.

Although emphasizing the Jewish immigration is necessary to depict the initial history of the village, Villa Clara's history is incompletely understood without first understanding the history of Entre Ríos, where many European immigrants settled in agricultural colonies well before the founding of the village. The history of the province, in turn, is inseparable from the history of the Argentine nation, including the global connections spurred by the transatlantic immigrations. However wide the lens for the story told here becomes, the focus is on Villa Clara within a larger context.

The Political Economy of Immigration Policy: From Cosmopolitanism to Nationalism in Reading the Nation's Past

This case study is framed by the changing political economy of Argentina and its intersections with ideological pronouncements about the foreign "other," which in turn offered political commentaries on the native populations. To clarify those intersections, I identify three stages relevant to the arrival of the immigration cohorts to Entre Ríos: the organization of the independent state, the imagined global nation, and the return to nativism.

Immigrants suffering from poverty, ideological and religious discrimination, and genocides in mid-nineteenth-century Europe who were fleeing to a country that was advertised to be freer found themselves in an Argentina that was far from peaceful. They arrived in a country in the throes of defining itself as independent of its colonial past and separate from its indigenous populations. Simultaneously with its need to define itself within the concert of nations, the new state also strove to define its national organization and identity. The first political issue that needed to be addressed after formal independence from Spain in 1816 was the polarization between the province of Buenos Aires and the rest of the country. Buenos Aires monopolized access to the harbor on the Atlantic and taxes on imports and exports, an issue that was not completely solved until the 1890s.

THE NATION IMAGINED BY THE LIBERAL PROJECT

The Constitution of 1853, the first proclamation of the nation imagined as a liberal project, started the process of legislating for the nation shortly after its ratification by all provinces.[3] The governing elite's discourse made evident its preoccupation with the size and ethnic composition of the native population. During the second half of the nineteenth century the liberal state embarked on the active promotion of white European immigration, viewed as an antidote to "civilize" the native populations, who were devalued as ignorant and backward. One well-known ideologue, Juan Bautista Alberdi, coined a popular dictum in 1852: *gobernar es poblar* (to govern is to populate). By overwhelming the native populations, the liberal project of the nation hoped to emulate Europe. Through a selective immigration policy (immigrants who planned to practice agriculture were preferred) and exposure to institutions such as public education, the military draft, and naturalization, the state planned to assimilate the newcomers relatively quickly. Another well-known ideologue, Domingo Faustino Sarmiento, extended the meaning of "populate" to "civilize" as he proposed a continuum of cultural and economic development: civilization characterized the progressive Europeans as heralding "progress" against the barbarism considered inherent in the illiterate indigenous population. That included the gaucho, the Argentine native whose role within the national political economy is admirably painted by Ezekiel Martínez Estrada (1942, 1: 58–59):

He did not have power [he did not own either land or cattle], though he faced the planet covered by animals who were wandering too . . . Thus emerged the gaucho . . . His vague aspirations fit a political program . . . [The gaucho] was never a poetic theme but an ethnographic type.

In addition to immigration, the expanding economy was fed by foreign investments, particularly British. Labor, capital, and goods interacted with each other to assure the stability necessary to continue attracting foreign investment (Rock 1985: 119). The British invested in transportation, particularly in the railroad, service, and financial sectors. It is not surprising that Baron Maurice de Hirsch of Bavaria, Germany, a wealthy banker who invested heavily in railroads in Europe and Turkey, registered his agrarian immigration company (the Jewish Colonization Association) in London, where he had numerous business contacts.

European immigrants might serve a dual purpose for the liberal project: as a cheap labor force for the growing agricultural industry and as a "civilizing" influence on the natives. Europeans were considered to be the most fit to populate Argentina's vast territory, promote sociability through the establishment of agricultural colonies in desolate rural areas, diversify economic productivity, and, in the long run, modernize Argentine culture and society. Fernando Devoto (2003: 31–32), a historian of Argentine immigration, notes the Constitution's hidden ambiguities:

> The preamble, in its generality, presupposed all types of possible immigration, since it offered the rights and guarantees of the Constitution to "all the men of the world with goodwill who wished to inhabit the Argentine land." More precisely, article 25, on the one hand, promoted immigration but only the European kind ["the federal government will promote European immigration"] and, on the other, also gave an extensive occupational definition of immigration, noting that entry could not be denied to "foreigners whose goal was to work the land, improve the industries, and introduce and teach the sciences and the arts."

Concurrently with policies favoring the entry of the much emulated Europeans, there was rampant discrimination against the "barbaric" indigenous and Creole populations: while these populations were obliterated through forced assimilation, relocalization, and genocide (or made invisible when counted as Argentines in population surveys),[4] the gauchos were marginalized as vagabonds, and their nomadic lifestyle was criminalized.

A political issue to be confronted by the new nation's landed elites was the need for agriculture as well as cattle raising to produce more export commodities (in addition to hides, salted beef, and tallow) to conform to new global market demands.[5] To accomplish this aim, the new immigrants needed some support to settle as farmers. The Immigration and Colonization Law (Law No. 817, known as Ley Avellaneda, after the president who signed it in 1876, Nicolás Avellaneda) approved the distribution of fiscal land to immigrants "who wished to work it."

Immigration was promoted throughout the process of active recruitment: the law authorized the state to appoint agents in Europe to attract immigrants and facilitate their travel, initial accommodation, and settlement and offered protection from exploitative practices. But a noticeable lag existed between the passing of legislation and its administrative implementation. According to Devoto (2003), the private sector had already implemented colonization programs, regardless of state legislation. In fact, many *colonias* had been founded in the provinces of Santa Fé and Entre Ríos between 1850 and 1870, well before the legislation was passed.

Excluding first-class passengers and immigrants from neighboring countries, an estimated 4,600,000 transatlantic immigrants arrived in Argentina between 1881 and 1914. By 1896 immigration reached massive proportions in the nation as well as in the provinces: 49.6 percent of the population of the city of Buenos Aires was foreign born, followed by the provinces of Buenos Aires (30.5 percent), Santa Fé (15.6 percent), and Entre Ríos (13.6 percent) (Devoto 2003). Two-thirds of real estate in Buenos Aires was owned by immigrants (Solberg 1970). While immigrants represented 25.5 percent of the total population of the country by 1895, they had reached 30 percent by 1914. The country's population composition was forever transformed with an increase of European immigration and a decrease in native populations as Argentine president Julio Roca embarked in the 1898 Campaign of the Desert to displace the indigenous population in the pampas and Patagonia. European immigration therefore played an important role in the construction of national identity. Within a few decades the country turned from a binary to a multicultural society.

THE RETURN TO NATIVISM

The Argentine population increased dramatically through immigration within four decades, doubling first between 1869 and 1895 and again by 1914. While immigrants kept coming, the nation experienced deep economic depressions in the 1880s. In addition, a growing working class was becoming unionized to demand better working conditions. These developments signaled the emergence of a cultural reevaluation of the Hispanic, indigenous, and *criollo* components of gaucho culture in the making of national identity. The earlier characterization of the gaucho as "barbaric" (Devoto 2003: 38) was transformed into a romantic vision, a "guiding fiction" of nationhood, "a glorification of the rural poor in which the gaucho, rather than a barbarian outcast, emerges as a prototype of authentic Argentine values and a victim of the oligarchy's selfish ambition" (Shumway 1991: 216). Both the defamation and the glorification of the gaucho as the embodiment of authentic Argentine culture were political projects according to Martínez Estrada (1942, 1: 59), who declared 1880 "the year of the death of the gaucho." Since the immigrant inflow continued to be related to economic development that supplanted the gaucho culture and lifestyle, "the reaction led not to restriction of immigration, but to defamation" (Solberg 1970: 65).

The ideological schism between the factions that supported either indigenous or foreign populations in the constitution of an Argentine citizenry became a source of contention for decades, dividing those who imagined either a more indigenous or a more cosmopolitan Argentina. In contesting the prevalent ideology of assimilation, another political issue that the evolving nation had to address was the nature of assimilation. What would the nature of the imagined Argentina that would erase differences between natives and foreigners be? If the Argentina imagined by the liberal ideologues of the mid-nineteenth century proposed the assimilation of the natives to the foreigners, the nativists reversed the equation, suggesting that the foreigners should assimilate to the natives, who were now considered the "real Argentineans."

The Invention of the Jewish Gauchos: Memories of European Immigration in the Argentine Pampas

Alberto Gerchunoff immortalized the metaphor in *Los gauchos judíos* (The Jewish Gauchos) in 1910. Gerchunoff was born in 1883 in Russia; his father had decided on emigration when his successful inn lost patrons with the arrival of the railroad. The family arrived in Buenos Aires in 1891 with the first Jewish independently organized immigration, which experienced a troubled settlement from the Hotel de Inmigrantes (Immigrants' Hotel) in Buenos Aires to Moisesville in the province of Santa Fé.[6] After Gerchunoff's father died at the hands of a drunken gaucho, the family moved to Colonia Rajil in the province of Entre Ríos and finally to Buenos Aires in 1896. There the author, naturalized Argentine in 1899, had a successful career as a journalist and a writer. Gerchunoff is best known for *The Jewish Gauchos,* which immortalizes the rural life of Jews in the Argentine pampas shortly after their arrival at the end of the twentieth century through twenty-three short stories based on autobiographical vignettes previously published in the prestigious newspaper *La Nación.* The book was written to contest the myth of cultural isolation of the immigrants popularized by the nativists, although it publicly accepted the axiom inherent in the gaucho literary genre (*literatura gauchesca*) that venerated the *criollo* native as the authentic Argentine.

While cultural nationalists were rehabilitating the Creole's reputation, they were denigrating that of the foreigner. The schools established by the immigrants were particularly attacked since they were the medium to disseminate this version of national history, though nationalists reserved their most virulent attacks for the Jewish schools of the Entre Ríos agricultural colonies. (Solberg 1970: 148, 153)

While epitomizing the much-expected acculturation of the foreign born, Gerchunoff's thesis in *The Jewish Gauchos* inadvertently set limits to the possibilities of advancement for the Jewish immigrants. In fact, by limiting their assimilation to the positive image of the gaucho, the Jewish immigrants were incorporating into a relatively powerless social group. Whether denigrated in the earlier "civilization" ideology or exalted by the nativists, gauchos were historically poor and marginal members of society. Upper-class *criollos*, however, made sure they were accepted as natives but not as gauchos. For example, the writer Leopoldo Lugones, a member of the intelligentsia who disseminated the notion of the gaucho as containing the seeds of national character (patriotism, loyalty, compassion, and elegance), made sure that he was not identified as one: "We are not gauchos, of course . . . but the Argentine of today, though racial mixture has changed his physical appearance, still bears the gaucho's heritage. When racial fusion ends, the characteristics of the gaucho will dominate" (quoted in Solberg 1970: 155).

In 1910, when *The Jewish Gauchos* was published, Argentina was celebrating the first centennial of its independence. As gauchos became the idyllic prototypical embodiment of the true Argentine melting pot, the riots that convulsed Buenos Aires in 1919 were blamed on foreigners and taken as justifications for xenophobic attacks on Jewish neighborhoods and the enactment of anti-immigration legislation. If Gerchunoff's motive had been to exalt the assimilation of Jewish immigrants, the symbolic referent did not seem to coincide with the immigrants' aspirations for their children, many of whom left the countryside. Why the gaucho and not the landed elite or the successful entrepreneur? Why refer only to the Jewish immigrants who settled in the agricultural colonies and not to their urban concentration, particularly in Buenos Aires, through both international and internal migrations? When the Jewish immigrants arrived, Argentina's guiding fiction (Shumway 1991) equated the gaucho with the barbarian. Clearly, it was not this image of the gaucho that Gerchunoff had in mind but the one prevalent at the centennial, when the marginalized gaucho had disappeared, leaving only a nostalgically imagined heroic native behind. Gerchunoff was probably just romanticizing the newly arrived immigrant, who needed to emulate the gauchos (real experts at dealing with the rural terrain) for instrumental reasons, though not as a path of downward social mobility.

The vision propagated by Gerchunoff was particularly effective because, unlike the other immigrants to Entre Ríos during the nineteenth century (Swiss, French, Italians, Spaniards, Belgians, Germans of the Volga), most Jews had not practiced much farming in the Old World. Gerchunoff must have thought of cultural pluralism (as different from a melting-pot ideology) and of assimilation in a narrow sense: instrumental and not class based.

In disseminating his powerful assimilation metaphor, Gerchunoff purposefully omitted the modes of incorporating immigrants in Argentina's social structure. Because the receiving society, despite immigration policies and ideological manifestos, did not nurture the European farmers, the immigrant colonization programs in Entre Ríos and most of the nation (with rare exceptions) were not sustainable. By the mid-twentieth century most projects would fail.

While the Constitution provided the legal framework for immigration, the newcomers were relatively on their own in terms of access to credit, police protection, access to naturalization, and land ownership. In fact, the expected democratization of land distribution did not occur. Rather, the large landowners' economic and political power was further consolidated through tenant farmers' revenues. By 1895 only about 8 percent of the immigrants (then approaching 1 million) were landowners (Solberg 1970). The metaphor of the Jewish gauchos is a paradox that will be unveiled through the mix of official and testimonial understandings of history.

By the end of the nineteenth century the rapid assimilation of diverse immigrant populations into a melting pot or *crisol de razas* had become accepted as a distinctive mark of Argentine nationality. As theories of cultural pluralism amply proved, however, immigrants in nations peopled by large immigrant stocks, like Argentina and the United States, proved to be more resistant to "melting" than expected: they eventually articulated with the larger polity as simultaneously nationals and ethnics. The cultural identity of a Jew, according to this theory, would not negate that of a gaucho. But the celebration of multiple cultural affiliations was not to emerge until 2000, when a federal program entitled "Mosaic of Identities" sought to promote the preservation of ethnic, cultural, and religious heritage. The first project of this program, "Shalom Argentina," focused on Jewish immigrations to Argentina, including the province of Entre Ríos, where Villa Clara is located.

Chapter Two

ENTRE RÍOS, MI PAÍS

Immigrants Becoming Argentine in a Province

Throughout the last half-century, hundreds of thousands of [people of] diverse origin have settled on the 75,759 square kilometers of the province of Entre Ríos: Italians who bring from their native villages the geometric notion of the furrow and who trace, as in a drawing, the ridge between two furrows; Andalusians who spread their song while they keep vigilance over the plough; Galicians whose coarse features on their Celtic faces resemble the contours of the clod they punish with the spade; Basques possessing a hard disposition but a soft heart; Germans who replicate with their gentle method and their inalterable sanity the old farm from the Rhine; Slavs, eyes lost in the horizon, who travel on flat carriages; Jews overwhelmed with antiquity whose flowering wheat Jehovah blesses during the Sabbath siesta as in the Jordan valley. They mix in those 75,759 square kilometers with the criollo mass under a favorable sky from one border to the other and integrate that mix of heterogeneous elements to make up the social and moral family and the uniform look of the Entrerriano man. There is an Entrerriano man ... The son of the German, the Russian, or the Hebrew already has in his facial features something of the native of Montiel[1] ... At the same time, one can find people with rigorous indigenous features.

(Gerchunoff 1973: 39–41)

To understand the social history of Villa Clara in the province of Entre Ríos, we need to cast a wider net, including the history of European immigration. Despite the enormous geographical distance from their countries of origin, newcomers grounded their linked histories of emigration and immigration in the province, adopting the region of settlement as if it were the country of destination. Nobody painted this phenomenon better than Alberto Gerchunoff, who coined the phrases "Jewish gauchos" to refer to the Jewish immigrants' symbiotic relationship with the indigenous rural population in Argentina and "Entre Ríos, mi país [my country]" as emblematic of the European immigrants' rapid assimilation to and identification with the province's local culture.

Entre Ríos and the Imagined Argentine Nation

Geographically, Entre Ríos is a *provincia,* the smallest political jurisdiction in the Argentine nation. Located in the country's northeast, it is nested between the Paraná and Uruguay rivers, which explains the literal meaning of its name in Spanish, "between the rivers."[2] It borders on the *provincias* of Corrientes to the north, Buenos Aires to the south, and Santa Fé to the west and with the country of Uruguay to the east.

As a political unit, Entre Ríos played a major role in four major nation-building processes in Argentina: subduing indigenous populations, framing political consensus about the nation, favoring European immigration, and promoting the settlement of immigrants in agricultural *colonias*. Given its proximity to the major harbor in Buenos Aires and its fertile land, it fit the national project of the new nation. It was to this region that many European immigrants, thirsty for freedom from religious, economic, and political oppression, would come. Together with the provinces of Buenos Aires and Santa Fé, Entre Ríos attracted the transatlantic immigrants who would help develop agriculture in Argentina between 1869 and 1914. The liberal administrators of the mid-nineteenth century lured them to the nation to comply with their dream to diversify both ethnic stock and the economy. The European immigrants arriving in Entre Ríos imagined the province as a nurturing country—and nurturing it was, but only toward the white European immigrants, not toward its indigenous populations.

SUBDUING THE INDIGENOUS POPULATIONS

Between the arrival of the Spaniards and of the newest immigrants, Argentina's history of civil wars and inequities had systematically destroyed the native inhabitants of Entre Ríos. Conquistador Hernando Arias de Saavedra was said to have been the first to arrive in Entre Ríos in 1607, in search of a trade route to link the city of Santa Fé, the province of Corrientes, and the powerful Jesuit-controlled mission complex in Asunción, Paraguay. Military service and self-interest triggered his travels and his capacity to recruit soldiers, who were attracted to service by the Spanish Crown's established practice of distributing land to members of military expeditions and colonial administrators in recognition of their labors. In fact, the large cattle ranches (*estancias*), the basis of the local economy, had resulted primarily from monarchic legislation that authorized land concessions (*concesiones*). Cattle raising became an investment with an excellent return rate, since cattle reproduced quickly and naturally. The Jesuit order (Compañía de Jesús), probably the largest landowner in the northeastern region of the country, shared political influence with stakeholders in the provinces of Buenos Aires, Santa Fé, and Corrientes. Spaniards, *criollos* (children of Spaniards born in America), mestizos (of mixed Spanish, Indian, and African ancestry), religious personnel, and indigenous people were the major populations in Entre Ríos by the mid-seventeenth century.

The eastward expansion of the province of Santa Fé, founded in 1573, was orchestrated as a military conquest. The military contingents subdued the indigenous populations, who lived by hunting, gathering, and fishing, in three ways: assigning them to Spaniards as free labor,[3] exposing them to new epidemic diseases, and annihilating those who resisted them in battle.[4] Between 1624 and 1750 frequent military expeditions were waged against the Charrúas,[5] reportedly the largest and most bellicose aboriginal population.

The Charrúas arrived in Entre Ríos between the beginning of the colonization period and the mid-eighteenth century, as they followed the increasing numbers of runaway cattle (*ganado cimarrón*), which they could easily capture on horseback. In the course of their nomadic displacement, these indigenous populations frequently attacked Spanish settlements, including those under Jesuit rule.[6] Although a military expedition dispatched from Buenos Aires formally defeated the Charrúas in 1751, the slow extermination of the indigenous peoples of Entre Ríos continued through the stress of forced labor and relocation in reservations (*reducciones*), vulnerability to new epidemics, and impoverishment.

After the indigenous populations had been stripped of military power, the province was now safe for newcomers. Landowners from Santa Fé and Buenos Aires, soon joined by concessionaries including the Compañía de Jesús,[7] were authorized to appropriate the runaway cattle through special permits (*acciones de vaqueo*) granted by the Spanish Crown through its administrative seats (cabildos) in Santa Fé and Buenos Aires. In addition to the legitimized users of this self-propagating resource, the marginalized (indigenous peoples, gauchos, and landless mestizos) also appropriated cattle, either for immediate consumption or for profit from the sale of hides or meat for the incipient curing industry (*saladero*) that emerged at the beginning of the eighteenth century.

Entre Ríos played a crucial role in the political organization of the country and was its political center from 1850 to 1860. After the 1810 Revolution against Spain, a succession of civil wars marked the provinces' contestation of the political hegemony of Buenos Aires and the location of the major harbor. Ideologically, the struggle opposed federalist principles—espoused by caudillos representing the provinces—against the centralism exercised by Buenos Aires. In Entre Ríos the factionalism between two caudillos, José Artigas and Francisco Ramírez, ended with the pacification of the province in 1822, as it established a centralized political administration.

In addition to this legitimized political structure, there were other social actors—indigenous peoples, runaway African slaves, and gauchos—all relatively uninvolved in the formal political process. Rarely the focus of historians' attention, these populations were marginalized by the new landlords of *estancias*,[8] who refused to acknowledge their presence, dismissed their nomadic lifestyle as barbaric, or attacked them. In fact, the historical appearance of the gaucho could be traced to the perceptions of "the other" held by the Argentine landed elite:

> Forced to satisfy his most elementary necessities, the man is a wanderer in the land. In his running he crosses the Uruguay and makes contact with the Portuguese possessions. There he is called a *gauderio*. The word signals that he is somebody dealing with cattle. Soon the word stops being used. Soon he is referred to as *gaucho,* with the same pejorative label. Intruder in the fields, without respect for authority or the existence of others or for fiscal prescriptions, the gaucho lives from smuggling, often from crime, often a deserter or a runaway from justice. He reigns sovereign from the margins of the Paraná to the margins of the Uruguay. The forest protects and hides him. Thus he is often also called *montaraz*.[9] (Bosch 1978: 14)

By the eighteenth century, when the cattle industry had decreased in importance (probably as a function of over-exploitation), foreigners used the word *gaucho* for anyone in the rural labor force:

> Robertson [a British businessman by the name of Juan Parish Robertson] calls the rural workers *gauchos*. This term is a misnomer used by travelers avid for local color and enthused by the exotic word. Those workers . . . were in fact settled farmers. The fair and current term of the times was *paisano*,[10] since the word *gaucho* has continued, for a long time, to be used to denote the

person who lives in the woods, is uncivil, errant, an enemy of work, without family. The city dweller applies the adjective exceptionally and, in that case, always in a pejorative sense. (Bosch 1978: 29)

In addition to the subdued indigenous populations, and the emergence of the gauchos, the labor force also included African slaves. This human traffic, which started in the mid-sixteenth century, had significantly increased by the eighteenth century.[11] Slaves worked primarily in the *estancias,* serving within the house and engaging in rural activities.

For two decades the province of Entre Ríos was placed at the center of ideological disputes and military confrontations between opposing factions regarding the relationship between Buenos Aires and the other provinces in the Argentine nation. Since the 1840s, the best-known *federal* in the province had been Justo José de Urquiza,[12] who established a unified federation of provinces in defiance of the powerful and separatist Buenos Aires in 1851,[13] deposed President Juan Manuel de Rosas in 1852, and assembled a national congress that authored the first Constitution in 1853. In Entre Ríos, Urquiza's administrations supported cattle raising, the traditional occupation of the rural population, but also promoted agriculture, practiced by the new immigrant population. The meat-curing industry, which generated an import-export economy, continued to be monopolized by businesses owned by Spanish, Italian, and French descendants. Economic diversification through the introduction of agriculture, colonization of immigrants, and education was a major preoccupation in Urquiza's administrations (Bosch 1978).

FAVORING EUROPEAN IMMIGRATION

After the claim of victory over the Charrúas by 1750, the 1810 Revolution proclaiming independence from Spain, the establishment of a political administration for Entre Ríos by 1822, and the adoption of a Constitution legitimizing a republican government for the nation in 1853, the province could boast the political stability conducive to attracting increased European immigration (other than the already established Spaniards).

Other Europeans had been lured earlier to these latitudes. In fact, an 1847 traveler's diary reported the existence of one hundred foreigners in Paraná ("most of them Italian, about a dozen French, a dozen English, and two U.S. citizens": MacCann 1969: 250). This report emphasized the importance of human stock to add to the advantages of the province's geography, which (with two major rivers and a myriad of streams) was decidedly favorable for commerce:

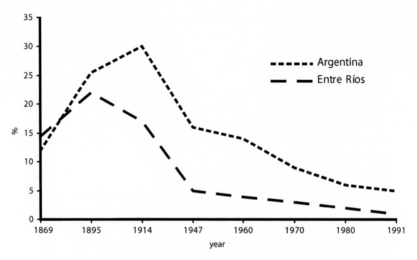

Proportion of foreign-born in the population of Entre Ríos and Argentina: 1869–1991.

The geographical position of Entre Ríos is definitely favorable to trade. In-terior navigation is possible for several hundred miles, and the ships with a European destination can load under the best conditions. But its political, commercial, and social relations are so disorganized that, for the time being, it seems impossible for the province to come out of the chaos in which it lives. (MacCann 1969: 253)

Much later, a French traveler noted the province's structure of opportunities for immigration:

Among all the provinces, Entre Ríos is the best prepared for spontaneous im-migration, that is, for all those agricultural immigrants who have some means to start working the land. Its climate is admirable and healthy, its soil beau-tiful, well watered by nature, very fertile, and dotted with frequent forests. All this promises the hard-working farmer a complete remuneration . . . Fast progress is to be expected as this province starts a rational system of coloniza-tion. (Napp 1888: 230–231)

PROMOTING IMMIGRANT SETTLEMENT IN AGRICULTURAL SETTLEMENTS (*COLONIAS*)

Although individual Europeans had arrived and settled in Argentina since the beginning of independence, the organized immigration of Europeans did not materialize until the institutional organization of the country was completed and ratified with the passing of the 1853 Constitution, which assured favorable settlement conditions for the newcomers. The national project to attract European immigrants was further solidified with the passing of the Colonization Law in 1876, which actively promoted settlement, particularly by those willing to settle in the immense and underpopulated countryside. To promote rural settlement, the state promised free transportation from Buenos Aires harbor to the immigrants' final destination, affordable land, and credits to facilitate their dedication to agriculture.

As Argentina debated its political mission and national identity, Europe was experiencing changes that affected the livelihood of many. They often improved their prospects in the growing Argentine economy, savoring freedom in the welcoming policies of the newly independent nation and construing emigration as an alternative to constraints in the Old World. The image of a freer and better life across the Atlantic was nurtured by letters or visits, by diplomatic envoys of the Argentine government, and by sailing or colonization companies. Many Europeans, seeking to escape restrictive economic and political conditions in their conflicted home countries, gladly accepted the challenge to make a new life across the Atlantic.

The province of Entre Ríos was a pioneer in the aggressive recruitment of settlers from abroad, using strategies such as legislation, resettlement policies, and envoys to Western and Eastern Europe. Keen on implementing colonization programs, the province passed legislation even before the federal government did. By 1860 Entre Ríos had approved its own Constitution, which included legislation that promoted agriculture and colonization. Following the lead of Governor Urquiza, landholders (both the government itself and private landowners) were stimulated to donate land to foreign- or native-born families with a commitment to farming for at least two years in exchange for tax benefits. A large landowner himself, Urquiza had established a military agricultural *colonia*, Las Conchas, as early as 1853 and had ceded part of his property to establish Colonia San José with Swiss and French families in 1857. Governor Urquiza's initial support of immigration was continued by his successor, governor Pascual Echagüe (1871–1875).

The combined effect of federal and provincial legislation and the large landowners' interest in devoting some of their huge unproductive lands to agriculture was soon reflected in the demographic changes in the province. By 1869, more than a decade before the passage of the 1976 Colonization Law, 10 percent of the province's population was foreign-born. By 1895 the proportion had reached 22 percent,[14] and 7,479 additional immigrants arrived between 1895 and 1897. By then, 38 percent of the immigrants owned their land, marking the appearance of an incipient middle class of farmers in the Argentine pampas. The social mobility imagined by the immigrants did have a real basis in Argentina at the end of the nineteenth century.

By 1887 Entre Ríos was second only to the province of Buenos Aires in cattle wealth. Agriculture had increased, and most of the cultivated land was located in *colonias*, which then concentrated the largest number of settled agriculturalists. *Colonias* quickly grew in number: from 11 in 1878 to 102 in 1888, 175 in 1893 (Devoto 2003), and 185 in 1898 (*Situación demográfica de la Provincia de Entre Ríos 1998*), when Entre Ríos ranked second in the country, which had 709 *colonias* distributed throughout 8 provinces, after the province of Santa Fé, with 363.[15]

European Immigration to Entre Ríos: 1850–1900

Evaluating the demographic record of this immigrant flow entails serious limitations.[16] First, it was difficult to record immigration by country of origin during the times of the Confederación Argentina.[17] Second, many transatlantic immigrants were actually recorded as nationals of neighboring countries:[18] when ships to Buenos Aires were full, some immigrants from Europe sailed to Brazil or Uruguay en route to Argentina. Third, natives from neighboring countries (primarily Uruguay) who immigrated to Argentina were often not recorded when crossing unregulated borders.[19] Fourth, gauchos in hiding and other marginalized populations remained invisible and thus uncounted. Fifth, some immigrant populations reported their country of birth while others reported their last country of residence: this applied to the Germans of the Volga and the Jews immigrating from Russia.

Despite these limitations, several demographic generalizations about the immigrant stock in Entre Ríos can be drawn on the basis of the Second Census of Population in 1895. First, although the proportion of immigrants had almost doubled since the First Census of 1869 (from 12 to 22 percent, though the population of the province continued to represent about 7 percent of the national population), their distribution by country of origin remained unchanged. Second, the majority of the population (67 percent) was settled in rural areas, primarily on the mainland (only a small minority lived on the riverbanks). Third, about a quarter of the population of Villaguay, the urban center closest to what would become Villa Clara, was foreign-born; the majority originated in Italy and Belgium, followed by smaller contingents from France, Spain, Germany, and Switzerland, in that order. Fourth, while cattle raising continued to be the major industry, agriculture was gaining in importance. Fifth, although only 422,647 (43 percent) of the 977,523 hectares set aside for agriculture were actually under cultivation, agriculture had already made an impact on the social structure: of 12,217 agricultural families, 8,496 (70 percent) were landowners and 3,724 (30 percent) were sharecroppers. Sixth, the agricultural methods were still labor intensive: over half the people working the land (55 percent) reported

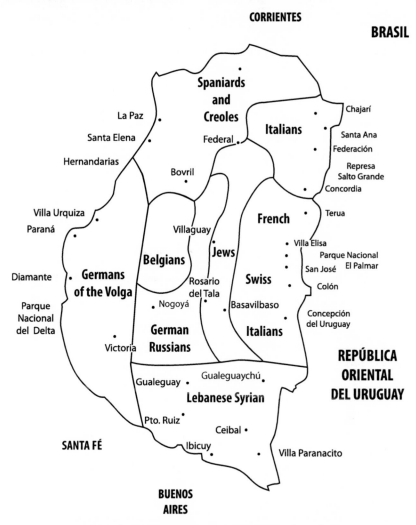

CORRIENTES

BRASIL

Spaniards
and
Creoles

La Paz

Santa Elena

Hernandarias

Bovril

Federal

Italians

Chajarí

Santa Ana

Federación

Represa
Salto Grande

Concordia

Villa Urquiza

Paraná

French

Terua

Villaguay

Belgians

Jews

Villa Elisa

Parque Nacional
El Palmar

San José

Diamante

Germans
of the Volga

Rosario
del Tala

Swiss

Colón

Nogoyá

Basavilbaso

Parque
Nacional
del Delta

Victoria

German
Russians

Italians

Concepción
del Uruguay

REPÚBLICA
ORIENTAL
DEL URUGUAY

Gualeguay

Gualeguaychú

Lebanese Syrian

Pto. Ruiz

Ceibal

SANTA FÉ

Ibicuy

Villa Paranacito

BUENOS
AIRES

*Location of major immigrant groups in Entre Ríos at the end of the
nineteenth century and first decades of the twentieth century. Map on permanent exhibit at the
Museo Histórico Regional de la Colonia San José; reprinted here by permission of its director,
Mercedes Vanerio.*

using plows as major agricultural tools. Demographic and historical analyses
are insufficient to portray the significance and diversity of immigration in Entre
Ríos. While some cohorts are analyzed in a voluminous literature (especially
the Jewish immigration), others (especially the Italians and Spaniards, numeri-
cally the largest immigrant groups) remain almost invisible to the historian's
eye. Finally, the written record tends to document the arrival and settlement of
the initial cohorts, with relatively little or no attention to the changes experienced by the immigrants or their children in the course of time.

Villa Clara's social history can best be understood through the combination of demographic, historical, and ethnographic perspectives. The province experienced three waves of immigration, each bounded by major historical markers. The first wave is flanked by two major events in the making of the state (the 1853 Constitution and the 1876 Law No. 817) and includes two organized migrations: Basques and Swiss. The second wave, containing organized migrations by Belgians and Germans of the Volga, ends with the second national census in 1895, when immigration reached its peak in the province. The third wave ends with the last organized immigration in the province, by the Jews of Eastern Europe.

THE FIRST WAVE OF EUROPEAN IMMIGRATION TO ENTRE RÍOS: 1853–1875

The first to arrive in the province were Spaniards, Italians, and Swiss-French. Like Italians, some Spaniards dispersed while others nucleated into *colonias*. A census of the inhabitants of the city of Paraná revealed that 3 percent were foreign-born in 1824, originating primarily in the Basque country, Catalonia, Galicia, Asturias, Andalusia, and Castile. The first organized immigrant settlement of Spaniards recorded in the province was the military and agricultural *colonia* Las Conchas, founded in 1853 by Justo José de Urquiza,[20] who organized the immigration of about fifteen or twenty Basque families. By 1858 Las Conchas had received German, Jewish, and Belgian immigrants and was renamed Urquiza. Spaniards continued to arrive throughout the century: by 1889 new *colonias* sprang up with people from the regions of Valencia and Catalonia. Spaniards arriving in the province of Entre Ríos came from across the Atlantic and from neighboring countries. In some cases immigrants undertook a two-step migration, settling in Uruguay en route to Argentina. A descendant illustrated the complexity of links when he recalled how his father immigrated to Uruguay with his father and siblings at the age of seven and then immigrated to Argentina on his own at sixteen. When his grandfather fell sick in Uruguay, he returned to Spain to join his wife, who had stayed behind with an older daughter. Escaping from compulsory military service was a prime motivation for male migration, forcing some immigrants to sever their links with their country of origin forever. The son of one of those immigrants mentioned that the fear of losing children to war was more agonizing than never seeing them again and that his grandparents sent off his father with a family sailing to Buenos Aires. Other immigrants, however, traveled frequently between Spain and Argentina to avail themselves of the best opportunities for work or to visit spouses and children.

According to the provincial census organized by Urquiza as early as 1849, the majority of the European immigrants in the province were Genovese, Neapolitans, and Friulians (Massoni n.d.). By 1872 there are records of two mutual-help associations founded by Italians, who followed two patterns of settlement. Some dispersed throughout the province, but larger proportions settled in a few *colonias*. Italians were the majority in some *colonias,* such as Colonia Caseros, which had 98 families (722 persons) by 1876, of whom 53 were Italian, 34 French, 5 Swiss, 2 Spanish, 1 Polish, and 3 Belgian. In others, such as Tres de Febrero and Santa Juana in Villaguay, all residents were Italian. In 1895 Italians continued to be the largest immigrant group (20,000) in the province.

Italian immigrants were primarily farmers, whether they settled in *colonias* or in dispersed settlements and whether they arrived spontaneously or through organized migrations. Some Italian descendants recall how most immigrants were orchard farmers (*quinteros*) all their lives.[21] Despite these nostalgic memories of a hard past, historical records indicate that other Italian families prospered in industries that employed new immigrants (for example, the Colombo family opened a quarry in San José that provided employment for many newly arrived Swiss). Finally, other Italians were very successful at fluvial transportation, the only means available at the time. The Genovese, in particular, owned most of the small ships. Less often recorded in print but vivid in people's memory are poor Italians and Poles who found employment in railroad and house construction (De Paoli de Bellman Eguiguren and Oyenden 1993).

As with other immigrant groups, the memory of the move was usually restricted to the saga of leaving the country of origin and resettling in the country of destination. Italian descendants remembered their ancestors' flight from wars, dramatized the long duration of the trip, and detailed the essential possessions that the immigrants brought with them. But when prompted to remember their ancestors' life in the country of origin, descendants proved how porous national borders were then and how regional loyalties often superseded the nation-state as identity markers. One woman, for example, first recalled that her great-grandfather was born in the town of Medici in the Lombardy region and her great-grandmother was from the Savoy before she identified those regions as part of Italy or France. Another salient theme was the transnational character of Italian immigration, particularly for the farmers. One man narrated that his wife's father and uncle came alone to work for a few months and then returned to Italy, where they worked before bringing their families. Other testimonies refer to several trips, which made the Italian immigrants, especially the farmers, truly transnational migrants. Benefiting from the opposite seasons and improved transatlantic transportation, the Italian immigrants grounded themselves simultaneously in both the country of origin and the country of destination. For that social system to operate smoothly, maintaining connections in Italy was crucial for immigrants, who often traveled back and forth until certain of success and used mail to stay in touch.

The second organized settlement during this period originated in the Alps, although it is remembered as the Swiss immigration and descendants in Villa Clara have grouped themselves as the Swiss-French collectivity.[22] Numerous pressures (resulting from the combined effects of impoverishment, high fertility rates, unemployment, and confrontations between Protestants and Catholics) made emigration an attractive alternative for residents of the Alpine region. The psychological and cultural distances to the major countries of emigration in , the mid-nineteenth century (the United States, Canada, Brazil, and Argentina) were minimized in the depictions provided by immigration agencies.[23] By 1857 General Urquiza had settled 100 Swiss families (530 people) on his property,[24] in what was called Colonia San José,[25] and hired French-born Alejo Peyret as its administrator.[26] The newcomers agreed to abide by a code of conduct and to carry out agricultural tasks. In exchange, the families were granted land (26–28 hectares each); their sons were exempted from the compulsory military draft; and the settlement was allowed some governance autonomy.

While most of the immigrants were Swiss (including people from the Canton de Valais,[27] currently located in Switzerland; from Savoy, currently located in France; and from the Piedmont, currently located in Italy),[28] others had French, German, or Italian origins, according to the political demarcations of the time. In fact, the descendants of this immigrant wave prided themselves on remembering the actual combinations of their grandparents' provenance in both national and regional terms.

General Urquiza was viewed as a benefactor and often visited San José to promote agricultural diversity. To facilitate marketing the colony's products,[29] he financed the construction of Colón harbor on the Uruguay River in 1863. This fluvial access contributed to further immigrant arrivals, both from neighboring Uruguay and Paraguay (which were experiencing political conflicts at the time) and from Europe. The circumstances of the trip, comparisons between the country of origin and destination as well as between spontaneous and organized immigration, and transnational connections are remembered today, after two generations. One man recalled being told that his grandfather had left France as a military deserter, fleeing twelve-year service in the Foreign Legion in Africa. An acquaintance worked on a ship sailing to Buenos Aires and helped him escape. Other testimonies point to hardships: one informant, for example, narrated the story of how his ancestors lost all their possessions when their ship sank in Uruguay, forcing them to beg for money there to be able to make it to Buenos Aires. Many mentioned how connections in the Old World were kept alive primarily through mail and how they saved letters in which those who stayed behind spoke admiringly of the wealth found in Argentina. While some arrived directly in Entre Ríos, others tried their luck elsewhere first. One example is a man's grandfather from the upper Savoy, who worked in railroads

The Swiss-French Delaloye family.

and mining in La Rioja:[30] "He got fed up; he couldn't take the heat anymore. To come from a cold area and go there!"

As major events convulsed Europe in the 1860s, leading to the annexation of the Savoy by France and the Piedmont by Italy, additional immigrants joined Colonia San José, which eventually branched into new agricultural settlements. Urquiza's colonizing mission continued unabated throughout his life. After his assassination in 1870, his widow and his first colonial administrator, Peyret (who had by then established his own colonizing company), continued his efforts and settled French, Swiss, Germans, Spanish, Belgian, and Italian immigrants in new agricultural *colonias* between 1872 and 1874: Villa Libertad, Villa Hernandarias, Tres de Febrero, and Colonia Caseros.[31]

The colonizing effort intensified in the province. In 1875 a law that authorized the donation of small plots of land to families (whether foreign or native) on the condition that they became farmers within two years of settlement was passed.[32] This legislation stimulated private landowners to settle immigrants on their lands.[33] The impact of this legislation in the Villa Clara region can be seen in the actions of private landowner Héctor de Elía. In 1890 Elía settled Belgian, Italian, French, Swiss, and Spanish immigrants and *criollos* on his property. His *colonia* was named Villa Elisa. Another law (passed in 1880) destined more land for colonizing immigrants, though payments were calculated over twenty years, since land prices had risen.

The economic crisis of 1880 both inflated land prices and decreased the viability of immigrant payments. Many *colonias* thus experienced high rates of desertion, for reasons ranging from poor harvests to high administrative fees, locust invasions, and cattle theft (Macchi 1977). Another unforeseen consequence was that, with the appearance of wired fences, "the modification of the landscape brings new social modalities. The itinerant gaucho, who rode across the fields through unlimited lands, disappears" (Bosch 1978: 244).

Probably the wealthiest immigrants to Entre Ríos were the British,[34] large landowners and industrial entrepreneurs (primarily settling on the Uruguay River coast) who employed both *criollos* and gringos. The traveler William Mac-Cann writes about an *estancia* owned by the firm Campbell, Wright & Parlane from Manchester, which "has its own harbor to send wool directly to Europe." MacCann cites many British landowners, including "the largest extension of land owned by a British subject in this part of the world" (Bosch 1978: 175). An Irishman by the name of Juan O'Connor expanded the operations of an Argentine packaged-meat company that he bought by founding a new town in 1863. Close to San José, Liebig housed the employees of the Liebig Extract of Meat Company. This packing house provided employment for thousands and exported most of its production to Great Britain directly from the plant. In addition to being large landowners and industrialists, the British were at first major lenders of capital for the construction of railroads and by 1892 owners of all provincial railroads in Entre Ríos.

THE SECOND WAVE OF EUROPEAN IMMIGRATION TO ENTRE RÍOS: 1876–1895

Scholars have understood what is known as the Russian German migration as a "double migration," because Germans lived in Russia for over a century (1763–1878) before their emigration to Argentina.[35] While in Russia, however, they continued to identify themselves as Germans and to replicate German lifestyles, agricultural practices, settlement patterns, language, and religion to a large extent. Several countries in the Americas—especially the United States, Canada, Brazil, and Argentina—had embarked on promoting European migration to the New World during the mid-nineteenth century. As early as 1847 Domingo Sarmiento, the opponent of President Rosas, had specifically urged Germans to emigrate in the belief that what he called proverbial honesty, hard-working customs, and peaceful and quiet character would be of benefit to Argentina.

The Russian Germans' experience with agriculture (developed over a century of residence in Russia) constituted yet another attraction for the government of Argentina, where cattle raising continued to monopolize production (93 percent of exports versus 2.3 percent for agricultural products at the time).

The German Meyer family.

But the self-labeled Germans of the Volga, who had experienced previously un-fulfilled contracts in Russia, weighed their choices first and sent a committee to Argentina in 1877 to explore the conditions of settlement. The relative peace reigning in the province at the time of the visit (after six years of political anar-chy following Urquiza's assassination in 1870) impressed the committee favor-ably. By the following year the committee had signed a contract with President Avellaneda, who has been remembered as a benefactor by this immigrant group. Having inspired the Immigration and Colonization Law (No. 817) in 1876, Ave-llaneda had expropriated land in Entre Ríos to accommodate the newcomers; with support from the province's governor founded Colonia Alvear in 1878;[36] and later accepted the colonizers' demands to settle in communal villages (*al-deas*), rather than on the 44-hectare individual farms allotted them. Although a contract dated 1877–1878 had stipulated the conditions for the settlement of 5,000 Russian Germans in Entre Ríos, by 1878 only 1,000 had arrived in the province's departments of Paraná, Diamante, Victoria, and Nogoya.

By 1882 Colonia Alvear had reached a population of 2,034. Since conditions were still favorable for land acquisition,[37] additional immigrants were settled in connected *aldeas* that sprang up in quick succession during the first decade after their arrival: Aldea Salto (1878), Aldea San Rafael (1887), Aldea Crespo (1888), and Aldea Santa Rosa (1893) and later Valle María, Spatzenkutter, Protestante, San Francisco, San José, Salto, Brasilera, María Luisa, and Santa Anita.[38] The administrations of presidents Nicolás Avellaneda and Julio A. Roca, at least initially, respected the original agreements: the provision of affordable land and exemption from taxes for the first two years of settlement. As land increased in value toward the 1890s, however, promises were not honored, forcing the second contingent of immigrants to form consortia of thirty to forty families to buy affordable lands.

The third contingent of Russian German immigrants settled in Santa Anita in the Department of Uruguay, closest to Villa Clara. The conditions for land acquisition were less favorable then,[39] but poor *colonos* felt protected by a Catholic priest of the Order of the Divine Word (Congregación del Verbo Divino). He had organized the settlement of this contingent on his own property, which he had bought from an English landowning family. At first the priest was apparently successful, since the new arrivals were able to clear their debts by 1907. As in other settlements of the Germans of the Volga, the cultivation of wheat was the most important occupation, though it was later supplemented with cattle raising, rice production, and chicken farming.

Shortly after the settlement of the Volga German colonies, *criollos* approached them to obtain employment clearing the Selva de Montiel, a job they knew better than the new immigrants. Social interaction was apparently restricted to work, according to testimony (Stang and Britos 2000). As minorities in the *aldeas,* however, *criollos* often Germanized, and many held the newcomers in great admiration:

> We kids did not have education and we grew up on the horse and you needed to gallop miles to find a mud hut; in the past, some people owned land as far as you could see. There were two or three immense ranches [*estancias*], and anybody could build a mud hut; nobody gave you a title or anything . . . Later, when taxes were required, nobody wanted to own the land and we *criollos* sought employment as *troperos* and *puesteros* . . . [40]
>
> The *colonos* are good people and I have many friends among them, but with the strange language they speak you cannot understand them . . . What great harvests they produced in those *colonias* that sprang up everywhere! What good bread their women cooked! And the way they changed things in a few years! They found a way for everything; they brought cloth and you could buy

clothing without walking miles and miles! They even tamed the horse for the plow . . . the roads they opened so they would not get lost. It was all for the good. (testimony of Don Benito Pérez, cited in Popp and Dening 1977: 173)

In contrast, ideologues of the Europeanized Argentina asserted that Germans were not assimilating and thus contributing to the country of destination. A vocal critic was Peyret, the French immigrant instrumental in settling the Swiss earlier (by then commissioner of colonies), who asserted that

> these individuals do not assimilate: they form a different national entity that remains isolated and that brings many problems. The proof is that very few of these [so-called] Russians, who were living in Russia for 120 years, speak Russian. (Peyret 1889: 164–165)

The Germans of the Volga, who had become expert at growing wheat in Russia, shared with the Jewish immigrants a history of discrimination and expulsion during the period of the "Russifying" tsars. Some came with their families; others married Argentines upon arrival. Not surprisingly, the wars and the transatlantic trip are well remembered, as are the difficulties inherent in making a life through agriculture in the first few years of settlement. The situation was even harder for sharecroppers, often prone to exploitation when land values increased. Those with a trade lived off it until they could make ends meet through agriculture. German descendants remember those times:

> When they arrived, the government promised so much land to some and so much to others and, since the land produced well, it was new, virgin land; at first they [the government] asked them for a percentage and afterward, when they saw that it produced so much, they charged them much more than what they had asked.

> He [the informant's father] continued in shoemaking, making shoes, boots, and had so much work that he would work until two or three in the morning, a lot of work! . . . And later he started leasing land, and had two wives, there are fourteen brothers, seven from one and seven from the other, and he bought about 400 hectares . . . he worked a lot on the farm . . . In Santa Anita, my dad grew up there.

Most informants attributed two characteristics to the Germans' work ethic: they were hard workers and they liked to work by themselves. A descendant of the Jewish immigration had this to say about the Germans:

Because the Germans . . . they like work, it doesn't matter to them, how do you say? Getting dirty . . . My husband was like a German. You weren't going to take him away from here; he worked by himself in the countryside. He set fences by himself; he fixed the mills by himself.

Germans very rarely employed people. [They lived primarily in Santa Rosa and Colonia Moreno.] This is pure German . . . And you should have seen how they worked! The women worked, on all the machines, with the bags, everything. Good-looking women.

Regarding their personal characteristics, the Germans are remembered as not very sociable and not open to assimilating through intermarriage or to teaching Spanish to their children. Extended families fulfilled an important role in preserving the German language and religion as markers of ethnicity, as one elderly woman explained:

I did communion, but all in German . . . the nuns [taught me] . . . In Santa Anita . . . They [her parents] sent me there. We would stay with our grand-parents. A month or two . . .

We left the countryside but we always would come to Santa Anita because it wasn't that far, how long it took I don't know, but from there we went to the farm, which was more or less a league and a half away. From there we went to school; to go to school we would stay with our grandmother who was in Santa Anita. And there I did up to the fifth grade.

Although they arrived later in Entre Ríos than the Swiss-French and the Germans of the Volga, Belgians settled closest to where Villa Clara is located today. In fact, they are listed as the first farmers in Villaguay (Ciapuscio 1973).

By 1880 the kingdom of Belgium was mostly populated by Catholic Flemish and Walloon ethnic groups, who eked out a living on very densely populated, over-farmed land and were thus unable to support their large families with agriculture. Their children tended to emigrate to Germany or France to work in mines or textile shops. Two events helped nurture the emigration dream: the first was President Roca's mention of benefits that the Argentine government would grant to immigrants during a talk he delivered at the University of Louvain in Belgium. The second auspicious event was the implementation of federal policy at the local level, as the city of Villaguay approved the adjudication of farmland for farmers. These events triggered the decision of Eugenio Schepens, a Belgian entrepreneur, to spend three months in Argentina during 1882 and to propose the establishment of a Belgian *colonia* in the city of Villaguay. His agreement with the Villaguay authorities stipulated that Belgian farmers would be granted

The Belgian Den Dauw family.

thirty-two hectares per family (or sixteen if unmarried), free transportation from Buenos Aires, and advanced credit to meet basic needs to establish a farm (such as a cow with a calf, a plow, farming tools, and seeds), a house, and a well.

Unlike the Germans of the Volga, the potential Belgian immigrants were hard to persuade, because they were concerned with the political unrest and frequent uprisings led by local caudillo Ricardo López Jordán. Committed to the plan, Schepens promised to finance their return if contractual conditions failed to be honored. Finally, about forty families sailed from Antwerp in Flanders (in present-day Belgium) in 1881, bringing with them furniture, tools, kitchen utensils, and some seeds. After a short stay in the Hotel de Inmigrantes in Buenos Aires,[41] they sailed to Colón. At the time, the population of Colón consisted of *criollos*, mestizos, and French-speaking settlers, who gladly shared their experiences in subsistence occupations that complemented farming with the newcomers. Specifically, the established immigrants advised the women to undertake chicken farming and the men to experiment with pig raising and honey making. Having stored the new knowledge, the new immigrants continued on their travels in wagons, arriving in 1882 at their destination, Colonia Belga in the woods of Montiel north of Villaguay.

But the political instability created by factions loyal to the late Urquiza or to his opponent López Jordán did not abate for much of that century. The *criollo* troops of caudillo Polonio Velázquez terrorized the *colonos*:

The *colonos* were astonished as they looked upon this elementary army, poorly dressed, trotting on their horses amidst clouds of dust and horse smell, some of whom in complete silence made gestures of repugnance to the gringos or jokingly tried to scare them by gesturing a possible beheading by passing a finger across their throats. (Beaurain Barreto 2001: 45)

As with the *criollos*, the reception of the established political authorities was equally ambivalent, adding fear to culture shock:

The political and military commander in charge was Colonel Polonio Veláz-quez, son of one of the most courageous men who had defended General Justo José de Urquiza . . . Like the majority of *criollos*, he loathed the foreigner. They saw the foreigner as a conqueror and enslaver. (De Grave 1966: 27)

Fortunately for the newcomers, other *criollos* and the foreign-born in the area assisted the first Belgians during their settlement, including many Germans, Italians (especially those dedicated to construction), and Swiss-French from the *colonia* of San José. Shortly after their settlement, the new immigrants originated the chain migration of additional Belgian families, who settled with other immigrants (for example, Italians in Colonia Santa Juana and Germans in Colonia Alemania). These diverse, multinational immigrant populations interacted through trade, barter, sharing of technological knowledge, and intermarriage, turning Villaguay into an important regional center.

Other entrepreneurs—particularly Germán Tjarks, who founded Nueva Alemania in 1887, and Héctor de Elía, who founded San Jorge and Villa Dolores in 1891—spurred the foundation of additional Belgian colonies in 1892.

The Third Wave of European Immigration to the Center of Entre Ríos: 1896–1902

Native Uruguayans would also move to Argentina. Their descendants explain how the poorly guarded frontier at the Uruguay River was symbolic of crossing over, not migrating:

At that time there wasn't a harbor. There was a ferryman who helped them [cross the river] . . . Nothing [bad] could happen. There was no documentation [required]. They had them, of course, but were never asked for documents, never.

Here there were people, who came . . . many Uruguayans who came to . . . Argentina, or to Entre Ríos, as they said. Because Argentina was legally organized before Uruguay . . . Poor people would defect [from the army] when

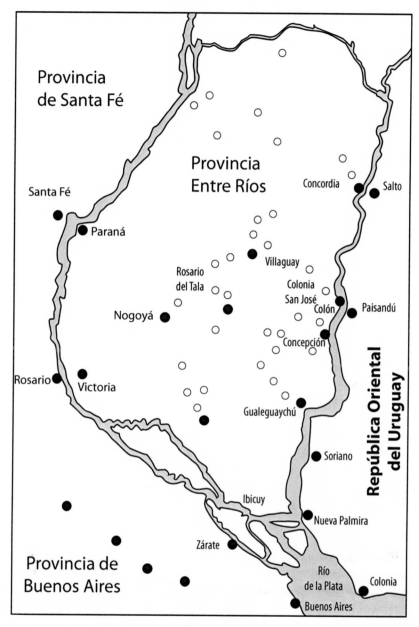

Provincia
de Santa Fé

Provincia
Entre Ríos

Provincia de
Buenos Aires

República Oriental
del Uruguay

Santa Fé
Paraná
Rosario
Victoria
Nogoyá
Rosario
del Tala
Villaguay
Colonia
San José
Colón
Concepción
Gualeguaychú
Concordia
Salto
Paisandú
Soriano
Ibicuy
Nueva Palmira
Zárate
Río
de la Plata
Colonia
Buenos Aires

References

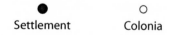

Settlement   Colonia

Map of colonias *in Entre Ríos in 1905 (modified from* Nuestros abuelos los pioneros: Colonos
europeos en la costa del Río Uruguay *[San José, Entre Ríos: Museo Histórico Regional de la
Colonia San José, 1999])*.

they could, somehow [they] crossed the river, and after they were here, there were no more problems. These people lived, got married, died, [had] children here without ever having it [documentation].

But the Jews from the tsarist Russian Empire were the largest organized migration during this period. Despite the image of the Jewish gauchos popularized by Gerchunoff, spontaneous individual migrations also occurred. Many arrived without proper documentation and then worked to support the immigration of family members. Some went to Brazil first. They did not all have a farm assigned to them upon arrival; many suffered long ordeals and ended up practicing agriculture as employees of established farmers. An elderly woman remembers her parents' immigrant career:

> They went to Brazil, to Rio Grande do Sul. They were in Brazil, worked a year with the coffee, harvested coffee; they didn't like Brazil because it's very hot there! They had come from very cold areas, so they didn't like the heat and came to Argentina . . . There were people in Brazil who knew Argentina; there were a lot of Poles . . . Dad and Mom knew Russian, Polish, and Portuguese, which they learned to speak there . . . They didn't know any Spanish, absolutely none! So speaking the language that was understood by the people there, those who worked there, they would communicate with each other and say: Oh! You have to go to Argentina, in Argentina there's a lot of work, a lot of harvest, the people are very different from here, they plant a lot of good wheat. They came, Dad worked in the harvests . . . because they said that here in Entre Ríos was the most planted part and since they were accustomed to these things, to farm work, they came directly to Clara.[42] Dad made ends meet at the railroad at first . . . he didn't like the railroad work, so he met a man here who was Jewish, I don't remember the last name . . . he was Jewish, so he gave him work on the farm . . . He worked on the farm, plowing and planting.

But it was the organized Jewish migration, the last such migration to Entre Ríos during the nineteenth century, that contributes most to our understanding of Villa Clara's social history. These immigrants shared three major preoccupations with their predecessors: access to land, education for their children, and freedom in religious practice. As Héctor Guionet (2001: 129), a descendant of the Swiss migration, put it: "Their language was the same as the pioneers' [in San José]: bread, peace, work, freedom. To be able to practice and educate their children in their own religion." Like the other immigrants, the Jews made special efforts to adapt to the new society while maintaining their traditions and understood early that adaptation is always a two-way street. Guionet illustrates:

Passport of Reisla Glatt from Kolomyi (Poland) with entry in Argentina in 1926.

The adaptation to the environment is rich in anecdotes: among them, one experienced by a teacher, around 1927, when classes were held on Saturdays. The farmers' children were not attending, and so the inspector was putting pressure on the teacher, Miss Teresa Maxit. To hold classes on Shabbat? Absolutely impossible! But then Teresa's imagination came up with a proposal. She suggested to the parents that on Saturday, after the service, they would come just to talk. With goodwill on both sides, they finally agreed that on Saturday the children would not come into the classrooms to do work, but under the shade of the trees they would freely read and talk about Argentine history and geography, each one bringing his own chair. (Guionet 2001: 132)

Despite these similarities, the experience of the last organized wave of immigrants was very different from that of others due to the Jewish people's history. If they shared with other European immigrants the attraction of Argentina in pursuit of a better quality of life, they were leaving for reasons of sheer physical survival. In 1791 the same Catherine II who had lured Germans to Russia had decreed the establishment of a Residence Zone for Jews, known as the Pale of Settlement, where all Jews born in Russia, Ukraine, Poland, Lithuania, Romania, Bessarabia, and Podolia (then under the Russian Empire) were interned. Their concentrated settlement magnified the destructiveness of pogroms, the impact of long military draft obligations on family life, and the restrictions on the household economy. Emigration was construed as a need, rather than as a choice, to escape genocide, occupational proscriptions, residential segregation, and long military drafts. The narrative of a survivor's descendant vividly illustrates the ordeals:

> They hid a few aunts, for example, under piles of straw, so that the Cossacks wouldn't find them, and she would say that she could feel the weight of the boots of the guys who were walking over her.

Unlike other organized migrations, whose members were experienced farmers in their countries of origin, most of the Jewish immigrants had never practiced farming, given the prohibitions in the Pale of Settlement. Another difference was the possibility of return. While other organized migrations maintained transnational connections in the event that their move proved unsuccessful or visited family and friends or returned seasonally to participate in harvests, immigration was forever for Jews, since their passports were granted on the condition of permanent exit. By contrast, approximately half of the Italians and Spaniards voluntarily returned to their home countries between 1861 and 1920, and Belgians traveled frequently between Argentina and the home country (Devoto 2003). Though the information was scant in comparison to the narratives of other immigrant groups, a few people told of correspondence with those who stayed behind. An elderly man remembered how his maternal grandfather, who arrived in Argentina late in life, looked forward to letters from his village that kept him abreast of "little things from everyday life, like the cow who had calves." In rare cases, immigrants also nurtured a dream of return, like the woman who remembered her mother repeating throughout her life: "I want to go to die in Lithuania."

After a particularly virulent pogrom, major Jewish organizations in Europe frantically attempted to find solutions for the Jews in the Pale. Private philanthropists supported various causes,[43] but it was Baron Maurice de Hirsch who attempted to address his co-religionists' misery permanently. The baron was born in 1831 in Munich, Germany.[44] He and his wife, Clara, were among the wealthy Jewish bankers in nineteenth-century Europe.[45] Hirsch had expanded the family's wealth through investments in railroads, copper mining, and sugar. He was also a well-known philanthropist, who donated significant amounts of money for good causes: for instance, he helped the Alliance Israélite Universelle establish schools for Jews in Turkey in 1873 and build hospitals for Turkish and Russian soldiers during the Russian-Turkish war of 1878. When their only son, Lucien, died in 1887, the Hirsches decided to donate a substantial portion of their fortune to persecuted Russian Jews. In the baron's own words: "I have lost a son but not my heir, because henceforth all humanity will be my heir" (quoted in Frischer 2002: 207). His first effort was to improve the Jews' education and vocational training in Russia, as a strategy leading to better employment opportunities. When the tsar accepted his funding without founding the elementary, technical, and professional schools as well as experimental farms that it was destined for, the baron opted to promote a grandiose emigration program for the three and a half million Jews from Russia and other Eastern European countries.

Three concepts coalesced in this Herculean program: belief, capital, and ideology. The baron was confident in the Russian Jews' ability to establish agricultural colonies. He optimistically believed that the agricultural practices of old Jewish colonies that he had personally observed during his long sojourns in Turkey carried over the experiences of the first Jews in Palestine. If the Jews were provided access to land, he reasoned, they would revert to their original ways of making a living: they would "return to agriculture" and become useful citizens of free countries. Thus in this formulation Jews were assumed to have a natural proclivity for agriculture, as an innate or genetic trait with more weight than the availability of fertile lands or the processes to make them productive. Based on that profound belief, the baron donated a large part of his extensive wealth toward the founding of the Jewish Colonization Association (JCA) in 1891 with headquarters in London,[46] funding the Alliance Israélite Universelle in Paris to provide educational support and intermediaries to secure passports and select the families in Russia for the organized migration.[47] His philanthropy was far from charity: he expected to help only those who helped themselves.[48]

On August 24, 1891, Baron de Hirsch made public the constitution of the JCA. Its initial capital resource amounted to two million pounds sterling, divided into 20,000 shares, 19,900 of which were controlled by the baron.[49] Article 3 of its statutes clarifies the JCA's mission:

> Facilitate and promote the emigration of Israelites from countries of Europe and Asia, where they are restricted by special laws and deprived of political rights, to regions of the world where they could enjoy these and other human rights. To that effect, the Association proposes to establish agricultural colonies in various regions of North and South America, as well as other regions.[50] (cited in Gutkowski 1991: 55)

Other statutes specified the institutional commitment to found agricultural colonies on good-quality land, to be distributed among families selected in their country of origin and, it was hoped, instructed in agriculture before departure. The trip was to be financed by the immigrant, but JCA would cover the costs if necessary. Long-term payment schedules at low interest rates were worked out to pay for the land, tools, and animals necessary for the practice of agriculture. Colonies were founded in Canada, Brazil and Argentina, and the United States.[51]

Enrique Dickman, one of the first immigrants,[52] provides testimony about the first contingent that left for Argentina. The JCA had opened a registry in 1890 in Constantinople for those interested in that destination of the colonization program. Five thousand persons signed up. Many were refugees who had been thwarted in their attempt to reach Palestine through Turkey. Several months later, seven hundred and fifty registered persons were selected and given a free ticket and some pocket money to travel from Istanbul to Marseille and then on to Bordeaux by train. The French ship *Pampa* departed from Bordeaux, after the immigrants were offered a respite in the castle of Baron Nathanaël de Rothschild. The ship also picked up Spanish and Italian immigrants in Genoa and Barcelona and crossed the Atlantic with three thousand persons. In 1891 the JCA signed a contract with the Argentine government, which stipulated the sale of land, tax-free for ten years. In 1892, a year after its founding, the Argentine government (then under the presidency of Julio Roca) granted the Jewish Colonization Association legal status and recognized its philanthropic nature.[53] In that same year the JCA had already bought a large expanse of land from Jacobo Spangenberg (later to be the name of one of the subdivisions of Colonia Clara).

The JCA would eventually own 617,658 hectares in Argentina, distributed in five provinces, and administer a sizable capital.[54] When the baron died in 1896, without having set foot in America, his wife, Clara, donated an additional one-third of her inheritance to the JCA.

Several explanations have been advanced for the emigration of Eastern European Jews to Argentina under the aegis of the JCA. One explanation refers to a conversation held in Paris in 1881 between the baron and President Roca's appointed agent of immigration, José M. Bustos, to confirm Argentine's support for steering this population to emigrate to the underpopulated pampas. Another explanation maintains that it was the intervention of Dr. Wilhelm Loewenthal, a Romanian physician on a public health mission for the Argentine government, that helped the baron make up his mind. During an exploratory mission, Dr. Loewenthal had found a group of Russian Jews in the province of Santa Fé, eking out a living close to a train station. The contingent had decided to emigrate from Kamenetz Podolsk (Ukraine) in 1887, originally to Palestine and then to Argentina, in order to escape the pogroms. When 836 persons of 120 families (Muchinik and Isuz de Schulman n.d.a) arrived in Buenos Aires harbor in 1889 on board the SS *Wesser*, they found no signs of the land they had been promised. An agent who had charged them exorbitant prices to emigrate (referring to the rumors that the baron was starting a relief effort in Argentina) had tricked them. A landowner in the province of Santa Fé, Pedro Palacios, eventu-

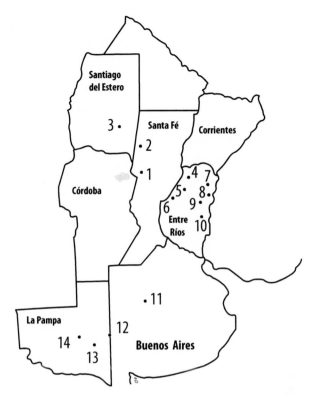

1: Moisesville; 2: Montefiore; 3: Dora; 4: Avigdor; 5: Leonardo Cohen;
6: Louis Ongre; 7: Santa Isabel; 8: San Antonio; 9: Clara; 10: Lucienville;
11: Mauricio; 12: Barón de Hirsch; 13: Narcise Leven; 14: El Escabel.

Map of the JCA colonias in Argentina.

ally sold them land, but they had no means of transportation. A descendant described their plight:

> They arrived in Palacios, just a rudimentary stopover. They did not find what they were promised there either. Destiny continued to play with their miserable lives. They had to camp next to the railroad tracks, in the middle of a desolate area, not knowing where to go, whom to ask for help, not able to go back, drowning in this immense land with no borders, where they had been abandoned to their bad luck. (Kreimer 1984: 5)

Forced to huddle in abandoned train cars, these unfortunate people were suffering from a typhus epidemic when discovered by Dr. Wilhem Loewenthal, who reported their poverty, high infant mortality rates, and lack of future prospects to the Argentine Ministry of Foreign Affairs and sent a proposal to settle them under an agricultural colonization program to Rabbi Zadoc Kahn in Paris. Kahn submitted it to the baron, who bought the land from its owner, Palacios.[55] There he founded the first organized Jewish immigrant settlement in Argentina, Moisesville, in 1889.[56] This historic epic has been glorified as proof of Jewish aptitude for agriculture and courage to withstand any difficulty in pursuit of freedom.

Bread and freedom have been two central themes recurring in both historical accounts and personal testimonies of immigration to Argentina regardless of national origin since at least the last third of the nineteenth century and even after World War II.[57] The Jews arrived in Argentina with the same desire for economic opportunity as other immigrants but with additional urgency. Their resettlement in a strange land was a matter of physical as well as religious survival, central to their identity as a people.

Chapter Three

COLONIA CLARA AND THE EMERGENCE OF THE "JEWISH GAUCHOS" (1892–1902)

I plowed the fields with my brother, led the harvester, and took care of the cattle. The cowherd [boyero], an old soldier of Urquiza, perfected my art of horseback riding and started me in the use of the lasso and the boleadoras.[1] *Like all youngsters in the* colonia, *I had the look of a gaucho. I dressed in a wide* bombacha,[2] *a wide-winged* chambergo,[3] *and boots with a jingling spur. The lasso with a shining ring hung from my saddle, and the boleadoras hung from my waist next to the horse. (Gerchunoff 1973: 25)*

This is the phenomenon: the children of the Israelites . . . are almost chauvinistic and even the oldest, those born in Odessa or Warsaw, are profoundly patriotic, they are deeply and sincerely Argentine. (Gerchunoff 1973: 35)

Colonia Clara was very progressive because there was a lot of work . . . There was work for everybody! . . . The Republic was made on horseback . . . the gringos, the criollos, there were no machines or anything. (criollo *informant*)

The Jewish immigrant settled in rural areas upon arrival in Argentina: 64 percent of the total Jewish population of Argentina lived in Entre Ríos in 1895 (Elkin 1978), and Jews continued to be in the majority until the early 1940s.[4] Colonia Clara and Colonia San Antonio, the first Jewish agricultural colonies in Entre Ríos, added 102,671 hectares to the JCA in 1892. While San Antonio specialized in fruits, dairy, and poultry, Clara concentrated on farming and cattle raising. A focus on Clara crystallizes larger contexts: events in Europe leading to the emigration of the Jews, the evolution of a philanthropic association created to help them, and the political economy of an Argentine province.

The history of the JCA needs to be understood within the two opposing alternatives open to those who decided to emigrate from the Pale of Settlement: the Zionist ideal promoted the return to the homeland, Israel, while Baron de Hirsch maintained that Jews could become agriculturalists anywhere and funded agricultural colonies in the Americas. The baron embraced the liberal Argentine discourse that promoted immigration and a reordering of social control over the major commodity (land) by large landowners. Immigrant colonization policies devised by the state and their implementation by colonization agencies such as the JCA were two of many factors that favored the immigrants' access to land, yet they changed little in helping the newcomers assert ownership. The state also downplayed the effects of land sales to accommodate the new immigrants, which further marginalized the *criollos*. In addition, concomitant with the state approval for JCA settlements,[5] the Argentine elites voiced opposition to renewed immigration after the global economic crisis of the 1890s. This was the political climate in Argentina that Baron de Hirsch's colonization program confronted as his association began settling the immigrants.[6]

Settling in Colonia Clara: From Shtetl to Pampas

By 1891 the JCA had purchased the Sociedad Anónima La Argentina (close to the railroad station of Domínguez), an unsuccessful colonization company devised for Western Europeans.[7] By 1892 the JCA had bought additional land from Jacobo Spangenberg and David Viñas (Estancia Los Naranjos, where the Colonia Balvanera had been established by the colonizing company La Agricultora). This colony had 459 inhabitants, a mix of immigrants (reported by country—Spain, France, Belgium, Holland, Luxembourg, Poland, Italy, Austria, United States—or region of birth—Alsatian, Flemish, Tyrol—or holding double nationality—Russian Germans) and Argentines (*Segundo censo nacional* [1895] n.d.).

Colonia Clara was founded on that land in 1892 in honor of the baron's wife, Clara Bischoffsheim. The largest of the JCA *colonias* in Entre Ríos (80,265 hectares), Colonia Clara was located mostly in the Department of Villaguay,

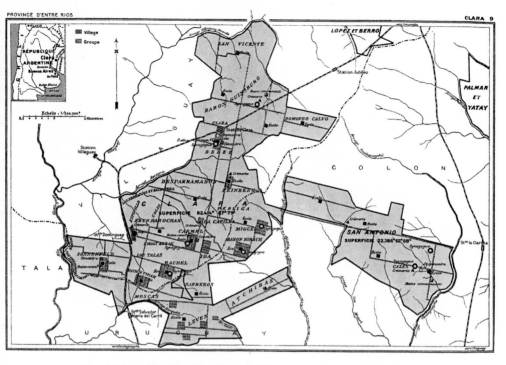

Map of Colonia Clara (modified from Atlas des colonies et domaines de la Jewish
Colonization Association en République Argentine et au Brésil
[Paris: Jewish Colonization Association, 1914]).

although its southern portion fell within the Department of Uruguay. Two railroad stations (Domínguez and Clara) and a small urban center (La Capilla)
would be located in the *colonia* within a few years.

The first JCA contingent (225 persons) to be settled in Colonia Clara arrived
in 1891 in Buenos Aires aboard the ship *Pampa* and, after an intermediate stay
in Mar del Sud (Armony 1998), was settled close to Domínguez and La Capilla. The second contingent was settled in Bélez, Feinberg, and Sonnenfeld.
The third contingent, with 150 persons, was settled in Perliza and Desparramados. Additional contingents continued arriving; by 1896, when the school and
the sanitation system were organized, 545 persons had been settled in Colonia
Clara. Although there were frequent busts and booms, population size clearly
increased, mounting to 743 persons by 1912.

Miguel Muchinik and Ida Isuz de Schulman (n.d.a) describe the first arrivals
in Colonia Clara very colorfully. Once the immigrants arrived in Buenos Aires
harbor, they were lodged in the Hotel de Inmigrantes, taken by ship to the harbor of Concepción del Uruguay, and then taken by train to Domínguez, the last

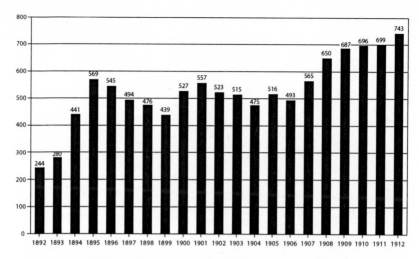

Population size in Colonia Clara: 1892–1912 (modified from Atlas des colonies et domaines de la Jewish Colonization Association en République Argentine et au Brésil [Paris: Jewish Colonization Association, 1914]).

stop on the Basavilbaso-Concordia line, which was under construction at the time. Finally, carts took the immigrants to their assigned lots (*chacras*),[8] where their houses were lined up in concentrated settlements or groups (*grupos*).[9] According to a descendant of one of the pioneers, the immigrants were located in concentrated settlements "because they were afraid of the pogroms and the attacks they had lived through, so as a means of defense they were all placed together just in case." The groups in Colonia Clara had names with diverse origins: some referred to the prevalence of a plant or an insect in the natural environment (Achiras and Las Moscas [literally flies], respectively); some honored a prominent Argentine figure or landowner (Domingo Calvo, San Vicente, Barreros); others memorialized the founder or supporters of the JCA (Barón Hirsch, Barón Guinzburg, Leven, Sonnenfeld, Feinberg); some used Hebrew names (Eben Haroscha, Kiriath Arba, Rosh Pina, Rajil); one group used the distorted name of a Russian village devastated by a pogrom (Bels). An elderly woman, the child of a settler, illustrated how the new immigrants found themselves in a geopolitical space occupied by Argentine landowners and earlier immigrants and were automatically articulated into an existing social structure that they knew nothing about:

> There were a lot of farms around here; all the land that Baron de Hirsch bought belonged to landowners. For this reason, a *colonia* was called Spangenberg because there was an *estancia* owned by the Spangenberg family,

which was a very old family from the time of Urquiza. The *colonia* that's farther, which was colonized by descendants of Belgians and Italians, which is called La Rosada, was the farm which belonged to Cipriano Urquiza, one of the sons of General Urquiza . . . The *colonia* San Vicente, it's called San Vicente because there was an *estancia* called San Vicente, the *colonia* Sandoval because there was a family where the owner of the *estancia* was Sandoval.

All groups followed a similar plan: the houses, a synagogue, and a school were built close together, while the fields were dispersed. But there were important differences among the groups. The largest group, Villa Domínguez, boasted a hospital as early as 1904. La Capilla, which became an important economic center, built a library and a community center. Some groups diversified their economy and monopolized an industry: the Feinberg group, for example, started selling milk to the Creamery Kleinman & Co. as early as 1905 (Muchinik and Isuz de Schulman n.d.a).

As they were settled in a group, the immigrants were allotted working fields, some land next to the house, housing, plows, oxen, and perhaps a cow to provide milk. Often the immigrants were first housed in tents upon arriving at their final destination, since their permanent houses were still under construction. All alike, the houses were made of brick and mud, with a slanted straw roof and a gallery. The few children and grandchildren of the original settlers in Villa Clara who had remained in the area remembered the small planned settlements of identical houses. Each family was given between 100 and 150 hectares of land to cultivate. Some *colonos* were fortunate enough to have been given land next to their house; for most, the working fields were a substantial distance away. The immigrants were trained to practice agriculture: they planted cereals such as wheat, maize (corn), barley, flax, rice, oats, and alfalfa.[10] Agricultural productivity varied in relation to natural and market forces and peaked in the early 1900s, probably due to the improved transportation provided by the railroad.

To a greater extent than in other colonies, the farmers of Colonia Clara experimented with the poultry and dairy industries and, in the course of time, with cattle raising.

In spite of the hard work, however, "the immigrants did not neglect spiritual and cultural life. Almost immediately, they started to build synagogues, social clubs, libraries, and schools" (Muchinik and Isuz de Schulman n.d.a: 3). Dr. Noé Yarcho, a physician assigned to the colony, resided in its epicenter, Domínguez. When he fell ill, the JCA sent a replacement, Dr. Jorge Wolcomich.

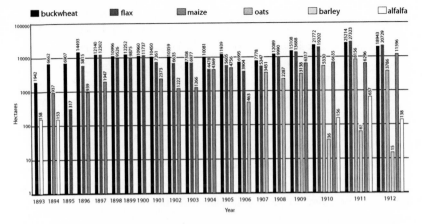

Cultivated areas in Colonia Clara by cereal in hectares, 1893–1912 (modified from Atlas des colonies et domaines de la Jewish Colonization Association en République Argentine et au Brésil *[Paris: Jewish Colonization Association, 1914]*).

Villa Clara's Region of Influence: Bélez, La Capilla, and San Jorge

Before making its appearance in the multicultural landscape of Colonia Clara, the future Villa Clara could be visualized as human settlements interconnected by the circulation of people, goods, and services. Within this region of influence, the largest human settlements in the vicinity of the contemporary Villa Clara were Bélez and La Capilla (established by Jewish immigrants), Colonia La Rosada (with a preponderance of Belgian and Italian immigrants), and the larger Colonia San Jorge (where the majority of the population was of Swiss and French national extraction). But Villa Clara's region of influence included a myriad of other settlements: the ones most often mentioned by the people I interviewed were San Vicente, Bergara Norte, Barón Guinzburg, San Ernesto, La Jerónima, Espíndola, Sagastume, Santa Rosa, San Antonio, Pueblo Cazés, and Jubileo.

BÉLEZ

One of the first groups founded in 1892 in Colonia Clara was given the name Bélez (a distortion of Bels) to memorialize the Russian village destroyed by a major pogrom. Seventy families were housed on both sides of the road (thirty-five on the right and thirty-five on the left) on farms of 7 hectares each. The working fields, ranging from 100 to 150 hectares, were located at variable distances from the living area. Bélez, the closest human settlement to Villa Clara, was inhabited

Threshing machine and harvest in 1927.

Horse-drawn plough.

by the first families honored by the local historians for their pioneer role in the Jewish immigration as well as for their participation in the first civic and social institutions.[11] One of them recalls that "the first immigrants to this area were my husband's grandparents; my father-in-law was twelve years old at the time. So there is experience from a long time."

Three alternative paths led to arrival in Bélez: original selection by the JCA in Europe; independent immigration, supported in most cases by social connections; and sponsorship by already established immigrants, who "called for" or defrayed the transportation costs of their relatives. In the second case, the new arrivals would approach the JCA to obtain colonization rights. These three patterns might coexist in one extended family.

Regardless of their mode of arrival, the new immigrants needed to be instructed in agricultural work on site. According to the now elderly child of an initial settler, Bélez "was like a camp to train the people. They were all immigrants, and most of them totally ignorant of rural tasks." Agriculture—the occupation the immigrants had contracted to practice—influenced the division of labor by sex and thus the social organization of the settlements. Here is a glorified description of an edenic communal life:

> Remembering the times of harvest is a special thing. As soon as the first rays of sun came up, the strong *colonos* and their oldest sons went to the fields to accomplish the hard tasks of thrashing, collecting, classifying, and transporting the produce to the barns. The mothers stayed home with their daughters, taking care of housework and preparing the meals, which we ourselves would take to the fields on foot, sometimes in a sulky, sometimes on horseback. We still had time to tend the garden, with its flowers, different by the season, the red roses, the geraniums and lilacs, pansies and jasmine, and decorate the yard. And we would also work in the orchards, those started by our grandparents, where the melons, watermelons, cucumbers, and pumpkins required extra work, since they were the primary food for the whole season. I will never forget the huge containers that were filled with cucumbers and watermelons and salted so they would keep until the winter. (Friedlander 1953: 15)

While men were expected to practice agriculture and women to fulfill housekeeping roles, everybody tried to diversify the family economy to make ends meet. Women often sewed for their family and for profit; men combined farming with other trades; young boys were sent to take food to the fields on horseback.

Jewish immigrants are often depicted as a homogeneous ethnic group, due to their immigration history and cultural characteristics such as religious affiliation and pervasive use of the Yiddish language. In fact, the Jewish immigrants

COLONIA BELEZ, Villa Clara - Entre Rios - R.Argentina

))) COLONIZADA MES ENERO L 8 9 2 (((

I - RESNIK, Jacobo (Enfermero)		24 - Comisaria (Hermela)- MUCHNIK, Iekil
2 - PALEY , Akiva		25 - GUENSELMAN...... / Reiguelman J.
3 - LEW , José		26 - MASS, Jacobo
4 - LEW , Motje		27- LEICACH, Gregorio / Isaac.
5 & KUSNAROFF,Jaim Itze		28- POVER, Mote
6 - BACOFF , Isrul/ Manuel		29 - MASS , Saúl
7 - KORACH , Herch		30 - GRABOIS, Samuel / Manuel
8 - GOLOMB , Aisik		31 - MASS, Abraham - Note
IO & COSTIANOVSKY, Chaie		33 - ESCUELA NACIONAL(Isher-Levi-Jofré-Nixil-Diaz)
II - LEIDERMAN, Iosil /Fridman,Manuel		34 -SINAGOGA:1892/912 .- 1912/72-Ieshiva 9o8/I3.-
12 - COSTIANOVSKY,Meirl./ Aarón		35 - COSTIANOVSKY, Schaie
I3 - COSTIANOVSKY, José		36 - SIJANOVICH, Jacobo
I4 - DIKENSTEIN, Abraham		37 - NAJEMSON,Rajmil/Jaime / Boris
I5 - GOLBERG, Abraham / Julio		38 - SIJANOVICH, Schulem / Simón
I6- HELLMAN, ...,/ TUBER Isaac L.		39 - SCHIJANOVICH, León
I7- YOGUEL,Abraham / Manuel		40 - SCHIRULSKY, Reful
I8- SCHULMAN, Jaime		4I - ANAPOLSKY, Ionte .
20- GAMIN, Jaim Leizer		42 - YOGUEL , Note Meir
2I_ SCHULMAN , Efroim - José		43 - KORACH, Gregorio (43)
22- Subovsky , Reisil		44 - PORTNOY, Meir — GOLONITZKY Efroim (44)
23- Arcavi		45 - TOU, Simón (Silla transa.lories) (45)
		46 - TOLCHINSKY, Oyer (46)
		47 - SUBOVSKY, - - KRAVETZ,Abe . (47)
		48 - DIKENSTEIN, Julio (48)

La Jewish Colonizattión Asociattión (I.K.A.) poseía en la provincia Entre Rios un total de /// 193.730 hectarías de campos.- En Villa Clara y alrededores 8.265.- hectarias.-

importante aclarar que nuestros antepasados,sustentaban de vivir agrupados en Colonias,por las siguientes razones: I) Fué hábito durante un siglo en Rusia de vivir en sociabilidad entre vecinos- Facilitaba la ayuda mutua yel auxilio solidario en caso de emergencia de cualquier tipo.- 3)Otorgar mayor seguridad a los colonos.- 4) La mayor cercanía a la Escuela y la Sinagoga permitía su asistencia aún en días lluviosos.- ///- Naturalmente,eran razones poderosas contra la oposición de / I.K.A. a buscar el trabajo más intenso de los campos,al estar cada uno radicado en su propia chacra.-

V:lla Clara - Marzo/ 89.- Eufemio Schulman

List of the first colonos in Colonia Bélez, prepared by Eufemio Schulman in 1929.

were quite diverse in terms of national origin, social class, occupational background, and degree of religious observance. The necessities of assimilating to the new setting pressured them to obliterate or soften these differences in pursuit of both individual and collective goals, as B. Sijanovich de Friedlander, who was born and raised in Bélez, tells us:

The *colonia* is a *mishpuje*.[12] Even the gauchos know of our friendship. Since we are a diverse idiosyncrasy, we can only live in peace by blending with one another. (Friedlander 1953: 15)

Solidarity also proved to be a defense mechanism against social isolation. The few *colonos* staying put a decade later shared baking ovens, farm tools, and rides to commercial centers. A man who grew up in Bélez enthusiastically described what it looked like during his childhood as he drove my students and I through what remained of the settlement. It was a sunny Sunday afternoon, but his voice was gray with sadness as he recollected details of people and places of a past that included his own:

Our *colonia* begins here. Matskin lived here, a tall man, very tall. There was a soap factory here, they would gather animal fat from all the butchers in the area and would make soap. All the *colonos* were here ... They were all concentrated because they lived in the *colonia* ... Ladies, you can't imagine Sunday afternoons, it was a crowd! Miguel Man lived here. This was called Colonia Bélez. Here we had the school up until third grade and here, in front where the tree is, stood the Hebrew school. I went very rarely. There was a synagogue here, remember that photo I showed you? It had two floors, wonderful! They should've left it as a relic. They demolished it and sent the money to Israel. A lady [named] Friedman lived here and was widowed with small children.

Daily life in Bélez was predictable, traditions were observed, and the interests of the community predominated over individual needs, according to the childhood recollections of a nostalgic woman:

How lovely was my adored *colonia!* Two lines of houses, about two kilometers long, with their wonderful plantations! Those famous and well perfumed *paraísos*, alternating with impressive *álamos*,[13] loyal guardians, tall and straight: as if they were a symbol for these saintly inhabitants, because that is how they lived their lives, like that of those trees, straight, noble, their vertical road toward the sky unencumbered by winds or storms. Their houses separated about fifty meters from one another ... they were like a large family, where everybody served and helped each other ... I still remember that symbolic door they had at the entrance to the *colonia*. To maintain the tradition, they exited through that door if traveling on Saturday. After a week of hard work in the fields, everybody yearned for Saturday—the day of rest—and, with their best and more luxurious clothes, they congregated in the synagogue, where they thanked God profusely for giving them their daily bread and then moved on to wonderful and friendly conversation. As they returned home from the synagogue, following those hereditary traditions of many generations ago, the mothers took good-smelling dishes out of the ovens . . . , which were truly delicious. Everything was eaten after the benedictions [*brujes*] with the silver [*bejer*] and the braided bread [*coilich*], which the crafty hands of the mothers decorated even with "little birds," made with the same dough to please the little ones. (Friedlander 1953: 12–13)

Daily life in Bélez was remembered with pride and nostalgia, though culture shock and miscommunication were not uncommon, as two descendants tell us:

My mother admired the floors at her mother-in-law's. They were nice and very smooth. She asked her what she was doing to have floors like that. So she said . . . you had to collect cow manure mixed with dirt and hay and you had to spread it with your hands to form a hard and even surface.

In Bélez next to my grandparents' house there was the engineer's tent. An aunt of ours told us that they were teaching her how to speak English . . . and at the same time the natives were teaching her how to speak Spanish.

The JCA had established schools that complied with the Argentine curriculum and taught the Hebrew language and Jewish culture. Despite the unpredictable absences when children could not attend—during inclement weather, harvest times, or religious holidays—the school was among the institutions that helped immigrants assimilate to regional culture and national history and nurtured the immigrants' dream for a different future for their children:

Remembering our lovely and loved school in Bélez, hidden between trees that provided shade during recess, I evoke the first and very dedicated teachers, promoters of civilization. Among them, the Cohen family.[14] (Friedlander 1953: 16)

What a beautiful image I have of that May 25 of 1910, centennial of our [Argentine] independence, when from early morning that long avenue was dressed up as the schools of *colonias* Perliza, Miguel, Espíndola, etc., paraded. They had to go through [Bélez] to concentrate in the village of Clara, as they sang: "One hundred years ago, sublime history . . . French, Berutti, and Saavedra, organized the victory." (Friedlander 1953: 17)

Impossible to forget the school, our beloved school which has given us the best teachers, whom we will never forget . . . they would most surely be happy to know their alumni are now men who serve the homeland, as physicians, lawyers, engineers, industrialists, businessmen, all good and hard-working men. (Aronson 1953: 25–26)

In addition to education, the JCA had also planned to meet health care needs. While schools were built in each of the *colonia*'s settlements, however, only one physician was stationed in the largest one, forcing the residents of Bélez to rely on traditional medicine:

Medical care was out of reach since the only physician in those times was Dr. Noé Yarcho, who lived in nearby Domínguez. For first aid help we used the elementary concepts given to us by the *felser* Resnik,[15] a nice and efficient person who alleviated pains and took care of accidents. I remember the quiet and efficient role played for many years by grandmother Heine Costianovsky. Without any pay, day and night, walking in the mud, the stones, tumbling and getting up again, always covered by her shawl and giving up her rest, she ran to take care of our wailing mothers not only for deliveries but also to calm any pain. Using her proven concoction of *lapacho* [a local tree] roots, she calmed those acute tooth pains, commonly suffered by pregnant women due to lack of calcium. After our infancy, the lack of medical attention was overcome thanks to the coming of our well-remembered friend Dr. Jorge Wolcomich, who fortunately settled in Villa Clara. With his intelligent partner, Mrs. Olga, they took care of many problem deliveries, saving mothers and children, due to their long years of study and practice. How many times the doctor visited all his patients in his *volanta* [horse-drawn cart], driven by his loyal chauffeur Florentino in the midst of rain or mud, storms or suffocating heat! (Friedlander 1953: 15–16)

In accordance with Jewish tradition, a cemetery and a *mikveh* were among the first requirements for a new Jewish settlement.[16] A cemetery opened in Bélez in 1892, the year of its establishment.

Ingeniero Sajaroff (Formerly La Capilla)

La Capilla (the chapel) took its name from a small church built at the site before the JCA settled immigrants there. This name has continued to be used in the region even after governor Ricardo Favre renamed the village Ingeniero Sajaroff in 1968 to honor the memory of the cooperativist leader.[17] Founded in 1892 with 100 families, it had only reached 390 residents by 2000, its economy having declined after the railroad was built too far away. Driving through this somnolent village today, it is hard to imagine a thriving immigrant settlement during the late 1890s. Yet the village housed the first branch of the Cooperativa Fondo

Comunal, which stored the farmers' harvests in its barns, and had a plethora of businesses (including general stores, a factory that made sulkies and carts, a creamery, and a slaughterhouse) and a variety of services (hospital, pharmacies, electrical plant, telegraph, civil registry).[18] A social club, a synagogue, and a library opened soon after the *colonos* were settled. An enthusiastic settler who drove me by the places where these buildings once stood nurtured an image of a vibrant and meaningful past:

> Capilla was one of the most important early settlements, more important than Domínguez and Villa Clara. The first civil registry opened here. There was a cooperative meat store. Imagine what the school was at this time! Imagine that each window [he points to a run-down and abandoned building] was a classroom, imagine the number of kids! The Historical Circuit remodeled the synagogue recently because there are practically no Jews left here.[19] The creamery operated under these palm trees. Look! You can still see a container there!

And one of the lay historians in the area, Miguel Muchinik, expands on what made the village stand out during those early times:

> It had a flour mill where one could barter wheat or flour that produced thirty-two bags of ninety kg daily. It had a community center, a library, and the first press in the area, which printed *El Colono Cooperador* [The Cooperative Colonist], the newspaper of the Fondo Comunal. (Muchinik and Isuz de Schulman n.d.a: 8)

SAN JORGE

Ten kilometers away from Bélez, San Jorge was a settlement with 150 inhabitants. The population was ethnically more diverse, with a mix of *criollos* and descendants of the Swiss contingent brought by Urquiza in the 1850s. More urbanized than either Capilla or Bélez, San Jorge hosted many businesses and institutions, though, as in the other settlements, its main industry was agriculture. My Swiss-descended landlady in Villa Clara, who was brought up in that area, recalls how her whole family worked on a farm. Although only 100 hectares in size, it seemed to produce large enough harvests to feed them all, something she claims could not happen nowadays.

As a politically recognized center with a mayor and a police station, San Jorge must have attracted enough attention from the residents of the nearby settlements of Bélez and Capilla to have them request the opening of a road to link San Jorge to La Capilla with an additional link to Bélez. Other testimonies attest to the interconnectedness of the three settlements through trade and education. San Jorge had a meat store, five general stores, and a blacksmith workshop. Adult education was provided during the evenings at the school where many of the immigrants learned to read and write "and, why not say so, to talk" (Muchinik and Isuz de Schulman n.d.a: 7).

Colonia Clara as a Case Study of the JCA's Failure and Success

An examination of the workings of the JCA administration in Colonia Clara between 1891 (when the land was purchased) and 1973 (when the enterprise came to an end) provides a good test of the implementation of the organization's mission. The conditions were auspicious for a successful operation: a solid endowment and government support. Yet, as in Woodbine in the United States,[20] several factors conspired against the sustainable implementation of the original mission, as enunciated by the philanthropic baron: the organization's administration style; the natural, social, and political environment; and the immigrants' aspirations for personal advancement.

After Baron de Hirsch's death in 1896, according to many critics, the JCA transformed its original philanthropic motives into a commercial focus. If, in founding the association, the baron was engaging in salvage philanthropy of a population that was discriminated against and under constant danger, implementing the association's goal was a trial and error exercise, given the physical and cultural distances. Charged with making day-to-day decisions, the administrators expected complete loyalty from those favored by the philanthropic initiative and lost sight of the constraints of acculturation. As a critic of the JCA administration stated:

> It was one thing to plan the colonization from a comfortable desk in Paris and another to implement it . . . in the uncultivated fields of Entre Ríos. Besides, the first designated administrators did not speak Russian, the language spoken by the majority of the immigrants. (Borche 1987: 10)

The JCA related to the *colonos* through the intermediacy of the administrators. The JCA was run as a rigid bureaucracy that tied the administrators in a vertical hierarchy. The *colonia*'s administrator, who visited the fields to evaluate the life conditions of the settled families, was expected to report weekly to the national office in Argentina's capital, Buenos Aires, which in turn reported at more infrequent intervals to Paris headquarters. In many cases, these three tiers in the line of communication understood little of the political economy of the region and its connectedness to the nation. Several structural characteristics conspired against implementing the baron's goals. One was the distance that needed to be traversed to implement this hierarchical style of communication: given that mail was the only mode of communication and transportation was slow, it often took months for a local request to go from a local administrator to Buenos Aires, from there to Paris, and then back to Buenos Aires and the provincial *colonia*.

A review of the correspondence (mostly in French) of administrators in the *colonia*, the Buenos Aires office, and the Paris headquarters reveals that the JCA administration construed *colonias* as isolated settlements located in the middle of nowhere. Little attention was paid to the *colonia's* interdependence with its neighbors or the constraints on immigrants' incorporation into the regional and national society and culture. Very scant references were made in these extensive letters to the daily life of the settlers or their interactions with other populations.[21] Rather, the content of the letters reveals a narrow focus on the productivity of the settlements. In the case of Colonia Clara, the letters refer almost exclusively to rains, storms, droughts, fires, and locust plagues and their impacts on harvests, as well as to the prevalent market prices for commodities.

Critics of the JCA have alluded to the social personality of the administrators as a negative factor. One critic remarked on the "arrogance, inflexibility, even the sadism that characterized the treatment of *colonos* by local administrators, without any involvement of Buenos Aires Directors to change their behavior" (Avni 2005: 152). Conversely, some directors in the Buenos Aires office, like Samuel Hirsch and David Cazés, blamed the "insatiable" *colonos* for the company's crises and used this characterization as rhetoric in their opposition to the expansion of the colonization program. This "blaming the victim" attitude was replicated at the local level. For example, administrator Abraham Sidi interpreted a considerable exodus from Colonia Clara in 1910 as natural selection in the annual report to the JCA: "We should not worry too much about their situation: the real farmers know they have to be patient and we settle a good number of them each year" (cited in Avni 2005: 169).

An opposing ideology within the JCA administration was more benign in that it empathized with the new immigrants and advocated additional support for them. Curiously, the tendency was for the administrators closest to the *colonos* to be the hard-liners and for those at Paris headquarters to notice the harshness of the immigrants' lives that was minimized at the Buenos Aires national office. In 1910, for example, Nandor Sonnenfeld (son of the ex–general director of the JCA), who visited the colonies during the winter, noted:

In Lucienville and Clara I found a desolate panorama: large families overcrowding small rooms, kitchens, and barns, living in mud and straw huts, exposed to rain and wind, and thrown by promiscuity to an antihygienic and immoral situation. (cited in Avni 2005: 166)

This report also cited the exploitative practices of settled immigrants, who often overcharged newcomers for rent.

Conflicts between *colonos* and administrators erupted with reference to payments. Each *colono* had signed a contract of purchase, committing to pay for the land in installments over twenty years and to repay loans advanced for the house, animals, and agricultural tools at 5 percent interest. These arrangements generated conflict when the *colono* was unable to honor these commitments, as a man who experienced this situation as a child recalled:

> I remember when the administrator of the Yevich would come in a tattered sulky to collect five pesos. It was just after the harvest; he would collect five pesos as a contribution to the payment for the land. Sometimes there was not enough money and he would only collect three pesos and fifty cents. I remember, because I lived through it. Do not think that it was a gift, there was nothing for free. Baron de Hirsch brought people here and gave them land, but they had to pay for it.

Another source of conflict between *colonos* and administrators was the contrast in their backgrounds. According to a JCA critic, the administrators frequently had different national, class, and cultural backgrounds than the immigrants. Their ignorance of the life conditions and cultural background of the Russian immigrants often made them insensitive to the constraints the immigrants faced in the new land:

> The JCA colonies went through crises, and not only due to the natural catastrophes. A main cause was the background of the administrators—French, English, or German—who did not understand the idiosyncrasy of the Russian Jew. These administrators did not sympathize with Jews in general. They could not understand each other. They were ignorant of agrarian economy or colonization. (Hojman 1964: 208)

Adolfo Leibovich, first president of the Fondo Comunal and later JCA administrator, expanded on this view:

> It is fair to recognize that the JCA was not very successful in orienting the *colonos*. The administration's personnel in the *colonia* had various nationalities, English, French, and Swedish. This was the first contact in their life with Russian Jewish immigrants. They communicated with them through signs

and interpreters. There was even an English administrator who, unable to pronounce the last names of the *colonos*, gave each a number to identify them . . . It should not surprise anyone, then, that the result of an inept administration, indifferent to the misery of others, and a mass of embittered people that had wandered in the world for a long time was not harmony but chaos. A remedy needed to be found. (Leibovich 1965: 52)

The clash was minimized when administrators had more cultural affinity with the *colonos:*

It was only in the 1900s that the administrators were Russian Jews. They were interested in the prosperity and well-being of the *colono* and the progress of colonization. They . . . focused on the creation of agricultural cooperatives, social centers, and social institutions. Little by little, the *colonos* started getting the idea of the economic benefits of buying agricultural tools and consumer items and selling their produce collectively. (Hojman 1964: 207–208)

In addition, the cultural misunderstanding between the local administrators and those staffing the Buenos Aires offices also influenced the daily life of *colonos:*

The agents who controlled the JCA headquarters in Buenos Aires were of German and Sephardic backgrounds and did not provide constructive initiatives. They gave the local administrators final orders to collect debts, without analyzing whether the *colonos* could pay them. (Hojman 1964: 207)

A pioneer settler summarized the relationship between the JCA and the settlers:

The first ten years it [the JCA] was of help; the next ten, the relationship was deteriorating; the last ten, there was eviction. (M. Lieberman, a *colono* who arrived on the ship *Pampa*, cited in *Fondo Comunal* 1965: 196)

The unpredictable relationship of the *colonos* with the natural environment added to their vulnerability. Natural catastrophes such as locust plagues, torrential rains, droughts, or fires suddenly interrupted the normalcy of a planned life and often ruined part or all of the harvests that the *colonos* had invested in, with so much hope and expectation. It is not surprising, then, that a common theme in the farmers' memories was sacrifice. They recalled how their previous occupations made the new life even harder:

Life started as a tremendous struggle: fields of thistle and grass. [And yet] we know that people who came were craftsmen, not farmers.

It was very difficult. Locusts invaded the fields and instead of a harvest we had the locusts. This happened year after year, so that people would fall behind in their payments.

We had a harvest, but the locusts came and ate it all. The horses ate wheat and they all died along with the cows and calves. We were ruined.

The difficulties often ended in the abandonment of the *colonia*. Although the reason advanced by the *colonos* was their difficulty in complying with contracts, the seeds of the problem might well be found in their country of origin.[22] While the JCA's mission was to settle immigrants in rural areas to practice agriculture, their most common occupations in the small towns and villages where they were concentrated before they migrated were commerce and crafts, according to their descendants:

There was a man who was a carpenter. Somebody else was a blacksmith. At that time it was necessary to have somebody able to repair a plow. People who came from Russia with skills could make a living.

My grandfather was a carpenter, and he made the windows and doors for the Yevich houses. When he had money he would use it to harvest the crop. Afterward he would go back to his carpentry.

Well, when immigration started here, in Argentina in the year 1900 more or less . . . the Yevich bought land and started to settle people. And with time they formed towns: Clara, Domínguez, and all this. And they started to ask for people with professions . . . Because then they started to look in Domínguez, Clara, they needed two carpenters, three carpenters, several masons, tailors, and they brought them from there. They would look for the profession there and bring them directly . . . And my dad was a carpenter.

These testimonies question the JCA administration's claim of a careful selection process during the recruitment of prospective settlers in regions of Eastern Europe where there were Jewish farmers (Poland, Romania, Lithuania, Czechoslovakia, Russia) (Jewish Colonization Association n.d.: 12). While many *colonos* had an agricultural background, according to the descendants' narratives, at the time of emigration Jews faced severe restrictions on practicing agriculture or could not make a living off agriculture,[23] and "the majority ignored agricultural tasks" (Isuz de Schulman n.d.: 3). The immigrants who had a trade, they asserted, were lucky, because they could take advantage of potential opportunities to earn a living outside of agriculture.[24] That paid off especially as Villa Clara's population increased and created a demand for goods and services that traders and artisans could supply.

An additional constraint for the new immigrants was the dismemberment of extended families. Relatives arriving together often were settled in different colonies. To make matters worse, according to many descendants, the JCA did not offer much support to settle the immigrants' children close to their parents once they married, which would have increased the potential of sharing tools and social support. That led some children to leave the JCA tutelage at an early stage to form independent farming settlements: Villa Alba, La Pampa, in 1901; Médanos, Buenos Aires, and Colonia Rusa, Río Negro, in 1906; and El Chaco in 1923. Other second-generation descendants born in Colonia Clara, for example, accepted starting anew in Avigdor, the new land acquired by the JCA in the north of the province, where many of the Jewish immigrants of the second wave in the 1930s were also settled.

Finally, other children became discouraged from continuing on their parents' path, either because they thought they could do better in trade or business or to follow their aspirations for higher education. In fact, a proverbial saying among Argentine Jews suggests that the immigrants settled by the JCA in rural areas interpreted the biblical mandate "you will educate your children" as a call to practice agriculture to allow their children not to: "you will sow wheat and harvest doctors." When opportunities for social mobility appeared, many parents followed their children on their own or were pressured by their children to move as well, either because they were aging or to support their children's careers.

The descendants of this immigration repeatedly told me that the land was not granted but sold to them. They did not object to the sale itself but to the strict and inflexible contractual stipulations. The land had to be repaid by income generated by the sale of harvests or other produce over twenty years in monthly installments, regardless of financial conditions. The resentment of what was labeled the philanthropic organization's insensitivity to their difficulties was voiced by the elderly descendant of a pioneer family:

When we moved here to the countryside they had assigned my dad his one hundred hectares . . . It was so difficult to keep ahead that my father spent his whole life paying the fees to the Yevich and never obtained the title for the land. It arrived several months after my father's death.

Despite the JCA plan, paying for the land in installments was not feasible for a good number of *colonos*, thus deepening the social stratification that had existed before migration. Some *colonos* were not able to keep the land or the tools to work it with.

> They would pay every year when they had the harvest. They would pay a portion . . . If the harvest was bad, they didn't pay. More or less it was twenty or thirty years. They took farms away from more than half of the people. The Yevich took the farms and gave them to someone else who was in a better economic situation.

> Look, my dad worked, say, thirty years and couldn't pay. When he reached old age, he couldn't work anymore and had to sell everything to pay the Yevich for the farm . . . For example, the machinery.

The JCA policy of redistributing the land that some could not pay for to new settlers often worked to the benefit of established *colonos*, who, in contrast, were able to keep their land and even buy additional land for themselves or their children.

According to many descendants, the philanthropic idea behind the JCA's founding was exemplary, but its implementation was commercial:

> The system of land-tenure system was imposed by the JCA, founded by the German Jewish Baron Mauricio de Hirsch as a philanthropic entity to settle Jews outside of the borders of the countries that persecuted them. In practice, his successors and administrators completely emasculated his purposes, transforming it into a commercial enterprise, which exploited the work of the peasants working on his lands. (Kreimer 1984: 1)

The result was often that the *colonos* could not pay their debts to the organization. Critics of the agricultural colonization program argue that the JCA administration did not provide enough to give the *colonos* a good start. While facing acculturation stress, the *colonos* placed high expectations on the harvests in order to pay their installment on the land and on the interest on the loans contracted with the JCA (to repay the construction of a two-bedroom house with a shed, a shared well, and the purchase of two oxen, four horses, and eight cows, for which they were charged 4 percent interest—which grew to 6 percent if they were in arrears). The *colonos* also contracted debts with local businesses that advanced credit to purchase seeds, food, and additional agricultural tools. Lacking knowledge of alternatives, the new immigrant was often prey to exploitation.

In Colonia Clara 1,399 *colonos* and their families abandoned their farms between 1895 and 1943, including 62 individuals with their families from Bélez and Guinzburg, the groups closest to the future Villa Clara (Museo y Archivo Histórico Regional de las Colonias Judías). Reasons for the flight varied: a prominent factor was bad harvests, like the one experienced in 1900, which pushed out 113 families. The attraction of better prospects was another; an example is the 43 families who left in 1901, attracted by an independent colonization company that offered them land in Villa Alba in the province of La Pampa. Economic conditions seem to have improved after 1902 with the opening of the railroad and the JCA approval of the *colonos'* request to forgive communal debts and increase their landholdings to 150 hectares (Cincuenta Años 1939: 176–178).

Reports on population size, abandonment, and ownership in Colonia Clara are hard to evaluate. Ownership could be a good measure of the colonization's success yet hard to ascertain since, as *colonos* abandoned the land or were evicted, others immediately took their place. For example, a letter sent to Paris headquarters in 1910 by the JCA reported that 269 families or 1,503 persons lived in Colonia Clara (YIVO Institute, N. Sonnenfeld Letter, p. 34). Yet a report issued by the JCA headquarters in Buenos Aires in 1941 maintained that there were 633 *colonos* in Colonia Clara, of which 401 (63 percent) were owners. A report based on JCA statistics on its program in Entre Ríos during the first sixteen years in operation (1891 to 1907) estimated that 82 percent of *colonos* had abandoned their land.[25] While some were unsuccessful at farming or rural life, others sold to settled *colonos* after obtaining ownership title, thus contributing to growing inequality; finally, some *colonos* abandoned farming but not the land, which they leased to sharecroppers. Perhaps the best indicator of the magnitude of the problem is provided by Haim Avni (2005), who estimated that by 1910 forty-eight of the farmers selected by the JCA had abandoned the dream of making it on their own in rural Argentina.

For a variety of reasons, then, the JCA was not successful in instigating rootedness or generational replacement, and the agricultural experiment lasted a little over a generation. While even settlers with agricultural experience found the farming conditions and methods difficult, the administrators' inexperience in agriculture was probably a more determining factor conspiring against the colonization program. This led them to fund the program inadequately or to be insufficiently sensitive to the farmers' claims.[26] But it is interesting to note that the literature (whether archival, scholarly, or testimonial) documents the rise and fall of the baron's overly ambitious vision to the detriment of its successes. The immigrants were snatched from a life of poverty, abuse, persecution, and possible death, and many of their children would have been exterminated in the Holocaust later. Instead they were able to experiment with agriculture and—if that occupation did not suit their aspirations for themselves or their children—were free to move elsewhere and change occupations. Although Baron de Hirsch had imagined immigrants settling in a country where they were free to farm, he had miscalculated the long-term goals that the immigrants themselves had for their children. The exodus of *colonos* to urban centers, usually taken as proof of JCA failure, is believed by many ex-*colonos* to be proof of success. A woman who migrated to Buenos Aires extolled the value of a farming past for a nonfarming present:

> What wonderful years! That colony formed by those people struggling for civilization so they could give their children and grandchildren their successful present, as they dedicate themselves to every activity, professional, cultural, industrial, commercial, etc. (Friedlander 1953: 14)

The child of an immigrant concurred:

> Thanks to the circumstances of the JCA colonies and due to the intolerance of several directors and administrators of the colonizing enterprise, . . . many *colonos* and their children abandoned the fields to settle in the large urban centers where they could enjoy a better lifestyle and as a result helped create and ensured the existence of many important institutions, publications, libraries, educational centers, social centers, etc., which are the pride of our community. (Hojman 1964: 198)

The view construing exodus from the rural areas as a measure of success espoused by the former farmers was eventually shared by the colonization program. JCA president Sir Henry Avigdor Goldsmit proclaimed after his visit to the *colonias* in the 1960s:

> I understand that the mission and goals of the Baron de Hirsch's enterprise were to found *colonias* in Argentina and transform them into the homes of persecuted Jews. If those goals were addressed through the personal effort of the *colonos* and their families and, throughout the years, conditions were ripe for them to settle in the cities and educate their children at a higher level, I—as president of this institution—am very happy with the work done. (cited in Zago 1988: 219)

The seeds for the rural exodus were planted as the Jewish gauchos felt recognized as Argentines, as they were transformed into *criollos* and claimed citizenship. During a visit to Colonia Clara with the governor of the province, Dr. Miguel Laurencena, in 1917, Dr. Antonio Sagarna said:

> The Governor . . . comes to tell you that the Promised Land is here . . . [that] you are no longer Hebrews, that is, foreigners of the other bank, you are Ar-

gentine citizens . . . We are all convinced that, when the time comes and attendance of the defenders of the nation is taken, the *Jewish Gauchos* of Entre
Ríos will not be the last in responding: Here we are! (cited in *Fondo Comunal*
1965: 111–115)

Another success, though unplanned, of the JCA program was the emergence of a cooperative movement under the leadership of the Jewish *colonos*
that devised coping strategies and protection mechanisms during agricultural
production and marketing. When ready to sell their produce, the *colonos* had
to contend with commercial monopolies (like Bunge & Born and Dreyfus)
that set the prices and with general stores where they were forced to buy all
their supplies. Since the immigrants had a history of community organizing in
their countries of origin, they founded agrarian cooperatives and credit associations soon after their settlement (Kreimer 1984). The cooperative movement,
which became emblematic of Colonia Clara, was "the daughter of necessity"
(Muchinik and Isuz de Schulman n.d.a: 5).

The first cooperative, however, was initiated by a progressive JCA
administrator:

> On November 21, 1904, the majority of the *colonos* of Colonia Clara got to-
> gether to discuss the proposal of the administrator of Colonia Clara, Don
> Adolfo Leibovich, to create a community organization with funding from the
> *colonos*, on the basis of shares and according to the means of each one, with
> the purpose of providing its members all items needed for the harvest (bags,
> thread, machinery, etc.) at low prices, introducing good seeds and other
> products necessary for the development of the best agricultural practices
> and cattle raising, granting loans against the harvest at a set interest, promot-
> ing savings and a healthy economy using all possible means, creating other
> industries, and watching over the community interests of the *colonia*. After
> exchanging ideas on the topic, the vote showed the unanimous resolution of
> creating such an institution with the name Fondo Comunal: Sociedad Coo-
> perativa, Agrícola, Limitada, for a period of ten years. (Foundational Act,
> cited in *Fondo Comunal* 1965: 7–8)

For the Fondo Comunal, "communal" or "community-oriented" meant
work contributed by every member to benefit the entire community and was
synonymous with "cooperative."

Some directors of the JCA fomented the practice of crafts, when they realized
the constraints faced by the immigrants to succeed in agriculture. JCA directors
Nandor Sonnenfeld and Louis Oungre both supported small crafts and trades

in villages that were growing either within or in the periphery of the Jewish colonies. While at first the JCA had opposed the sale of lots in what was to become Villa Clara (fearing the settlers might prefer business to agriculture), after 1907 the organization adopted more liberal policies regarding the rental or sale of lots close to railroad stations. An additional, yet insufficiently unrecognized, success of the agricultural colonization program was the transformation of the region into a center of economic development and intercultural relations.

Chapter Four

From Jewish Gauchos
to Gaucho Jews

*Regional Economic Development
and Intercultural Relations at the
End of the Nineteenth Century*

> In that incredible nature, under a unique sky, in the vast calm
> of the land traversed by rivers, my life was full of fervor, and
> that [feeling] obliterated my origins and made me Argentine.
> (Gerchunoff 1973: 26)

Through this expression of devotion to the new land, the man
who coined the phrase *gaucho judío* (Jewish gaucho) revealed
how the natural environment of Entre Ríos inspired awe for
the new homeland and helped effect the transformation from
foreigner to national. But what are the links between citizenship (a legal status of belonging to a nation-state), immigrant
identity (a sense of belonging to a diaspora), and nationality
(a civic right conferred by birth or naturalization by a nation-
state)? How do social actors construct those links over time?
The social history of Villa Clara, or the biographical and historical past of an immigrant village, can contribute to exploring
these questions by interweaving the oral memory accumulated
by informants (a private realm accessed through ethnographic
interviews) with the archival record (a written and thus public historical repository contained in newspapers, community
organizations' minutes, and manuscripts written by residents
acting as local historians). Though to a large extent these two

histories complement each other, their focus of interest is completely different. While the informants remembered the history of the village by accessing their own life-course, the archival record reflected what the writers (whether representing themselves or an organization) considered relevant or worthy of being noted by the larger public, including their descendants and reference group.

Memories need to be understood in the context of "larger histories" (regional, national, international) and "smaller histories" (archives of local institutions, experiences transmitted in oral or written form). It is the larger, official history of immigration that glorifies the benefits of immigration—peace, land, and freedom—and contrasts these conditions with the immigrants' hard life in Europe. But the experiences related by people I interviewed, as well as written documents left by their ancestors, helped to portray daily life, including the difficulties the *colonos* had to face, such as acquiring land ownership, learning a new language and customs, and overcoming their ignorance of the local terrain. For example, the immigrants needed to learn locally validated strategies to defend their land from natural disasters: they had to learn to defend themselves from locust invasions capable of destroying a field in the course of just a few minutes and to protect themselves and their crops from floods or droughts. But they also needed to learn the social structure and political discourse of the new land and become proficient in intercultural and political communication.

European Immigrants Becoming Argentine in Entre Ríos: Factors in Assimilation to the Nation

Immigrants holding a regional (in the case of the immigrants from the Alps), a binational (in the case of the Germans of the Russian Volga), or a multinational (in the case of Jews from Eastern Europe) sense of self were pressured to adopt the identity of their chosen nation-state upon arrival. The major mechanisms that facilitated the articulation with the new land were intermarriage and universal education.[1]

Many of the people I interviewed (second- and third-generation descendants of the original immigrants) reported the intermarriage of their European ancestors before their transatlantic relocation or their marriage to *criollos* upon arrival in the country. Although the historical records document immigration from individual countries, I was referred to numerous cases of intermarriage before immigration (the usual combinations being French and Italians, Swiss and Spanish, Spanish and Belgian) or after settling in Argentina (mostly marriages of Germans, Belgians, Italians, or French to *criollos*).[2] Often the European side would prevail; as a leather artisan whose mother was German married to a *criollo* explained, "When we came from the countryside we didn't know how to speak Spanish." Intermarriage between Christians and Jews, however, was rare in the past. If Jews were seldom identified by their national origin, Christians were always identified by nationality. While Christians referred to Jews by their religion rather than their national origin, Jews generalized all non-Jews by using the Yiddish term *goi*. The two religious categories maintained an "equal but separate" position concerning intermarriages: in the past "you did everything to avoid them." According to people's memories, both parties were to blame: "the Jew didn't accept them, but the *criollo* didn't accept the Jew either." To some extent, this applied to marriages of Europeans to *criollos* as well. An elderly woman recalled: "when I was a girl, when a *criollo* married a Jew or a German married a *criollo*, it was a battle. The family declared war on the children."

A second mechanism of assimilation was universal education. While complying with Argentine legislation to conduct education in Spanish, many immigrants also established private schools so they could provide religious instruction in the language of origin. By 1882 the province had 124 schools, of which 60 were private. As immigration declined during World War I, the number of Argentine-born children increased, bringing assimilation to the private realm of the family. In 1895, almost two decades after the passage of the Avellaneda Law, immigrants represented 22 percent of the province's population.[3] By 1914 this proportion was reversed, with the foreign-born declining to 10 percent of the province's population at a time when the foreign population of the country had risen to its highest proportions: 30 percent in the country and 50 percent in the capital city of Buenos Aires. Finally, a third mechanism that increased similarity and assimilation was the compulsory military draft for males.

But to understand cultural assimilation in Entre Ríos at the beginning of the twentieth century we need to understand social interaction and the ways in which the various social groupings perceived each other.

ASSIMILATING TO THE LOCAL SOCIAL STRUCTURE AND CULTURE

All organized migrations settled in relatively isolated rural ethnic enclaves or *colonias*. Both historical renditions and contemporary celebrations of heritage treat these enclaves as if they had little or no connection to the larger society, including other similar entities and the inhabitants that the immigrants encountered as they settled in the new land. Becoming Argentine in Entre Ríos, however, was based upon communication, rather than isolation.

Cultural assimilation is predicated upon understanding the individual's place within the local social structure, which can be discovered by learning how individuals perceive each other. At the turn of the twentieth century, when

European immigrants settled in *colonias*, the social world was constituted by three social classes well defined through property: large landowners, immigrant farmers, and *criollo* workers.

Members of the landowning *criollo* elite were ethnically descended from Spaniards born in Argentina, who were themselves the offspring of previous immigrants who had been granted large extensions of land as a reward for their participation in either conquest or nation-building and had later extended their holdings through purchase or marriage.[4] In contrast, landless *criollos*, who were the result of interbreeding between the Spaniards' descendants and indigenous peoples in either Argentina or Uruguay, worked as peons hired for farm work and were often called gauchos.

According to *criollo* informants, the state either did not distribute land to the poor *criollos* and descendants of indigenous peoples or made it impossible for them to hold onto property. Being illiterate and ignorant of the structure of private property, such as claims to titles and taxes, they felt vulnerable and powerless when the state expropriated land from both the indigenous peoples and the gauchos. They felt that the state only granted land to the European gringos because they complied with contractual agreements. A man who worked as a *tropero* in his youth and still dresses as a gaucho in Villa Clara told me this story:

> I had a field of 50 hectares. We *criollos* didn't know anything about getting a land title. They would come and they would say: put a fence over here and here and over here. What if a *criollo* was locked inside the fence? Well, hire him as a *peón*, they would say. The land was not his anymore. Eh? That was the way it was.

Later in the interview the same man acknowledged that the *criollos* accepted the changes because, being illiterate, they felt inferior to the immigrants. He said: "They still got along well, the Jews and the *criollos*. Do you know why? Because the *criollo* was so, I'd say, so ashamed that he didn't know how to read. They were almost fearful of those who knew how to read."

The term *gringo* was reserved for the immigrant farmers. Gringos shared characteristics that differentiated them from both landowners and gauchos: rudimentary mastery of the Spanish language and local culture and reliance on the culture of origin, which they continued to hold onto in the host country through their adherence to religious rituals, family economy, education, and trades. Soon after their arrival, gringos became an incipient middle class of small producers.

The perceptions that these social classes had of each other help explain their interaction in the course of daily life. The response of the *criollo* landowners to the arrival of the gringos varied: at one extreme, some landowners failed to comply with commitments (the case of Moisesville is an example); at the other extreme, some landowners promoted immigrant settlements (Urquiza was a prototype) by granting, selling, or leasing land to the immigrants.[5] The landless *criollos* also expressed ambivalent reactions to the newcomers, perceiving them in a continuum from benefactors to usurpers. On the positive side, immigrants were perceived as potential employers: after the local landowners dismissed *criollo* employees as they sold or leased land to the immigrants, the immigrants themselves employed the *criollos* as permanent (*puesteros*) or transient (*peones*) rural labor, as employees in rural or village businesses, or as domestics or handymen in the villages. On the negative side, the *criollos* perceived immigrants as usurpers taking over the open land that the nomadic gauchos had been able to travel freely, without the barriers of fences. There are records of threats (such as a gaucho mimicking slashing a throat as he swiftly galloped past the precarious hut of a terrified Belgian *colono*) as well as actual assassinations of Jewish *colonos* who tried to protect property granted by the Jewish Colonization Association. Some *criollos* believed that the gringo farmers replicated the exploitation by the previous employers, the landowners. One of them explained:

> The worker, or the *peón*, didn't earn money, he earned vouchers . . . Yes. They were always asking the *patrón* [landlord] for money because they didn't keep receipts for what they were given. As the end of the month arrived, they were not paid, and they were told: "Oh, you already cashed everything you earned!" Or they gave you a crumb, saying, "I don't owe you more than this!"

Curiously, whether perceived as usurpers or benefactors, gringos were never seen as competitors for land ownership by the *criollos*. I have not found any case of social movements of landless *criollos* struggling for land or attempting to reproduce the immigrant programs established for Europeans at the time, although this might result from the *criollo* informants' own weak social consciousness. According to most people I interviewed, European immigrants were considered to be hard-working and to have sided with *criollos* in the process of nation-building. One *criollo* man married to a German woman who baked the bread that he sold door to door proudly asserted the benefits of immigration, for both newcomers and the nation:

> The province of Entre Ríos is hard-working, the gringos came, the Jews, Belgians, Germans, Swiss, Poles . . . These people are very hard-working! All hard-working! And the government began selling land because it wanted to have a harvest . . . Here there was work for everyone . . . Everyone made the Republic on horseback, the gringos and the *criollos*, when there weren't machines or anything.

Gringo informants remembered that *criollo* gauchos, though occupationally diverse, were uniformly poor. But the people I talked to disagreed on the causes of *criollo* poverty. Some gringo descendants thought that gauchos were poor because they spent their salaries on instantly gratifying activities. One asserted that "until not very long ago what the *criollo* and the gaucho liked was *joda* and *chupa*, and they ate and drank what they earned and they didn't care about anything else." [6] Others believed that gauchos were poor due to their nomadic lifestyle. Most viewed them as honorable, as in the lyric of a folk song that talks to the gaucho thus:

> You never had a *querencia*,[7]
> You were poor among the poor,
> But rich in behavior, honor, and decency.

The *criollo* informants, however, had a different perspective on their poverty and the social type they embodied (the gaucho), which slowly disappeared with the changes brought about by the immigrants. They remembered gauchos as honest workers, whose passion for freedom and lack of education caused their displacement, both physical and social, as gringos arrived. One of them, who barely knows how to read and write but has dictated two books on this culture to his daughter, generalized his experience, saying that his "life is like that of many *criollos* that grew up around here. We were almost always marginalized." And he proceeded to link marginality with lack of education:

We kids did not have education and we grew up on the horse and you needed to gallop miles to find a mud hut; in the past, some people owned land as far as you could see. There were two or three immense ranches [*estancias*] and anybody could build a mud hut; nobody gave you a title or anything . . . Later, when taxes were required, nobody wanted to own the land and we *criollos* sought employment as *troperos* and *puesteros* . . .

And yes, some *criollito* always had some land, since there wasn't documentation, there wasn't anything, the government was in charge of it [the land], held onto it for the colonizer that was coming, and it [the land] ran out . . . And sure . . . I had 50 hectares of land, right? . . . And when I was older I was supposed to be given a paper [property deed] . . . And we didn't know anything about having a land title.

Through an often difficult assimilation process, the immigrants were transformed into Argentines in the course of social interaction at sites of employment and education and in the context of the intercultural family. Their national or religious background continued to be acknowledged. In the words of my Swiss-descended landlady, the Swiss would say "the German who lives in such and such a place" or "the Jew who is in such and such a place."

Immigrants rarely viewed either themselves or their ethnic group as an isolated grouping. Rather, they found ways to integrate with each other, since they were already a part of a regional economy. A descendant of a German *colonia* resident remembers that her co-nationals were more interested in farming than in commerce and that the businesses were owned by Jews. Yet either this report is inaccurate or the heavy out-migration of Jews from rural areas diminished their control of business, since "in 1943 five of eleven stores were owned by Israelite families" (Honeker de Pascal and Jacob de Hoffmann n.d.: 218).

The views that the two groups held of each other varied, depending on whether assimilation mattered to different stakeholders. Although the social interaction of *criollos* employed in the Volga German colonies was restricted to work,[8] many *criollos* viewed the newcomers with great admiration:

> The *colonos* are good people and I have many friends among them, but with the strange language they speak, you cannot understand them . . . What great harvests they produced in those *colonias* that sprang up everywhere! What good bread their women cooked! And the way they changed things in a few years! They found a way for everything, they brought cloth and you could buy clothing without walking miles and miles! They even tamed the horse for the plow . . . The roads they opened so they would not get lost! It was all for the good. (testimony of Don Benito Pérez, cited in Popp and Dening 1977: 173)

In contrast, other stakeholders whose job was to promote acculturation to Argentina asserted that the German immigrants were not "benefiting the country" by refusing to assimilate, which prompted the commissioner of colonies, a Frenchman, to assert that

> these individuals do not assimilate: they form a different national entity that remains isolated and that brings many problems. The proof is that very few of these [so-called] Russians, who were living in Russia for 120 years, speak Russian. (Peyret 1889: 164–165)

Immigrants also worked for other immigrants. During idle or hard times many Germans, for example, accepted employment in the Swiss colonies of Villa Urquiza and San Benito as well as in the Jewish *colonias*, which was sometimes viewed as exploitation:

Honor diploma awarded by the JCA to a colono *for the quality of his harvest in 1939.*

Yes, and in general the Jew was the one who always had land, the German [immigrant] was always exploited the same as us [*criollos*, natives] here. At the time they would husk corn . . . in full frost with a bag thrown over their shoulders . . . the difference [between the Germans and the Jews] was that one was the boss and the other a *peón*. One lived in a mud hut and the other in a solid house.

In addition to labor, the *colonias* exchanged technical knowledge of agriculture and the concept and practice of cooperativism. For example, the Jewish *colonos* were acknowledged as experts in the cultivation of linen and sunflower, the use of horses rather than oxen for plows, and "Russian carts," which they popularized. Conversely, the administrators of the Jewish *colonias* are known to have sought the advice of Belgian and Italian immigrants to build their houses and wells.

But it was not until the *colonos* created associations to protect their interests that they became Argentine stakeholders themselves. Shortly after they were settled in productive units (*colonias*), immigrant cohorts responded to JCA suggestions to associate. The first agricultural cooperative in Entre Ríos was born in 1900 in Lucienville, and the cooperative movement extended to Colonia Clara in 1904, as the Fondo Comunal made its appearance. Cooperative movements sprang up in other colonies as a survival strategy to protect the in-

Fondo Comunal shares, 1925.

terests of the new farmers from commercial monopolies through collective association. The first credit associations, meat and bakery cooperatives, and dairy (cream and milk) cooperatives were founded by one or more ethnic groups: Belgians started La Augusta by themselves and La Cosmopolita with Germans and Italians, while Jews created the Fondo Comunal. The cooperatives stored the *colonos'* cereal production and negotiated sale prices and commercialization agreements with the largest buyer firms.[9] The major advantage for farmers associating with a cooperative was that members could buy tools, household goods, clothing, and other goods at the local cooperative store on credit against their upcoming harvest.

Cooperative associations sprang up in the immigrant *colonias* as land became a prized commodity to be distributed among additional immigrants as well as their children. The Jews were the first immigrant group to use agrarian cooperatives as a political strategy for social advancement.[10] German cooperatives were more oriented to creating internal community solidarity than to exerting pressure on outside stakeholders. In the early 1930s two cooperatives were established in the German colony closest to Villa Clara, Santa Anita: Comuna and Cooperativa Agrícola Ganadera Santa Anita Limitada.

A decade after the arrival of the Jewish immigrants, cooperatives founded by different immigrant groups sought to help each other and cemented bonds of solidarity that extended across the immigrant *colonias*. In the course of time, cooperative associations grouped individual cooperatives based on their shared interests as producers, independently of ethnic or national origin. Cooperatives boomed during the administration of governor Héctor Maya (1946–1950), who passed Law No. 3430 to exempt cooperatives from taxes; but the reversal of this legislation in 1976 resulted in the disappearance of all cooperatives in the province during the following decade.

ISOLATION AND INTERDEPENDENCE: THE NEW SETTLERS OF COLONIA CLARA AND THE "OTHERS"

Like the other *colonias*, Colonia Clara inherited the human geography preceding its establishment: descendants of indigenous populations, native Argentines (both the Spanish-descended landowners and the *criollo* laborers), and European immigrants. The discourse of interaction evidenced ethnic and class distinctions within the immigrant groups. The Jewish immigrants originating in northern Russia, for example, considered themselves of a higher social class than those they called Besaraber (originating in Bessarabia in southern Russia), though they were forced to learn agriculture from them.[11] There were also marked class differences between all Jewish farmers and the JCA administrative cadre as well as with the native inhabitants that preceded them in the countryside. Ethnicity was the explicit social category defining relationships both within and among the first immigrant group in the area (the Jews) and the indigenous population already living there (the *criollos*). Though the discourse was ethnic, their daily interaction was class-based.

Like other immigrants (and despite the picture painted in the correspondence of JCA administrators in the *colonia*, Buenos Aires, and Paris headquarters) the Jewish newcomers were certainly not alone; nor was the *colonia* an isolated enclave grafted onto the land. Rather, the immigrants interacted with *criollos*, Argentine clerks in small administrative centers, the landowning elites of large *estancias*, and immigrants with diverse national origins, among others. For example, Don Julio Aletti (an Italian mason) and his *criollo* employees who lived in the small settlement nearby which would become Villa Clara were said to have been contracted by the JCA to build the identical brick and mud houses and the water tanks. Jewish *colonos* also employed German men in the harvest and German women as domestic help (Bargman 1992: 54). But most often, according to the descendants of the Jewish settlers that I talked to, the Jewish *colonos* offered jobs to the *criollos* when they could afford to, even though in principle the JCA did not support this practice. Whether *criollos* were employed or just interacted amicably with the new settlers, there is consensus that the two groups established a symbiotic relationship, with some mention of *criollos* speaking Yiddish. While some *criollo* informants claim that the Jewish employers had high expectations and might have been exploitative, others point out that *criollos* benefited overall from employment.

On their part, the Jewish settlers' descendants agreed on the central role played by *criollos* (usually referred to as gauchos) in their adaptation, particularly since the natural environment, language, and occupations differed so drastically from those of the countries they had left behind. They characterized the gauchos as good, generous people, open to sharing their experience-based knowledge:

> *Criollos*, natives, all who worked in the fields, they already knew how to do the hard work, because that was the way they were making a living. When the new people arrived, the *criollos* helped them to learn how to yoke an ox to the plough, to lasso. People from here, *criollos*, natives, and Indians, when they saw the people that did not understand the language, very spontaneously, with gestures and symbols helped them to clear the land of trees and undergrowth, to get the most useful part of the land.

> They planted ten hectares of flax and they did not know how to thresh. There was a *peón* who was teaching them. They [the Jews] learned from the *criollos*.

While some *criollo* men were hired seasonally or part-time, often whole families moved to the *colonia* to work with the new landowners, the Jewish immigrants. Thus, in the course of daily life, the *criollo* workers were probably the most immediate social referent of Argentine culture during the first stage of the Jewish immigrants' acculturation. Not everyone admired their qualities, however; some elderly Jewish gauchos recognized their help but said that "gauchos were poor because they were lazy, they only worked to get housing and food in exchange." Yet they needed each other, since they were both vulnerable and destitute in their own specific ways. Abraham Schejter, a descendant of the Jewish immigration and one of the popular historians of Villa Clara, said:

> There was a symbiosis between the immigrant who arrived and the *criollo* who was abandoned when the landlord sold the land. There were no social laws to protect him and he was left drifting, so when the gringo came, the *criollo* found work, protection, and bread. They started helping each other: the *criollo* teaching the immigrant how to cultivate the land and how to com-

The Lipcovich family dressed as Jewish gauchos.

municate, the gringo gratefully giving him whatever he could. My grandfather said that *criollos* were very good people and very intelligent. Many of them even learned how to speak Yiddish.

This understanding was shared by *criollos*, some of whom felt they were becoming as much gaucho Jews as the immigrant Jews were turning into Jewish gauchos. In the words of an elderly *criollo* who grew up and then worked among Jews throughout his life, "They were like my second family. I can say I am more of a Jew than anything else." They learned from one another's culture. If, for example, "the *criollo* liked the bread that the Jewish women kneaded," the "*criollo* would tan the leather to make the saddle, and make the harness to tie the horses to the plow, and make the lassos, and nail the posts for the first fences." In the course of time, the gringo and the *criollo* established a symbiotic relationship.

This symbiotic relationship replicated the relationship experienced by the children of the Jewish immigrants, who fully identified with their closest Argentine model: the gaucho. According to a Jewish gaucho, the term designates Jews who adopted gaucho customs, such as occupations, clothing, and language. While this transculturation applied almost exclusively to males (because women were less involved in outdoor lifeways), the phrase became a metaphor for the rapid and successful adaptation of Jewish immigrants. But while most recall the goodwill of the natives, some remember animosity toward the newcomers, who were considered intruders. Before the arrival of the immigrants, the gauchos freely appropriated land. Private landowners accused the gaucho of being an intruder, because "he moved the fence over and that was it, since he did not pay taxes." According to informants of gaucho ancestry, gauchos had reasons to resist the foreigners: while the few who had owned land or had permanent jobs as *puesteros* had been forced to relocate when the lands were sold to the JCA, most—who worked temporarily for the landowners as *peones*—had lost their jobs. There are some references to threats and even killings by "ignorant people who didn't like them because they came to settle and had another religion."

Many descendant narratives included comparisons of social milieus in the country of origin and destination: the immigrants, who were "doctors, tailors, people with titles," used to running water, electricity, and other amenities, moved to a barren place where they had to "open up land for cultivation, make houses from mud, ride on horseback." In their new home, they had to behave like gauchos if they were to tame the natural environment. The essential features of the new cultural type—gaucho culture—were defined for me as a cowboy lifestyle (where the horse is indispensable in daily life) and adherence to a code of honor based on courage, honesty, and reciprocity. An elderly resident of Villa Clara continues to refer to himself as a Jewish gaucho because he is the only Jew in Villa Clara who still rides on horseback and belongs to an Asociación Tradicionalista (an association that promotes the preservation of gaucho culture through, among other things, participation in patriotic celebrations). He reasserted his identification as a Jewish gaucho when he spoke about his youth, saying that he "tamed thirty-two horses by myself, by myself! During idle times we tamed horses . . . I didn't charge."

As a social type, Jewish gauchos emerged from a combination of factors: a vital need to adapt to new life conditions, daily exposure to gaucho culture, and the Argentine-born generation's profound desire to assimilate and break away from the strict rules imposed by their immigrant ancestors, such as the adherence to food habits prescribed by religious codes. One of them explained how "our immigrant grandparents and parents respected these food rituals [kosher].

Meeting at a local bar.

Rural gathering in front of a commercial establishment.

We were born in Argentina and we socialized with the *criollos,* whom we tried to imitate in everything and who were excellent at grilling meat. We ate the barbecue they shared with us" (Kreimer 1984: 1).

Like recollections, versions of the gaucho result from both social constructions and selective memory. But the image of the gaucho is also part and parcel of a political poetic invented by the landed *criollos* to legitimize their authenticity as Argentines and their social distance from the immigrant farmers. Folklorist

Ana María Dupey explains that there were at least three incarnations of the gaucho after the nativists claimed the gaucho's centrality in Argentine identity: as the hero who opposed the large landowners, as the patriotic citizen who fought in Argentine wars, and, finally, as the assimilation referent for the children of immigrants.[12] To understand the embeddings of *criollo*, gaucho, and gringo in Argentine history it is useful to think of the cultural politics in different historical periods. The Jewish gaucho, like other terms designating the gringo imitation of the *criollo*, was a hybrid identity that confirmed assimilation to Argentina within the political canons exalted at the time: the immigrants gave birth to the first generation of Argentines. These hybrid identities were the inroads into Argentine citizenship, but the transformation of immigrants into ethnic social groupings and their primacy as social actors in the organization of development centers are best understood in the foundation and institutional establishment of a small settlement such as Villa Clara. The Jewish gauchos moved there on their way to becoming more Argentine than Jewish: gaucho Jews.

Chapter Five

THE RISE AND DEMISE OF JEWISH VILLA CLARA (1902–1930S)

The Jewish gauchos were the founders of this village. This village was founded by the Jews. (criollo *informant*)

And these Jews are the founders of Clara. (Swiss *informant*)

That febrile little village stuck in the center of Entre Ríos, where almost all the inhabitants were Jewish, youth with iron will, with few possessions primarily of kitchen utensils, some of them really useful, without which their adaptation would have been even more difficult. (Tepper 1990)

Two major sources of information to reconstruct the early history of Villa Clara are historical documents and recollected life histories, which generate two separate thematic data banks. While historical documents represent scholarly renditions of past facts, the testimonial record expresses how historical facts were experienced, what they meant to real people, and how facts were perceived as changing or otherwise affecting daily lives. In a word, the memories of the informants provide meaning for the documented past. Neither historical documents nor memories of the past present a full picture; however, both are indispensable for establishing a chronological periodization

Muddy Avenida San Martín.

for Villa Clara. While I was compiling sources for this case study, it became apparent that triangulating sources of knowledge is not synonymous with merging: sources often paint the past with different colors as they emphasize different aspects. In addition, because both scholarly historians and informants as lay historians are part and parcel of the civil society of their times when they provide information, their retrospective gaze necessarily contains elements of the present.

An example of the similarity and difference in the information provided by these two sources of knowledge about Villa Clara can be found in their description of initial village life: while there is consensus about the foundation of Estación Clara, only testimonies describe how the village actually looked and who lived there. Informant recollections referred to themes associated with the early days of the village, which were depicted in contrasting terms. One theme was the rudimentary conditions of life, termed *atraso* (backwardness) and believed to be evidenced by the mud streets and the lack of electricity (although Villa Clara was not in fact any different from other villages in Entre Ríos at the time). A contrasting theme was *progreso* (progress), evidenced by a thriving economic life, nascent cooperativism, institutional growth, and the economic impetus brought about by the railroad. Two lay historians eulogized:

> Clara, how much have you progressed! I remember your past, your antiquity, soul of crickets and moon, when you breathed the peaceful provincial air with your bare low houses, and your muddy streets, surrounded by *paraísos* playing with bounty. (Muchinik and Isuz de Schulman n.d.b: 1)

In turn, in clear contrast to the informants' memory, the archival record focused solely on the development of civic associations, commercial establishments, and public services, with particular emphasis on dates and names. Since neither historical nor testimonial sources provided a full picture of the past, remembering Clara holistically tapped both.[1]

Unlike historical records, memories play a vital role in actualizing the past. So it comes as no surprise that the people interviewed about how their own biographical past interlaced with the village's would emphasize Villa Clara's social composition throughout time and be concerned about my correct understanding of who was who in Villa Clara during different stages in its history. Both institutional history and ethnographic themes are important to reconstruct the phases in the social history of the village in a regional and national context.

Phase 1: Who Was Here First? (before 1902)

The historical record concerning the origin of human settlement in contemporary Villa Clara refers us to the region it was part of (Colonia Clara) and the JCA. Current residents of Villa Clara dispute whether the actual land where the village sits was a wasteland or a hamlet before 1902, when the precursor of Villa Clara (Estación Clara) was established. These two versions of Villa Clara's initial population history illustrate the interplay of ethnicity, immigration, and class in the construction of identity.

One version advocated uniformly by gaucho-descended informants as well as some immigrant-descended informants asserted that "Clara existed before it was founded." Providing memory-based evidence about the existence of a human settlement at the site before the opening of the station, an elderly woman who had raised her children there disputed what she called the Jewish version and established differences in timing, size, socioeconomic status, and occupation between those already at the site and the new arrivals:

> When the Jews arrived in Clara, there was a small *caserío*.[2] And they say they were the first to arrive! . . . Yes, there was a small *caserío*, and the Jews arrived in large numbers later. So first there was a *caserío criollo*, very poor, and economically dependent on the immigrant as temporary workers.

Moving further back in time, the proponents of this version recognize the precedence of indigenous peoples and Africans in support of their argument that the area was not a wasteland.[3]

The informants argued that *criollos* living in the *caserío* either came by themselves, since some had always lived a nomadic life, or were forced to relocate when the JCA acquired the rural establishments (*estancias*) where they worked as *peones*, working-poor survivors of an almost feudal stratification system:

> In those times, an *estanciero* was like a governor . . . [4] When they rode their horses, the *peón* rode behind the *patrón*. The *patrón* was well dressed . . . the *peón* was poorly dressed, he was as they said a *tape*, a *criollo* from the hinterland, poor . . . the *criollos* were never rich, but they managed to survive.

Few in number, the *criollos* grouped themselves in *caseríos* consisting of *ranchos* (mud huts) in an area owned by the JCA; but, in the words of a descendant, "it was an area that nobody claimed," a no-man's land. They lived off the land, which they knew well, or from temporary employment with the new farmers in the area, supplementing their diet with leftovers from a slaughterhouse. The narratives of the *caserío* version argued that *criollos* both anteceded the immigrants and knew how to make a living in that landscape, as evident in the following quotation:

> The *criollo*, the local native, all those who did the field tasks, all the hard and rudimentary tasks, knew how to work the land because they already supported themselves that way.

A contrasting version of Villa Clara's social origins was promoted by many JCA farmers' descendants, who asserted that the site of the future village was a wasteland and that "there was nothing there before we arrived": "the first to come here were Jews." Even if there had been a *caserío*, they assured me, it would have been too insignificant to play any role. In addition to disputing the relevance of the *criollos*, indigenous peoples, and Africans to the new settlement, the Jewish version concerning the populations in the area before the arrival of the railroad also failed to acknowledge the existence of other immigrants at the site (for example, the mason Aletti, who had helped build many of the JCA houses).

Phase 2: The Foundational History (1902)

There is consensus about the official foundation date for Villa Clara on January 27, 1902, the date on which it has since then celebrated its anniversary. Dr. Leónidas Echagüe, the governor of Entre Ríos, inaugurated Estación Clara on the Villaguay-Concordia railroad route in the JCA's Colonia Clara. The event marked the incorporation of Villa Clara into the region and the nation: since then, the political economy of Estación Clara has been intertwined with the history of the railroad, ranging from its establishment by the British to its nationalization by the Argentine government to its privatization and final ending of passenger services in 1994. Villa Clara was one of a myriad of villages that experienced a boom with the railroad and a bust without it, so a review of the role of the railroad in Argentine history is in order here.

In 1852 Argentine ideologue Juan Bautista Alberdi had hailed the railroad as an instrument of national unification. His plea was institutionalized in the Constitution of 1853, which authorized Congress to build railways and waterways to implement economic development. It was during the presidency of Bartolomé Mitre in the 1860s, however, that the first concessions to foreign capital to build railroads were made. By the 1870s the largest investors were the British, who continued to expand during the 1880s. Between 1880 and 1914 Argentina represented 8 percent of total British overseas investment, which signaled the start of a dependent mode of development:

> The railway proved the key feature in the export-based economic development of Argentina by transforming the fertile *Pampas* from an unused resource into a factor of production, and was financed almost entirely from abroad, with the British share dominant. (Ford 1971: 652–653)

The success of British investment in railroads was facilitated by two historical developments in Argentina. One was the defeat of the indigenous populations, which assured investor safety. The other was the national promotion of European immigrants willing to settle as permanent agriculturalists who would produce for export (Ford 1971: 651). By the 1930s the British had successfully bargained for a monopoly in railroad equipment sales to pressure Argentina, which had a trade surplus with Britain, to sell it grain and meat (Wright 1974).

British investors built the Entre Ríos Railways in 1882. By 1901 efforts for expansion were underway as manager Sir Follett Holt signed a contract with Governor Echagüe to link Villa Domínguez with Concordia, thus joining the Entre Ríos Railways to the Argentine railroad, the Ferrocarril Este Argentino or Argentino del Este. Apprised of the extension, the London Board shared the news with its shareholders on December 31, 1901:

> The line proposed will join two railroads and will run for a considerable distance across the property of the Jewish Colonization Association . . . We are convinced that this railroad concession in the north of the province of Entre Ríos and Corrientes will have a favorable effect on the future development of these companies. (cited in Chiaramonte et al. 1995: 273)

Share (in English) issued by British Railroads in Argentina.

In fact, both the Entre Ríos Railways and the JCA, which was interested in transporting exports and people, profited from this extension.[5] As a prominent British investment in Argentina, the railroad also symbolized the strong European influence—in both ideological and political economic terms—on the new nation-state, as reflected by Villa Clara at the local level. For example, the British enterprise strengthened the capital city's role as a seat of political and economic power by starting and ending all major rail lines in Buenos Aires. Two other examples are the railroad's focus on exporting products to international markets (particularly to Great Britain) and its transportation of the immigrant protagonists of this story from Buenos Aires to their destinations in Entre Ríos.

The opening of additional railroad stations helped to mitigate the isolation of the new immigrants in rural areas and helped them market their products. Estación Clara was emblematic of Villa Clara's economic progress, centralizing the trading of regional goods and increasing social diversification as it attracted internal migrations. In fact, the opening of the station in Villa Clara simultaneously linked the village to the region (which explains why an informant referred to the railroad as "the life of the village") and led to the slow death of neighboring San Jorge, at the time more urbanized than Villa Clara and a likely candidate for the station. A controversy about the selection of the site for the railroad station still endures, with some stating that the final location was technically more favorable while others speculate that it was because the British engineers' *estancia* was located closer, in Jubileo. Some Villa Clara residents, originally from San Jorge, complained about the impact on their lives of this apparently last-minute change of mind by the British investors, which they perceived as benefiting Villa Clara at their own cost:

> They say that when people realized that the railroad was coming they moved closer and closer to what became Villa Clara . . . They also say that in Colonia San Jorge, which was ten kilometers away from Clara, there was a large population, a lot of Jewish immigration, also *criollo*, Swiss, French, there were Germans too, and this Colonia San Jorge is now deserted, which is to say that almost everyone came to Clara.

> Clara was supposed to be located in San Jorge. San Jorge was a *colonia* ten kilometers from here and my mom's uncles had stores there . . . Here there was pure *cina cina*. Do you know what that means? It means that there were only nasty thorny trees and nothing else. The train was fundamental!

> And this little village [San Jorge] disappeared, because the train didn't come through . . . I've read that there was a butcher, a school, and a police station in San Jorge.

When the train arrived, Villa Clara became important. Just imagine, even the teacher who was in San Jorge was transferred to Villa Clara!

The railroad's history provides the backbone for many personal biographies. Immigrants from various nations (Yugoslav, Polish, Russian, Czech, and Italian) worked on railroad construction, including many Jewish *colonos* of Colonia Clara, like Schejter's grandfather, who used his Russian cart to transport rails. Informants reminiscing about life in the village of their childhood remember the railroad fondly for providing an outlet for socializing and entertainment in addition to travel and trade. Many of the older Clarenses recalled with nostalgia their teenage years, when they would hang out at the train station and gossip about who was arriving and who was leaving. And the arrival of the first train at the station left an indelible mark in villagers' minds:

> Everything started in the year 1902. On January 27 of that year the first train arrived along the steel road that links the cities of Villaguay and Concordia, vomiting steam and smoke, a gray and thick smoke wrapping this simple village in a hug, a reciprocal arrangement. This was the first step . . . to progress. (Muchinik and Isuz de Schulman n.d.a: 2)

Phase 3: The Jewish Village (1902–1930s)

Progress, however, was a function of people. Two immigrant streams arrived in the village during its two first decades. Some were *colonos* of the Jewish Colonization Association who moved with their families because they preferred commerce to agriculture, seeking a lifestyle more attuned to their work experience in the Old World, where many had lived off self-employment as artisans or traders. Jewish gauchos, attentive to the opportunities created by the establishment and consolidation of Estación Clara, told stories as part of their life-course in both continents:

> The first artisans—shoemakers, carpenters, saddlers—appeared here in the village in 1902. Some Jewish settlers left the fields and started commercial enterprises because they realized that they were obtaining a greater benefit. Besides, it was more fitting to their way of life.

> Many people came to become merchants. After they got the land they opened a small store, a meat market . . . In the meantime the railroad was being built . . . Polish workers were hired to work on the railroad, and when those people arrived there was a need to establish more or less formal businesses.

Other Jewish immigrants, arriving independently of the colonization program, constituted the second immigration stream to the nascent village. A woman born in nearby Colonia Carlos Calvo who settled in Villa Clara when she married explained:

Artisans settled in Clara almost simultaneously: blacksmiths who fixed agricultural tools, replaced tires, etc.; masons who helped to build houses; tailors, carpenters, and also merchants.

As the village became more established, additional JCA farmers realized that living in a more concentrated settlement provided two important advantages: proximity to the railroad (at the time the closest outlet to market agricultural products) and to emerging civic institutions and public services. Some *colonos* found it possible to continue farming while commuting between the village and the fields, leaving a *criollo* worker overnight on the farm and returning during the day. An elderly man recalled:

I never abandoned the field. I worked there all day with the workers and I came here in the evening and stayed overnight. You have to work the land. If you do not, nothing will come of it.

A *peón criollo* related the opposite experience:

My father worked in the fields, with one of the Jews . . . as a *peón* . . . His boss lived in the village and they lived on the land.

The arrival of the railroad provided the impetus for the institutional organization of civil society. By 1905 a branch of the Fondo Comunal Cooperativa Agrícola (Community Agricultural Cooperative Fund) opened in Villa Clara, renting the warehouses (*galpones*) alongside the railroad tracks to the prestigious Bunge & Born, which monopolized the marketing of agricultural production in the region. The warehouses were used to store cereal, sell bags and thread, and exchange wheat for flour. Most of the members of the cooperative were from the rural area. The Fondo Comunal was one of several cooperatives established in the province by *colonos* who associated to counteract the pressures imposed on them by the JCA and the buyers of their produce. According to David Kreimer (1984), ex-president of the Instituto Movilizador de Fondos Cooperativos (Institute to Mobilize Cooperative Funds), Argentine agrarian cooperativism was born in Entre Ríos, more specifically in Basavilbaso, where the first cooperative (named Lucienville, to honor the baron's son Lucien) was founded in 1900.

Fondo Comunal on Avenida Hirsch in 2002.

When the Fondo Comunal opened a branch in Villa Clara, it had already achieved success in its headquarters at Villa Domínguez, where it had started in 1904. Kreimer, a former *colono*, remembers that members bought food or farm equipment and brought in their produce, cereals, cream, and eggs, to entrust the co-op to market them. He describes the meat section, where they would discount the members' expenses and provide vouchers that indicated their choice of kosher or nonkosher meat.[6] There was also a bakery section: in exchange for a bag of flour minus the cooperative's operating expenses, the members were given vouchers for bread or crackers. The cooperative soon captured 50 percent of the commercialization of the local produce, acquiring its own building by 1926 and reaching 467 members by 1941.[7]

Civic institutions thrived and combined ethnic and national themes. For example, the celebration of the first centennial of Argentine Independence Day coincided with the inauguration of the Jewish cemetery:

Let's remember the Centennial in 1910, which was a patriotic act and a great dance, and where possibly the first popular *asado con cuero* was served,[8] and when an elderly Jewish immigrant ate it hair and all and died of indigestion, and he was the first to be buried in the Israelite Cemetery Clara Bélez. (*El Pueblo*, January 21, 1992, 3)

We wish to point out an important fact in the institutional life of our village and its neighboring colonies. We refer to the constant preoccupation that the residents and the authorities have had to preserve and increase the public and cultural institutions, such as schools, the municipality, the Caja Rural, the Casa Social, the libraries in the village and the colonies, the first aid clinic, etc. We also need to point out the progressive work of the consumer, production, and credit cooperatives, which are notorious in the important social role they play and in showing the organization and solidarity of the farming population of the area. (Smuckler 1953: 29)

Since their arrival, a central preoccupation of the Jewish *colonos* had been providing education to their children. The Yevich built a school in Colonia Bélez staffed by Sephardic teachers, so the children could get used to Spanish where classes were taught in Yiddish or Hebrew. Some parents also sent their children to an Argentine school in San Jorge. But with the new settlement in Estación Clara, the villagers requested their own school. Escuela Nacional Río Negro No. 84 started operating in 1911 under the direction of Adolfo Pascadore, "a very much appreciated, intelligent, simple, and kind-hearted man" (Muchinik and Isuz de Schulman n.d.a: 20), who was transferred from neighboring San Jorge. As with trade and entertainment, the advancement of education was also credited to the railroad:

First board of the Fondo Comunal, 1922. The first on the left is Dr. Wolcomich.

We waited anxiously for the furniture and supplies to make our dream a reality. Finally, the railroad, the village's founder, brought the elements that were ecstatically received by the residents and taken to the teacher's house, where the school operated at the beginning . . . Many of the students of the School No. 37 or the present one, No. 84, became professionals, some well known businessmen, farmers, workers, or housewives, but in every case the school tried to train good people. (Isuz de Schulman n.d.: 1–4)

Many children had to travel extensively from the surrounding JCA *colonias* to attend the new school in Villa Clara. Recalling his childhood, lay historian Schejter illustrated in an interview how school attendance became integrated into the household economy:

We traveled in winter, and we had to be in school at seven-thirty in the morning, so we left at six in the morning on horseback. School ended at approximately twelve-thirty, and we not only had to pick up what we were told but also the food that was needed and some other stuff from the village which we bought at various stores; we used a saddlebag, a special bag made with two openings which we secured to the saddle, and there we stuck bread, food, fruit, whatever, and the mail, and we returned home.

Health care institutions also provided services that a growing village deserved: Dr. Jorge Wolcomich and his wife, Dr. Olimpia M. de Wolcomich, arrived in Villa Clara from Villa Domínguez in 1913. Dr. Wolcomich was praised in both the archival literature and the ethnographic interviews for his civic participation. Among many other roles, he was a physician on staff at the First Aid Clinic and a member of the Board of Directors of the Casa Social. While Dr. Jorge Wolcomich replaced a Dr. Irigoyen, who actually had not yet been licensed to practice, his wife was the village's midwife until 1950, aided by midwife Ite A. De Schnitman, known as the Bobe Ite. One can only imagine the respect, and often awe, he commanded in the region:

During the difficult years of the First World War, he was the physician of a poor colony, taking care of all kinds of patients and illnesses: a long line of sulkies and carts could be seen every morning on the other side of the rails in front of his house; sulkies and carts that, in many instances, had covered long distances, transporting patients who wanted a physician who could assure them their illnesses could be cured. As an instinctive attitude, we children remained silent and walked on tiptoe when we had to go by the doctor's house. (*Nuestra Clara* 1, no. 1 [1953]: 8)

School in Colonia Bélez in 1928.

Villa Clara soon became the shopping center of the region, where regional farmers at well-populated *colonias* traded their products (such as poultry and eggs) for manufactured foodstuffs (such as flour) or brought their harvests to be loaded on the trains. Yoine Paikovsky, a Polish Jewish immigrant who arrived independently of the JCA and made a living loading and unloading the trains, explained in awe that "you would be out looking in the direction of the warehouses and see a line of carts loaded with wheat or flax, packed in bags. Cart after cart all day long!" The village's economic boom, however, was related to the productivity of the countryside, so, as a *criollo* expressed pensively, "there was work when the harvest was good. If the harvest was not good, there were no jobs."

As was to be expected, periods of economic boom were permeated with busts. The particularly rainy year of 1914, for example, ruined many residents, one of whom shared a reminiscence that showed the power that nature held over household economies:

> I will never forget the famous year 1914, with its storms that made it impossible to use the streets and go to school. I still remember that sad day when my father was forced to exchange the piano for ten bags of flour to cope with the misery of that unforgettable rainy year. (Lemelson 1953: 18)

Despite economic problems, the village experienced continued growth in public services: a judge was appointed, and private electric factories (*usinas*) were installed. Yet daily life was both very hard and unpredictable: the *colonos* were vulnerable not only to adverse impacts of the natural environment (too much or too little rain, invasion of locusts, etc.) but also to the political economy of the region (the obligation to pay a fixed annuity to the JCA after the harvest or to sell the harvests to large companies, such as Bunge & Born).

Having reached a population of 1,500 inhabitants by 1920, Estación Clara (District Bergara) applied to Departamento Villaguay (equivalent to a U.S. county) for authorization to have its own Junta de Fomento (equivalent to a City Council in the United States). The village was granted the rank of *municipalidad de segunda categoría* (a small city government), although the provincial government in Paraná continued to consider it a rural center, given its small size (75 square kilometers). Despite its humble beginnings in a resident's home, the Junta de Fomento was extremely productive during its first years in operation: it set up a tax structure, acquired equipment for garbage collection, installed a new slaughterhouse, explored options for lighting, bought trees for streets and a plaza, started building a road to the closest *colonia* in order to transport products,[9] and opened a library, the Biblioteca Popular Clara (Clara Popular Library), which offered reading material, literary evenings, and theater shows. If the library replicated the social gathering places of the JCA *colonias* and honored the founder's wife, the tree-lined plaza firmly expressed the immigrants' desire and right to be Argentines: it honored the major political figure of the province, Justo José de Urquiza.

A succession of bad years and the double dependency of the JCA farmers on both the administration and the marketing monopolies instigated a group of artisans, farmers, and small storeowners to create "a society for borrowing and savings with the purpose of helping each other," soon to be transformed into a banking cooperative. Referred to as Caja Rural de Villa Clara, Cooperativa de Crédito, it obtained legal recognition from the provincial government by 1922 and, like the Fondo Comunal, symbolized the discrepancies between the goals of the JCA and the need for protection as perceived by *colonos*. The society aimed at being representative of the social structure of the Jewish *colonias* and stipulated that four agriculturalists, two artisans, and two merchants would constitute the board.

By the time it closed in 1951, the Caja Rural was used by most of the *colonias* of the JCA in the province:

> The sphere of influence of the Caja was the area that goes through Villa Clara, including the Bergara District of the Department of Villaguay and the Third and Fourth Districts of the Department of Colón, with the following groups and *colonias:* La Capilla, Bélez, Feinberg, Perliza, Miguel, Desparramados Norte, San Jorge, Carlos Calvo, Domingo Calvo, Pueblo Cazés, Hambis,

Board of Directors of the Caja Rural of Villa Clara, 1929–1936.

Jubileo, Barón Guinzburg 4, 5, and 6, San Vicente, and Bergara Norte, notwithstanding its extension by resolution of the General Assembly (Article 4). (Muchinik and Isuz de Schulman n.d.a)

While the Caja Rural and the Fondo Comunal were founded by the JCA *colonos,* the cooperative ideal was a socialist not an ethnic idea. There were other cooperatives in Villa Clara at the time. On the ninetieth anniversary of the foundation of Villa Clara, a journalist urged people to:

> remember the unionization of the workers of flour mills and the stevedores who formed a Workers' Union of Diverse Trades and opened a cooperative bakery and a meat store inspired by the Uruguayan union organizer . . . and the organizer of Despertar del Obrero. (*El Pueblo,* January 21, 1992: 3)

Despite a growing diversity in the village, JCA ownership continued to be pervasive; for example, the Junta de Fomento asked the JCA to advance 115 hectares (to be paid in two years) to establish its jurisdiction and needed permission from the JCA to install a slaughterhouse on its land. In 1919 the JCA assessed its holdings in Villa Clara since 1895, a step conducive to either selling or donating land

Workers in the sheds, who took turns baking in the Panadería Obrera (Workers' Bakery).

to facilitate the establishment of the village's government and civic institutions. The JCA leased land to the Junta de Fomento in 1921, but it donated eight hectares in exchange for tax concessions in 1923. The JCA also donated land to establish an "Israelite" cemetery, to eradicate mud huts (*ranchos*), to open a new slaughter-house in 1921, and to establish a Municipal (or Catholic) Cemetery in 1927 and a Catholic Chapel in 1936 (Cristo Rey), among many other donations.

The survey that the Junta de Fomento carried out during its first year of opera-tion also provided a sense of the economic, political, social, and cultural life in the village in the 1920s and early 1930s. At that time there was a tannery, a tin shop, a saddler, a blacksmith, a carpentry shop, a soap factory, an auction house, cereal si-los, and a flour mill, which attested to the role that the village played in the region. A car rental business, hotels, and a gas pump indicated that some people needed to stay overnight. Some establishments offered entertainment, such as a bocce court, a billiard hall, a racetrack, an opera, and a cinema. A photographer was on hand to cover social events (Muchinik and Isuz de Schulman n.d.a: 27–32).[10]

Although in 1920 the Junta de Fomento symbolized the political participa-tion of Villa Clara in the province and the department, and its boom in central-izing the regional economy, it was not invulnerable to crises. By 1922 the Junta de Fomento had to approve the opening of biweekly Ferias Francas, fairs that lowered costs of basic foodstuffs (such as sugar and flour) by rationing them into small packages. An idea originally developed by the union organized by the workers of Ortelli & Brothers (the first flour mill) to lower living expenses, the

Ferias Francas would become the second cooperative experience in the village, in this case unrelated to the European immigrants. The workers' union eventually acquired a building, opened a library named El Despertar (The Awakening), offered a loan system to members, and opened its own bakery in 1925.

Life went on despite the ups and downs of the economy, and socializing seemed to be a high priority for the residents. As early as 1922 there was a café used as a meeting place, where people played dominos and cards. The village also had an orchestra, which played at social events attended mostly by immigrants:

> The parties and weddings at the Villa and the colonies were animated by an orchestra composed of aficionados, people who followed the tunes, the *freilachs*, *schers*, valses, *lanceros*, polkas, mazurkas, kept the spirit until sunrise. (Muchinik and Isuz de Schulman n.d.a)

> I remember very well the social and family festivals and the happy weddings, with their dances and traditional rondas, which I will never forget. I also remember the rehearsals of the National Choir of Clara, surrounded by hundreds of children . . . they would look at me and smile when I taught them the National Anthem and the school songs. (Lemelson 1953: 19)

By 1923 the well-respected Dr. Wolcomich had opened his own clinic, where all births of the village and its area of influence took place. In addition to his pro-

President H. Yrigoyen greeted at Villa Clara during a brief stop.

fessional role, he was very involved in civic life and during his lifetime became president of the Junta de Fomento and the school cooperative and a member of the Board of Directors of the Fondo Comunal and the hospital. In 1924 a private electric enterprise owned by a former *colono* started selling lighting for the streets, partially paid for by well-off residents and by the Junta de Fomento. By 1928 the service was extended to include paid home delivery. Although electricity continued to be privately owned until the late 1930s, the state telephone company set up its operations in the village in 1931.

The interconnectedness of Villa Clara and the closest settlements in the region was omnipresent. Colonia Bélez's geographical proximity, accentuated by economic and social interaction during the first two decades of the twentieth century, resulted in the creation of the Comunidad Israelita Clara-Bélez in 1925, to avoid replicating activities of the Jewish populations in the two localities. A direct road replaced an older one going through Bélez to shorten the way to the cemetery. These changes showed that Villa Clara was growing at the expense of Bélez (as it had done earlier with San Jorge) and was increasing its connectedness to the region; one of the first projects of the Junta de Fomento was to open a road to connect Capilla with Villa Clara. The continued growth of the village was evident in the opening of a police station in 1923, although the police commissioner still lived in San Jorge and only came to Villa Clara to get major news:

> He could read and write and came to town to get the news; he wrote down in the store on wrapping paper the news related to his service, so that after several days he could bring the birth certificates, many with names changed forever since he had already written down the information in the books. (*Gacetilla de los Clarenses* [January 1994])

By 1927 there were three hotels: Central, Entrerriano, and Sr. Darchisky (Muchinik and Isuz de Schulman n.d.a: 43), and in 1929 the village inaugurated its own band:

> [Let's remember] Don Hernani B. Nery, musician from his heart and composer, who came around 1929, teaching music to many youngsters: he funded a municipal band, which trained many well-known [musicians]. (*El Pueblo*, January 8, 1992)

The village experienced a substantial demographic increase in the 1930s. Most of the newcomers continued to be JCA farmers. As described earlier, it was difficult to predict good harvests that would suffice to meet the payments required by an insensitive JCA administration. An ex-resident of Bélez remembered:

In truth, we have to admit that the *colonos* were not always compensated for the sacrifices they made to work; sometimes this was due to the fluctuations of the international market where their products were placed; at other times it was due to climate changes. We also need to add the amortizations and expenses related to the exploitation of their lands. Starting in 1930, that caused a marked drop in their production and their move to the urban centers that affected the evolution of our colonies that lacked the necessary support to keep them. (Smuckler 1953: 29)

After thirty-five years of colonization, a large number of JCA farmers abandoned the rural project in the provinces of Santa Fé and Entre Ríos during the 1930s (Weinstein and Salomón 1991). By then the restlessness in the JCA *colonias* had been exacerbated, as the *colonos* found a referent for new possibilities of making a living in Villa Clara. The pull to the village was probably more complex than the reasons advanced by Salomón Smuckler, since, according to the people I interviewed, both those who were successful and those who had failed as *colonos* were attracted to the village as it grew into an economic and social nucleus.[11] The contingent of JCA farmers that moved from the *colonia* to the village during the 1930s included some who could not meet the payments expected by the JCA and others who gave up on agriculture altogether, selling their farms and buying a store in the village with the capital obtained. In addition to keeping house, women also sold handcrafts to help provide for the family.

It is not surprising to learn that in the early days of the village its population was predominantly Jewish, estimated at 300 families:

Well, the butcher was a Jew, the baker was a Jew, the milkman was a Jew, the owner of the general store and the owner of the warehouse were Jews, and most of the members of the cooperative were Jews, because they were the people who brought the concept of a cooperative here.

I remember that when I was growing up this town was Jewish more than anything else.

As the JCA farmers kept coming, this predominantly Jewish village became a center of regional trade. Although most of the stores were owned by Jews, most of the employees were *criollos*, with a minority of immigrants of other ethnic extraction who also owned property and practiced trades. In addition, there were marked social differences among farmers, artisans, and learned people within the majority Jewish population. As early as 1904 the landless Jewish immigrants had begun congregating for religious ceremonies in what was called the Synagogue of the Artisans in Colonia Bélez. Soon, however, the wealthier group

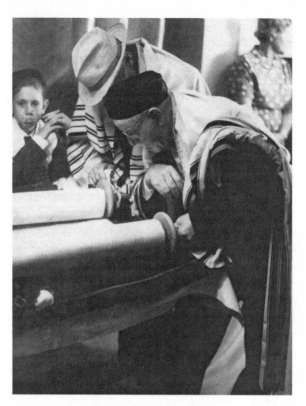

Religious ceremony at a synogogue.

started building a two-story synagogue, Beith Jacob, which was opened in 1917 in Villa Clara. The Portuguese builders Correia and Silva together with the Italians Visiconti and Aletti constructed most of the solid buildings in the village.

In the early days the village was small and the streets were muddy, making transportation difficult. Combining what he was told by his family with what he learned at school and through his own reading, a middle-aged *criollo* man told me:

> Look, I'm going to tell you what my father and my grandfather told me. From 1901 to 1909 there were two or three houses in the village of Clara. I was born in '27 but, of course, I read a lot also. There was this street in the center, straight out of the Municipal Building. In 1902 there was no asphalt, there was no gravel, nothing, nothing, everything was mud.

An elderly man who worked for the Fondo Comunal during those times was more specific:

People would come from the *colonia* and *peones* and *colonos* would have to leave their horses and their sulkies in the outskirts, because the mud would be up to the horses' chests. There was a little path close to the wall, but that was all . . . only mud.

The Municipality of Junta de Fomento would close San Martín Street with wire so it would not be damaged, because there were too many carts.

The village's economic and cultural boom attracted still more migration from the neighboring areas (this time not Jewish), particularly during the 1930s with the arrival of several farmer families from the areas of San Jorge and Villa Elisa, descendants of the Swiss colonized by General Urquiza. Additional farmer families from diverse national and ethnic backgrounds also arrived from Santa Rosa, Hambis, San Ernesto, and San Jorge. Some of this migration was the result of the economic depression of the 1930s, to which Villa Clara was not immune. Both the Junta de Fomento and the residents had to cope with it:

> The crisis of 1930 was felt in the village, and the wages of the municipal employees were decreased in October. The crisis continued, and the Junta reported a deficit of 3,749 pesos generated by unpaid car registrations. After discussing the gravity of the situation . . . the Junta decided to request a loan . . . A fixed price for meat was established . . . The bakers also offered bread at a lower price. (Muchinik and Isuz de Schulman n.d.a: 47–50)

To make matters worse, the rural economy continued to suffer from natural disasters. By 1932 the Junta de Fomento was so concerned about a type of locust known as *saltona* that it requested provincial funding to extend existing protection and to purchase additional equipment to combat the invasions. Yet, despite the economic depression, businesses continued to be established in the 1930s, including shoemaking, tailoring, and sewing shops, hair salons, a mechanic shop, a carpentry shop, brick factories, general stores, bakeries, several meat stores, and even a street ice cream vendor who went from house to house with a wheelbarrow.

According to the last names provided by Schejter (1986), most storeowners in Villa Clara continued to be Eastern European Jews, but Italians owned the two flour mills in town (Ortelli & Brothers and Marini & Castiglioni). The two commercial establishments most remembered by the informants are Casa Kleiman (hardware store and fuel sales, cereal storage, and cattle auctions) and the Fondo Comunal.

By 1942 Villa Clara had major public services: a civil court and civil registry, police station, post office, telephone, telegraph, and electricity, although that service was unpredictable, as a descendant of Italians told me: for six months "there was only electricity in the Centro. But many lived in the outskirts, in the barrios."

Because the village offered a range of facilities, services, and community activities that provided more comfortable living conditions for the aging immigrant population, many retired, elderly, and disabled people moved there, either leaving their children behind to work the land or having their children also move to the village.

Rural Depopulation and the Emergence of a Multiethnic and Socially Stratified Landscape in Villa Clara (1940s–1990s)

We can say that . . . this village . . . was a result of the influence of the Jewish colonias. After a confluence of immigrant waves and together with the French, the Belgians, the Germans, the Italians, and with the contribution of the criollo, *it has truly become a melting pot today. (Schejter 1986)*

There is nobody in the countryside now! Pura tapera.[1] *(Swiss-French descendant)*

In the past, the colonia *was a small village, and now there is nobody there.* (criollo *woman)*

There is nobody in the land, neither in my colonia *nor in any* colonia. *(Volga German descendant)*

In the postwar era Argentina experienced a decrease in the size of European immigration and a decline in its international role as a major exporter of basic foodstuffs. Although its status as a "promised land" or a "mill of the world" became untenable, images of infinite wealth were still crafted in political discourse, particularly during the presidency of Juan Domingo Perón (1945–1955). During this populist decade, the image of unlimited Argentine economic potential underlined an apparent shift in the concentration of power, from a landed bourgeoisie to a new middle class, and nurtured the emergence of a highly politicized working class brokered by a cadre of trade unionists who negotiated a new paradigm for the distribution of wealth, rights, and benefits.

To explore the impact of the international and national economy, it is useful to examine the demographic, economic, political, and social changes at the local level. Particularly relevant here are the dates 1947 and 1994, which marked two significant events in the natural history of the railroad, which continued to act as a proxy for the history of Villa Clara. In 1947 the railroad built by the British in Argentina was nationalized by President Perón to prove the country's capacity for endogenous development. Perceived by his supporters as a strong commitment to nationalism and by his detractors as a populist strategy (one JCA farmer pointed out that the British were pulling out of the investment anyway), the nationalization of the major transportation system was one among many policies, such as industrialization, labor legislation, and political participation, intended to modernize the country.

From 1950 onward the state-promoted industrialization process attracted many Argentines to urban centers. The impact of these policies on Villa Clara and its area of influence was significant. On the one hand, the centralization of industrialization in a limited number of large towns stimulated rural-urban migration and added to the multicausality of rural flight. On the other hand, smaller towns and even villages like Villa Clara also became the destination for those unwilling to migrate too far from home. The most formidable pull factor lurked in the distant lights of Buenos Aires: according to many informants, the baron's dreams were turned around as rural and village desertion of the Jewish settlers of Entre Ríos became normative. Soon their flight was replicated by other European immigration waves. Internal migrations, and particularly rural-urban migration and urbanization, became natural correlates of the process of import-substitution industrialization.

In 1994 the neo-Peronist government of president Carlos Saúl Menem privatized the railroads as a move to restructure the economy and negotiate payment of the country's external debt. When the railroad station ended passenger service in Villa Clara, a heavy blow was dealt to both the economic and the social life of the village and nostalgia tinged the collective memory of the past.

Phase 4: The Incorporation of Bélez into Villa Clara (1940s–1950s)

Villa Clara was a vibrant village during the mid-1940s, as attested by the existence of four soccer teams as well as strong commercial, civic, and social institutions. There was the café of Suse Goldman, for example, which was "the social gathering place of merchants and professionals and that—and why not?—was like the political headquarters for any party" (*El Pueblo*, February 1, 1992). A retired teacher, very active in the Asociación de Jubilados (Senior Citizen Center), recalls the time when she was taken there during her first visit to her boyfriend's family in 1943 and had the distinct feeling that she was being introduced to the whole of Clarense society.

The village also boasted major health services (a hospital, three pharmacies, three physicians, one dentist), public services (a notary, post office, and police station), educational and technical institutions (a grade school and a sewing school), and the railroad, local government, two cooperatives, businesses that marketed a variety of regional products (hides, cereal, chicken, eggs, dairy products, fruits, meat), and even a cinema.[2]

The residents of Villa Clara continued their high level of civic involvement, and two major institutions emerged in the 1940s through their fund-raising efforts: the Hospital General San Martín, which opened in 1942 and extended inpatient and outpatient care for low-income inhabitants in the village and neighboring *colonias*, and the Casa Social Barón Hirsch, established in 1947, whose goals were to "endow the population with a building for public cultural and social and events that enhance spiritual brotherhood" (Casa Social Barón Hirsch 1947 [Statutes]). Although its by-laws state that "all persons . . . with no distinction of race, belief, sex, or nationality as long as they are persons of moral and good manners" could be members, the perception of many non-Jewish informants was that it catered to Jews (referred to collectively as the Colectividad Israelita) and prevented access to non-Jews through the high rental fees of its facilities. This view is not supported by the many programs that document the numerous national commemorations, school events, weddings, birthdays, concerts, theater performances, graduation parties, and political meetings that took place there.

Concomitant with Villa Clara's growth was Bélez's decline, symbolizing the end of *colonia* life in the region and the JCA program as short-term colonization. Although at first Bélez was larger than Villa Clara, soon the pattern was reversed. And in the course of time Bélez and Villa Clara merged through the schools and the synagogues. At most only two generations of immigrants remained there, as this JCA resident who stayed put explained:

Musician playing the accordion.

My parents lived at my grandparents' home since they weren't alive anymore. All my dad's brothers went to Buenos Aires. My sisters got married: one went to Concordia and the other to the province of Buenos Aires.

The original family could only hold onto the land if the children stayed or returned to the village to take care of production. There are several cases in Villa Clara of children who, after years of living in large urban centers pursuing higher education, came back to replace their parents as they aged or became disabled. One, a veterinarian, was able to find a direct application of his studies to his new occupation in the village. A computer specialist could not and opened a meat store in the village to supplement profits from the farm he came back to exploit. When his father fell sick in the mid-1970s, his mother asked for his advice: if she leased the farm, she said, she feared that

> the old man's sacrifice was going to go into the hands of a tenant. And after a week of thinking about it, I talked to her or I wrote to her, I think, and said that I was coming. That I was coming to live here. We only had about ninety hectares and some cows. I lived in Clara and did the same as my dad, but I replaced the horse with a motorcycle. I went to the farm by day and returned at night on my motorcycle.

The primal relationship of Jewish *colonos* with the land was radically transformed within their first decade of settlement in Argentina, generating a decline in the rural population that can be understood as a function of land tenure and residential changes. Some stayed on the farms that the JCA originally allotted them. For those who were drawn to the village to avail themselves of educational opportunities for their children or start their own business, there were several possibilities. One was for the original farmer to sell the farm: some farmers, including their children who wanted to continue with the family operation, were unable to hold onto the land for lack of capital or credit. A son of an original *colono* explained that "you could only continue to be a farmer if you had a lot of capital. You could not continue with the little that your parents left you because there wasn't any more credit, your old machines didn't work anymore, and you couldn't buy new machines." Additional factors that made farming unprofitable and pushed farmers to sell their JCA farms during the 1940s were the new municipal taxes, labor legislation for rural employees, and their hopes for another lifestyle for their children. Several JCA descendants mentioned the inability of *colonos* to afford the new social benefits awarded to the *peones* (the *criollo* hired workers) by President Perón's legislation and assured me that the implementation of this policy simultaneously harmed two stakeholders: older Jewish *colonos* whose children had left and the *criollos* they employed. While *criollo* unemployment was seen by some as the result of Jewish farmers' lack of social sensitivity, others understood the positive and negative impact of legislation for rural employees on the regional economy.

Another reason for rural desertion by *colonos* lay in their beliefs about the best future for their children: some saved money to send some of their children away to be educated or supported the decision of other children to enter business in an urban location. This decision often resulted in two, possibly unforeseen, consequences: the children were not around to help aging parents with seasonal work and the children's move often became permanent. Some *colonos* even dissuaded their children from continuing with their parents' rural occupations. I often had the impression that many among the original settlers had lost the confidence that the baron had vested in the fruitfulness and moral call for a "return" to agricultural work, as this man narrated in obvious frustration:

> I was already older and had the intention of continuing to work my parents' land. I didn't have money, but my parents had money, so one day I said to my mom and dad: "Let's buy a harvester and a tractor. Let's continue working the land." My mother was a very intelligent woman, but not for certain things, and said no, no, and no. I don't know why she was so opposed, but it hurt me very much because I wanted to continue with the farm.

Many sold their farms to existing JCA farmers and thus contributed to land concentration in fewer hands. Three JCA descendants in Villa Clara successfully extended their holdings from the original 100 to 150 hectares allotted by the JCA to more than 1,000 hectares. One of them recalled this was not an easy process:

> We kept struggling, fighting to make a living and doing everything we needed to do to make our lives better, like taking the milk to the creamery. That way we made a few pesos and we bought another farm, next to ours. When my parents were alive we bought land, because we saw that the people were leaving for Buenos Aires, where people made a good living! Yes, they were selling, and some of the wealthier ones started to extend their parcels.

The lack of generational continuity in farming activities combined with the natural aging process of the original settlers contributed significantly to rural desertion. Consider this: an immigrant arriving at age forty in 1892 would already have turned eighty by 1932. Thus normal aging, fear of isolation in *colonias* with high rates of desertion, and the real possibility of death of a spouse, illness, or having their children leave were all factors weighing on the decision of *colonos*, or their children, to leave agriculture by either leasing or selling the farms. A major reason to move to the village was illness of a family member or death of a spouse. One woman explained that she had "to sell the land when my husband died to pay for the costs of his illness"; another narrated the family's story of selling the farm and buying a small house in the village when her father became very sick. Staying alone during rural flight pressed elders to leave, since "nobody was living at the house or around and you were scared." In fact, some planned their old age around living their retirement years in the village. One JCA descendant told the moving story of his father buying a house in the village by 1945 (when he finished making his installment payments), moving there, and leasing the land in 1956, when he already "was sick and didn't want the land so he sold the farm equipment."

Maintaining ownership and leasing the land to others was another alternative chosen by those unable to farm due to advanced age, illness, or disability. A man who traveled frequently for dialysis treatment to a hospital two hours away from Villa Clara explained to me that he had leased his property of 168 hectares (his father had bought additional land for him) for the last twenty years to a descendant of Volga German settlers who has a veterinary business in the village. Soy cultivation provides him better profits (22 percent of the harvest) than cattle raising (only three pesos per head).

These alternative land tenure arrangements facilitated different relationships with the land, the major factor in production. In addition to changes in land tenure, it is instructive to examine changes in patterns of home ownership. Once Villa Clara boomed, some Jewish *colonos* bought homes that they rented out while they lived on the land and later occupied as they became too old to farm the land. Though nostalgic, the aging *colonos* who moved to the village could socialize with other pensioned workers and access more services. They contributed to reenergizing the institutional and social life in the village. In fact, Villa Clara's social life was culturally Jewish for the first three decades of the twentieth century.

The total population of Jewish *colonos* in the rural area declined with their move to the village shortly after its foundation in the early 1900s, and the total population of Jews in the village decreased after the 1950s: Comunidad Israelita de Villa Clara's estimated 200 Jewish households by 1947, 137 by 1960, 92 by 1970, and 57 by 2008 (of those, 22 were mixed, with one non-Jewish spouse).[3] Between the 1940s and the 1960s the Jews became a minority and other ethnicities moved in. Daniel Bargman (1992: 55) calls this "a process of ethnic substitution within the same structure: *chacras*, cooperatives, villages, and institutions endure; the ethnic ascription of its members has changed."

Phase 5: Regional Migration to Villa Clara and the Process of Ethnic Substitution (1950s–1960s)

Rural desertion has been concomitant both with the increase of cattle raising since the 1940s and with industrialization, at the expense of farming. Jews were far from being the only population groups settled in *colonias* to abandon the rural areas for more urban locations, though their emigration took place later, between the 1940s and the 1960s. The child of a pioneer Jewish immigrant and high government official during the 1950s, Benedicto Caplan, summed up the return to earlier forms of production in these terms:

> Between 1945 and 1955 there was an important economic and sociological change: industrialization. The countryside started to collapse as the manu-facturing suburbs started to appear in the large cities. The Jewish peasants were not the only ones to leave. They only left earlier. Afterward everybody left. (De Paoli de Bellman Eguiguren and Oyenden 1993: 181)

Bustling with commercial and artisan shops and concentrating agricultural production for marketing and transportation, Villa Clara continued to be a vi-brant village during the first half of the twentieth century. While the major-ity of the resident owners of land and commerce were Jewish, the village also attracted residents of neighboring *colonias* with diverse national and ethnic backgrounds, who came to buy and sell produce, deal with bureaucratic tasks (*trámites legales*), and socialize. The residents of many of these *colonias* (such as San Jorge, Santa Rosa, Villa Elisa, San José, La Capilla, Santa Anita, Bélez, San Salvador, La Rosada, San Gregorio, Bergara Norte, Lucas Norte, Lucas Sur, Carlos Calvo, and San Antonio) had populations with Jewish, French, Swiss, Belgian, Italian, and German backgrounds who, as in Colonia Clara, had also experienced a rapid assimilation process. Their children, by then *criollos* claim-ing birth "in the Argentine," were there to stay.

Other European farmers were suffering from the same factors that pushed the JCA farmers out of the countryside and had also experienced a dependent relationship with landowners, though in their case the land was owned by wealthy individuals who profited from colonizing landless immigrants rather than by a philanthropic organization. A German descendant explained how wealthy landowners implemented colonization programs:

> The family was very rich. They would place some animals on the land, mea-sure it, and it was a *colonia*. Then they would put *colonos* to take care of mat-ters, and to plant wheat, oats, flax, and corn, everything. Well, they would bring those of us who wanted land and didn't have it. Then the *patrones* [bosses], these people who were so rich, would be notified; then you would go and talk to them and they would say: Yes, go have 50 hectares, move here. Then the *colonos* would plant and give a percentage to the *patrón* and the rest was the *colono's*.

As in the case of the Jews before them, one of the factors that attracted the Western European descendants to the village was their changed relationship to the land. Although the children of the original settlers had obtained land through inheritance, large family size often resulted in parceling the land into small plots, nonsustainable for agriculture. That is why those arriving in Villa Clara were often called *colonitos chiquitos* (little *colonos*). One of them explained that "grandfather had two wives and fourteen children. He had about 400 hectares. Each one inherited his part, but there were a lot of them."

The opposite pattern, experienced by more successful Western European farmers, was the purchase of land for their marriageable children. Even if these properties were not too large, ranging from 70 to 100 hectares, the fact that the new immigrants were able to make a living for themselves and leave a sufficient inheritance to their children within one generation was a marvel to some of the people I talked to. Comparing the economic situation at that time to the present, a retired seamstress of Swiss descent enthusiastically affirmed that it was easier to make money then, mentioning as an example that "my father worked as a carpenter all his life. And he was able to give 100 hectares to each of us, nine kids!"

Even if they had inherited land, the farmers tried every possible strategy to avoid losing it. One was mortgaging the lands when interest was high; another was to lease them and live off sharecropping income, as these descendants recall:

What happened here was that they were paying whatever amount of interest. You would put 10,000 pesos in the bank and you would make a fortune with the interest. After the interest fell, these people were left on the street and had to sell the farm because they didn't have anything to maintain it with.

All my life we'd plant *cosecha fina*, like wheat and flax.[4] But since the prices wouldn't cover all the expenses we had to stop doing that and focus on planting *forraje para animales* and lease some to people to plant on a percentage basis.[5]

These farmers also recalled a life of hard work and little predictability, often referring to the lack of time, since "farming is from sunrise to sunset," and noting that "the weather doesn't cooperate, either it doesn't rain or it rains a lot." Some of the people who were unable to keep their farms remained in the agricultural industry as contractors: "they take five hundred or one thousand hectares and work them for others, charging per hectare." And those who were able to keep the land managed to extend their landholdings through purchase from those who needed to make a quick sale, since "there was always someone to buy, always a buyer; it was land that was idle. People always want more land."

Thus population streams other than the neighboring Jewish farmers, including both immigrants and *criollos*, were also drawn to the village by the railroad, at the expense of La Capilla, Bélez, San Jorge, and many other settlements in the region. Some of my informants' recollections referred to the arrival of people from diverse backgrounds, yet all hopeful of making a better life in Villa Clara, to the extent that some of the other settlements virtually disappeared. As a previous resident of San Jorge told me, "almost everyone came to Clara. San Jorge is now deserted."

The German *colonia* of Santa Anita provided a moving example of repeated relocations. The torrential rains of 1929 in the region, the world crisis of 1932, the droughts of 1934–1935 and the frequent locust plagues forced many debt-ridden *colonos* off their lands. By the 1940s many young *colonos* were also forced to abandon Santa Anita, transforming a self-subsisting village into an area of out-migration. During the 1950s and 1960s the emigration of sharecroppers reached massive proportions. The land had been too subdivided to be productive, the prices for cereals were not as profitable as during World War II, and there was less need for workers, given technological advances in agriculture. Many *colonos* were evicted for failing to meet the payment conditions. Changing government policies worsened the situation:

> The first president that extended the sharecropping contracts was the conservative Dr. Ramón Castillo in 1939. By 1939–1940, when World War II was declared, Argentina supplied meat to England and its armies. Cattle raising took on extraordinary value. It was sad to see many *colonos* leaving, their furniture piled up on their little carts. After Castillo, Perón continued with the extensions, but later Presidents Aramburu and Onganía reversed the situation by approving a decree favoring the landowners. (an informant quoted in Honeker de Pascal and Jacob de Hoffmann n.d.: 234)

Many residents of Santa Anita moved to Villa Clara, either directly or after trying their luck at other sites first, and continued to remember their *colonia* nostalgically. An elderly woman descended from the Germans of the Volga remembered the family saga:

> I was born in Santa Anita and from there we came to San Salvador, the *colonia*, and from San Salvador to *colonia* Lucas and then to a *colonia* called San Gregorio . . . My dad was only one year old when he came from Russia with his father. When there was that big war, many people fled to Argentina. So my great-grandfather, my dad's parents, lived on the water for a month.

But in Santa Anita, as in many previous *colonias*, the only ones who can make sense of what is left of the European colonization period in the region are those with either personal or passed-on experience of the immigration and emigration narratives, who tap their memories to understand the ruins. As a chronicler of the German colonization wrote:

> Today the *taperas*, surrounded by *paraísos* and fruit trees, remain as silent testimonies of that exodus. Often one sees a car with some of those *colonos* or their descendants visiting, with nostalgia. (Honeker de Pascal and Jacob de Hoffmann n.d.: 235)

While most of the *colonias* came to an end, the actual reasons differed, as in the case of the Belgian immigrant settlements in Villaguay. Colonia Belga was expropriated by the military during the 1940s to establish housing for their families, accelerating the process that this *colonia* was experiencing, similar to that of other immigrant groups. While some descendants of the original settlers stayed put (a few as medium or large landowners, most as sharecroppers or rural employees), the majority emigrated to Villa Clara or larger urban centers.

Criollos were also dislocated by changes in the rural economy and the concentration of jobs in Villa Clara and settled on the outskirts, in La Clarita. One leather artisan pointed out the differences between the past and the present housing styles:

> Now there are only houses built with concrete, only nice houses, but in the past there were only small *ranchos*, made of weeds, aluminum. The *colonos* lived in the center of town. In La Clarita there were poor people, poor *criollo* people . . . who came from Villaguay, from Lucas, from Mojones, they would come looking for work. Colonia Clara was very progressive because there was a lot of work . . . not like now when the people are dying of hunger. There was work for everyone!

While some immigrants' children owned either small holdings or larger holdings obtained through inheritance or through their own investment practices, the original *criollos* had rarely owned land. Although there are some accounts of people who owned land or had sharecropping arrangements and were subsequently dispossessed when the new immigrants arrived, most *criollo* informants tell stories of working as hired hands or contract laborers. As we have seen, the *criollos* and the Jewish *colonos* had developed a symbiotic relationship by being embedded in an economic and social system, as temporary or permanent workers. Whether living in the *colonia* or in the village, *criollos* continued to work for the settlers of Colonia Clara; thus, not surprisingly, they were the first to suffer the impact of rural desertion. Other *criollos* arrived later from other areas, attracted by the economic boom in the village that generated predictable sources of employment and housing.

Unable to become landowners, some *criollos* became homeowners. Some were able to buy land in town, building on the lot themselves or becoming beneficiaries of municipal housing programs for low-income persons. These strategies helped them partially offset the loss of employment either on the farms or in businesses that closed down with the recession in agricultural productivity. A woman who bakes bread that her husband sells door to door told me the following story:

> We came afterward, while we were working for this boss and were earning in good proportion to what we were producing. We would put a little toward food and would save a little for the land. We planned well. At the time, they gave you opportunities so for a few years every month we'd have to pay thirteen pesos, every month . . . And one day my husband said to me: "We're going to work and dedicate ourselves to having a little piece of land, we're going to build a house because sooner or later the boss will throw us out, and we'll at least have somewhere to live." The two of us reached an agreement and, well, we have been here for five years.

These regional migrations helped Villa Clara attain the required population size to be considered a *municipalidad de segunda categoría* (second-rank municipality) in 1943, a status it retains to this day.

Phase 6: Social Class Stratification—El Centro and La Clarita (1970s–1980s)

Simultaneously with the continuing process of rural desertion of immigrant settlements in the 1970s, the village financed additional public services, attracting still more newcomers. Some examples are the opening of the Cooperativa de Agua Potable (Cooperative for Drinkable Water) in 1969; the improvement of the road connecting the village with the highway; and the operation by a major bank (the Banco Comercial del Norte) of the first financial institution, Caja Rural, in 1973. A long-awaited high school, the Instituto Delio Panizza, which awarded a business degree, opened in 1972 on a lot donated by the Fondo Comunal and became an important attraction for future migrants who preferred the village to agriculture.

While the village appeared to be insulated from the outside world, there was political proof of its connectedness at the individual and institutional level. Local events in Villa Clara also mirrored those of the nation. For the first time in the village's history, the highest administrative position was appointed rather than elected in the 1970s. When a military junta representing the three branches

Multiethnic group of musicians playing at a wedding in 1957.

of the armed forces in Argentina seized power in 1976,[6] municipal employee Leopoldo Baldoni was appointed mayor, a position he retained throughout the junta's period in government, the Proceso de Reorganización Nacional (Process of National Reorganization), 1976–1983. Strangely enough, I found no references to the impact of the military dictatorship on daily life in Villa Clara in either the testimonial or archival sources, although Baldoni's administration is hailed for its public works. Looking at the last names of the members of Mayor Baldoni's administration in 1976, when he was named delegate of the military intervention, it is clear that Villa Clara was already a multiethnic locality. Last names such as Baldoni, Arlettaz, Muchinik, de Heer, Fontana, Wouterlood, Schulman, Coduri, Birocco, Mendelevich, Kler, Blanc, Schejter, Den Dauw, Roude, Catvin, Marinelli, Becker, López, Elstein, Fontana, and Hermosa reflect Baldoni's administration; there was an expansion of public services, including forestation, asphalting and providing sidewalks for the major avenues in the Centro (downtown), building playgrounds and a sports center equipped with a swimming pool, and installing a garbage collection and sewer system, among other improvements to the village.

But the public service that Mayor Baldoni is most remembered for is the public housing projects in new neighborhoods that expanded into La Clarita, concomitant with his program to abolish the mud huts (*abolición del rancho*). The drive, however, was to make housing available to all rather than only as a welfare program for the poor. Conscious of its popularity because of these major public programs, the Municipality started a *Boletín* (Bulletin) to inform

New government housing in La Clarita.

the population about its accomplishments. In *Bulletin 6* (1978) we are informed of the inauguration of the Housing Plan Alborada, where houses were given to members of various ethnic groups (Carlos Hermosa, Carlos and Neris Lugren, Salomón Kusnir, Gladys Zermatten, and Gregorio Vara, among others). It is not surprising that so many people admire Baldoni's public works program, which benefited so many.

A *criollo* woman authored Baldoni's eulogy, using her biography to document his multifaceted support for her family:

> In the eighties, you, our Mayor, helped us settle in a municipal neighborhood and visited us from time to time to see our progress. Little by little, we recovered our material life. But the most important thing for us was feeling worthy of your concern. You also gave me the possibility to work in the municipal government; I felt so proud that I promised I would not let you down. (Reynoso de Fleitas n.d.: 12)

While this tribute is about personal help, the document also praises Mayor Baldoni for his many projects to benefit the village: a school of folk dances and sports, a crafts school, music bands, a nursery school, and, of course, the museum.

Symbolic of the ethnic transformation were changes in the visibility of the Jewish and Catholic religions: in 1968 a synagogue was demolished and a new Catholic church was built. The synagogue built in Colonia Bélez in 1912—the last icon of Jewish community life in the JCA *colonias*—decayed beyond repair after a storm. Opposing factions debated over two options: restoring the synagogue (which, as Eufemio Schulman and other members of the community reminded people, contains the history of the initial times of the Jewish colonization in the Argentine Republic) or demolishing it to raise money for Israel. Proponents of the latter option prevailed in 1972. While the Jewish presence was still very prominent in the village (an informant recalled that there was still a Jewish school in 1977), the Municipality financed a Catholic parish to replace a smaller chapel dating from 1936,[7] a move that some consider emblematic of the military government's rampant Catholicism and well-known anti-Semitism.[8]

Probably more important than religious differences were the extreme social distinctions that could be mapped in the village landscape, where one could identify a center and a periphery as a proxy for social stratification. While the historical records documented a village where social differences were based on ethnicity, oral histories painted a picture of social class distinctions that had deepened over time. In fact, a clear physical and cognitive separation between the haves (in the Centro) and the have-nots (in the barrios) had been established. The Centro, located around the Municipality, was characterized by the concentration of housing from the early times (usually built at the owners' expense) and had become more visible as the contrasting public housing appeared in the periphery, the barrios. Generically labeled La Clarita, the name of the first neighborhood, the barrios included many poor and lower-middle-class neighborhoods. Characteristics of the barrios include location in the outskirts of the village and housing provided at reduced cost and built by the government. The contrasting physical landscape of the Centro and the barrios was reflected in the relative perceptions that their populations had of themselves and of each other.

Harvest.

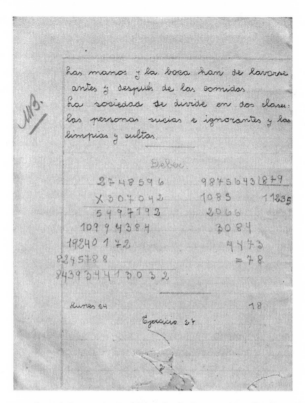

The concept of social class as perceived by a schoolgirl in 1930. Translated into English, the text says: "The hands and the mouth need to be washed before and after meals. Society is divided in two classes: persons who are dirty and ignorant and those who are clean and educated."

The increased occurrence of begging and petty theft in the Centro, attributed to the poor residing in La Clarita (the periphery), helped nurture a public discourse that explained socioeconomic differences as educational deficits. These, in turn, were related to ethnic background, thus adding another feature of comparison between the past and the present. Social stratification was visible: the Centro had electricity, and the barrios like La Clarita did not. In time, "La Clarita" became a generic term for the poorer part of the village, now a myriad of new barrios. The stratification became even more apparent when more *criollos* came to live in Villa Clara as it became the commercial center of an agricultural region in full development.

The increased ethnic and social class diversity in Villa Clara since the 1970s was reflected in three housing types: *casas grandotas* (huge houses) in the Centro, *piecitas de alquiler* (small rental rooms) in several places close to the Centro, and *ranchos* (mud huts) in La Clarita. The Centro continued to be the preferred location for the descendants of Europeans. As soon as the newcomers could, they moved from renting to purchasing existing houses or building their own.

While the Centro did not have much space to expand (only north of the railways and close to the municipal building), La Clarita, the poorer part of the village, continued to expand toward Villaguay, the closest town. According to an informant, the periphery had grown fourfold since the mid-1930s. Almost 45 percent of the population of the village had arrived from the rural areas be-

High society.

Mud hut.

tween 1968 and 1970 and built *ranchos* in the barrios. A former mayor of Belgian descent ironically referred to Villa Clara at the time as "the capital of the *rancho*."

While some residents of La Clarita reported having moved to Villa Clara from the countryside for personal security reasons, most claimed lack of employment and access to services as the major reason. With unemployment and underemployment running high in the barrios, many people do short-term jobs, as cattle transporters (*troperos*), workers at the storage sheds (*galpones*) behind the railroad tracks, store clerks, and temporary peons in the fields (*peones de campo*) during the sowing and harvest periods, or perform infrastructure tasks, as fencers (*alambradores*), waterhole diggers (*poceros*), and—the lucky ones—permanent overseers (*puesteros*) on the few farms surrounding the village. Others attempt to make a living at anything they can think of, which includes begging or holding onto municipal welfare programs. New survival strategies have emerged to face everyday needs in the periphery, some supported by residents of the Centro as philanthropic movements. Examples are a biweekly *trueque* (barter of cooked food), a weekly *ropero familiar* (family closet, where used clothing is distributed), and *comedores comunitarios* (community dining rooms that provide free meals for infants, school-age children, and seniors and are funded by the Municipality, the state, cooperatives, and the Catholic parish).

Many institutions from the early years persisted. The Fondo Comunal continued to be a vibrant cooperative association through the 1980s. It approved new laws in 1984 to promote both agriculture and cattle raising and offered technical assistance to producers, including providing them with fertilizers, seeds, and tools and continuing to market the members' products. Cooperativism was alive and well in the region, and a rice cooperative emerged in Villa Elisa, with a large population of descendants of the Western European immigration. The Fondo Comunal in Villa Clara was selected in 1990 as the site for the commemoration of the International Day of Cooperation. And, as the JCA deviated from its original plan, it donated many of its lots to the Municipality to build social or administrative institutions or housing for the poor. By 1978 all the donated land was legally owned and titled. The railroad was still strong and provided employment for ten people from the village in 1976.

Some reverse migration emerged: several informants who had moved to Buenos Aires returned during the 1970s to live closer to their families. Some with connections in the village could find work. But the trend was for outmigration rather than in-migration. Most of those who had left Villa Clara never returned in person, though their memories were tied to the village of their childhood and youth. Some nostalgic émigrés founded an expatriate association in 1951 and a periodical publication in 1953: *Nuestra Clara, ¡Patria Chica! ¡Rincón Querido! Organo de Difusión de la Asociación de Ex Residentes de Villa Clara y sus Alrededores, Entre Ríos* (Our Clara, Small Motherland! Beloved Corner! Official Publication of the Association of Ex-Residents of Villa Clara and Its Surroundings, Entre Ríos). The first issue described the mission of the association: to promote a "spiritual link between the ex-residents of Villa Clara and its surroundings, stimulate the love for our native heritage and the spirit of social solidarity that developed in the colonies, and contribute to the progressive development of cultural and social activities." In the second issue, the conditions for membership were outlined: a prospective member must be a native or resident of Villa Clara's region of influence and must be accepted by the Board of Directors. The activities of the Association of Ex-Residents were diverse and drew on the members' needs to ritualize the past in Villa Clara to establish a connection with each other in the present. For example, the second issue of the periodical announced the constitution of a Subcommittee for the Pilgrimage to Clara to plan "a trip to our beloved village, addressing one of the most important wishes of many of the members." As many transnational immigrant associations do today, the association supported several institutions (such as the Casa Social, First Aid Clinic, and School Cooperative) and funded repairs to the synagogue.

In addition to institutionalizing memory outside of Villa Clara, the municipality triggered remembrances of village anniversaries. In 1977 the celebration of its seventy-fifth anniversary was covered by *El Pueblo*, the Villaguay newspaper. The celebration paid tribute to the early beginnings: after singing the national anthem, the political authorities rendered tribute to Independence leader and general José de San Martín, unveiled a bust of Baroness Clara de Hirsch, visited the first houses built in the village, and watched a parade on horseback honoring the gauchos and folk dances. Both the municipal (Catholic and Protestant) cemetery and the Israelite cemetery were honored.

By the eightieth anniversary in 1982, the organizing commissions were not ethnic: they were called Ceremonies and Tribute (Ceremonial y Homenaje), Celebrations (Festejos), and Sports (Deportes). The president of the organizing committee was Abraham Schejter, a descendant of the Jewish immigrants and a representative of the Jewish gaucho generation, who had written about the history of the village. To commemorate the event the elementary school and high school also held competitions for manual work, painting, history, and anecdotes of Villa Clara. The celebrations opened with a theater presentation. A descendant of the pioneers set the tone:

The people of Villa Clara participate with pleasure in a sacred ceremony, a transcendental ceremony to evoke the eightieth anniversary of its foundation. This ceremony will be the best homage to those struggling pioneers of those generations who bestowed on us multiple manifestations that will not erase the shadows of times past. Let us close our eyes. It was 1898, and thousands of oppressed immigrants were arriving from tsarist Russia.

A significant population decrease and decline in services has reversed the role of the once thriving province of Entre Ríos. In 1869 the province had ranked third in the nation, concentrating 7 percent of the total population due to transatlantic immigrations between 1869 and 1895 and the development of agricultural *colonias*. As a result of the massive emigration from the rural areas since the mid-1940s coupled with the industrial development of the urban centers (particularly Buenos Aires), the population of the province dropped to 3 percent of the national population by 1991. And the immigrant population of Entre Ríos fell from 23 percent in 1895 to 5 percent in 1947 to 1 percent in 1991 (*Situación demográfica de la Provincia de Entre Ríos* 1998). Moreover, the ethnic distribution of the immigrants has changed dramatically: by 1977 those who reported being descended from the Volga Germans in Entre Ríos accounted for 25 percent of the province's population; and, while some descendants remained in the fifteen original *aldeas*, many had spread all over the province, including Villa Clara.

These demographic changes do not by themselves account for the increase in inadequate services: 23 percent of households had some unmet basic need, 19 percent of households lived in overcrowded housing, and Villa Clara had the highest dependency index relative to the working-age population in the province by the 1990s (*Los municipios de la Provincia de Entre Ríos: Estadísticas básicas* 1991). The increasing income disparity, rampant unemployment, and deteriorating public services were reflected in the social and economic life in the village.

The rise, the flowering, and the decline of Villa Clara are part of Entre Ríos and the nation's history. Since people continue to call Villa Clara home, this history is still being written, on paper and in the hearts of the inhabitants. Which part of this past would be deemed important in the present? How has the past been remembered in Villa Clara more recently?

Chapter Seven

THE PRESENT AS POLITICIZED PAST

Legitimizing Social Structure through Heritage
(1990s–2000s)

*In spite of demographic growth, cultural changes, and the techno-
logical revolution of the last few years, Villa Clara continues its
loyalty to village traditions: siesta,* mate, asado,[1] *the daily greet-
ing, all small things that contribute, together with the tolerance
and respect that different resident collectivities show one another,
to having reached its centennial. (Nuestra historia [Our History],
Museo Histórico Regional de Villa Clara, 2005)*

*To our village! This bouquet of memories exhumed from the mess
of His Highness Time, so history does not become legend. (dedication of manuscript, Muchinik and Isuz de Shulman, n.d.b)*

A social history of Villa Clara as a memory site and the examination of cases that illustrate the process of producing heritage
through memorializing activities and invention of traditions
are in order. Whether private or public, does the process of
heritage production, dissemination, and use contribute to
reifying and legitimizing the current social structure through
created versions of the past? The village has visibly changed,
transforming its public persona from a producer of goods and
services at the start of the twentieth century to a producer of
heritage by the beginning of the twenty-first. What has in fact

changed, and how have different stakeholders assessed this change? While the population has continued to grow through regional migration and increased fertility (from 2,358 in 1991 to 2,794 in 2001, according to the census, to 3,200 inhabitants in 2005, as reported by the Municipality), the sources of employment have in fact diminished, and there are frequent complaints about unemployment and poverty. Rural industries (agriculture and cattle raising) that were important in the past are currently exploited by only a handful of residents, most of whom lease their lands to outsiders and thus no longer provide local employment. Some previous landowners who provide services to rural industries (such as planting, harvesting, fertilizing, and transportation) offer a limited source of employment.

But technological advances in rural work increasingly deprive the village's growing population of unskilled laborers of predictable employment. In the outskirts of the village, however, relatively new industries—rice (fields and a mill), poultry farming, and a slaughterhouse—provide additional job opportunities. In the village, particularly in the Centro, the Municipality offers about a dozen white-collar positions for social workers and clerks. Many retail businesses tend to be family operated, and some of the latest to appear are in living rooms opening on the sidewalk to save on rental costs. Rampant unemployment in La Clarita seems to doom the area's large families to poverty. In 2001 the village was ranked among the localities with the most unmet needs in the province. A federally funded program, Programas de Jefas y Jefes de Hogar (Programs for Household Heads), partially mitigates income disparity through the provision of a monthly stipend to poor families in exchange for some hours of work at the Municipality. Workers in this welfare program are a common sight in the Centro, picking up garbage or sweeping sidewalks, which the residents of this area contemptuously refer to as "pretending to work." The children of La Clarita knock on Centro households to beg for food or money. Additional survival strategies employed by residents of La Clarita are the exchange of labor for goods, bartering, and dependence on charity. As the children of the poor increase, many children of Centro families leave the village to study or work elsewhere. Is this the Villa Clara that the Centro residents wish outsiders to see?

When I began fieldwork in 2002, I invited residents to discuss how best to write the history of Villa Clara. I asked them to visualize Villa Clara and describe it to an imaginary outsider. The railroad and population diversity were distinct central themes, though described differently by the younger and the older people. About the railroad, the younger informants said: "It is a village with a small population, with a plaza, a hospital, a school, a police station, a bank, running water, a museum, one rail,[2] a library, a radio station." The older informants said: "It is a village that lost a lot of economic and social movement due to the lack of a railroad"; and "On Sundays, we went to watch the train to have fun." About the diversity, the younger informants said: "Here there were *criollos*—who are rural people—and immigrants, who are Turkish, Polish, Russian, German, Italian, Spanish, Jewish, Swiss, French. Some continue living here." The older informants said: "We are like a big family, there is a lot of friendliness"; and "The Jews go to the Catholic celebrations and vice versa." Individual interviews added other themes to visualize the history of the village: the municipal involvement in providing low-income housing, the out-migration and in-migration, the increase in unemployment and poverty, and the centennial celebration. Rarely would the railroad be omitted from accounts about how to tell the history of the village.

In fact, the railroad's closing of passenger services in 1994 epitomized the end of what, for many informants, was the golden era of the village and the beginning of an era of negative change, ushering in a decline in rural productivity, unchecked population growth, and lack of work opportunities, even for the self-employed. People remember the railroad nostalgically, and symbolic representations of the railway figure prominently in the logo chosen for the centennial celebration, woven together with symbolic representations of work, immigration, prosperity, and freedom. After all, as the winner of the logo competition explained, the train is closely associated with the village: the village's foundation date is taken to be the date of its arrival, many immigrants arrived through this mode of transportation, and the village and regional economy flourished during its operation.

The history of the railroad, emblematic of Villa Clara's history, also mirrors that of the nation. Argentina moved from a foreign investment policy that included building railroads to nationalization to privatization. As foreign enterprises were nationalized when the nation embarked on an independent development path, the railroads were owned and operated by the state from 1947 to 1994. By 1992, during the administration of President Menem (1989–1999), economic restructuring, including the privatization of public enterprises, became the policy to appease both internal opposition and external pressure to pay off Argentina's external debt (Llanos 2002). Passenger services were terminated in Entre Ríos in 1994, and freight companies were offered concessions. Villa Clara was one of many settlements whose economy suffered in the process.

While memory is private, and inherent in the human condition, the creation of a public version of memory for outside consumption is a political construction of power-holders with "the resources and power to promote a particular past" (Shackel 2001: 655). Memories ground personal identification in the present, but collective identities rarely emerge naturally. Yet the private and the public are interlinked realms of experience. How is this process accomplished? And how can we arrive at "a better understanding of the relationships between public heritage and private inheritances" (Chambers 2006: 42)?

The written historical renditions of international immigration epics recon-struct the saga of a particular group with little or no reference to other popula-tions sharing geographical and social space. The human settlements are repre-sented as ahistorical enclaves locked in the past and isolated from one another. The framework for historians to understand the past is often the past, although in practice accessing the past can only be done retrospectively and thus from the vantage point of the present. Together, written renditions about the past often privilege an "official" history rather than a "history of the people."

A "true" history is unachievable since a myriad of histories, often disparate, usually exist simultaneously. Establishing the degree of agreement between and within histories that have been officially sanctioned as true and the histories that people tell on the basis of their experience contributes to understanding how and why history is created. For example, I found a tendency toward in-creased consensus in the official histories and more variation in popular histo-ries. Popular histories, told from the perspective of everyday life (work, family, institutions), make allusions to social stratification and conflict. Several ver-sions of village history in Villa Clara exist, showing that ethnic origin and social class played important roles in accounting for diversity. These versions of his-tory vary, depending on spatial localization (as a proxy for social class) and tem-poral localization (as a proxy for ethnicity). In Villa Clara it is possible to map ethnic and social class in space: the farther away people reside from the seat of local government (the Municipalidad building), the poorer and more *criollo* they are, the darker their skin, the larger their family size, and the greater the number of unemployed family members and female-headed households and teen pregnancies. In contrast, the closer the residence to the Municipalidad, the higher the representation of wealthier families, with more chances of hav-ing immigrant ancestors, lighter skin, single-family households, employment, and smaller families. Naturally, these are generalizations, since intermarriage and social mobility have occurred. But the histories that are grounded in the space of the Centro are the ones that have transcended the individual level to become public for both the village and outsiders, the ones projected to the out-side world and marketed to lure cultural tourism. They are, without any doubt, the visible histories: those preserved and officially endorsed.

If the "official history" (whether written or material) is intent on crafting consensus and homogeneity, thus often romanticizing the past, the versions of history passed on orally refer to the past while also in a way referring to the pres-ent status of the narrator. The storytellers are popular historians. What is the difference between a scholarly historian and a popular one? The first interprets facts on the basis of documents, the second on the basis of lived experience (whether personal or narrated by an older individual with direct access to such experience). The tool to access that experience is memory, while the historian validates facts by comparing and contrasting documents. Yet both historians and popular storytellers need facts as truths to create the past, so they are bound to be selective as they transform facts into a version of history.

But why use memory to access the past? No published history books on Villa Clara existed by the time of the centennial celebration in 2002, when the local historians leaving their accounts in manuscripts feared that "the past will become legend" (Muchinik and Isuz de Schulman n.d.a): fairy tales with no actual grounding in historical truth. Recovering memory became crucially important in 2002 because the populations that arrived in Villa Clara after the Jews who founded it had a political need to be publicly recognized and have their story told as well. Finally, another important question is why memory needs to be collectivized. Although there were many individual testimonies to draw from, the goals of the ethnic groups who mobilized during the preparations for the celebration of Villa Clara's centennial were representative of the whole ethnic group, the collective.

Memorializing Patrimony: Present Commemorations of the Past

In 1996 the government of Entre Ríos passed legislation creating a new division, the Area de Comunidades (Community Area), and assigning it the task of "the recovery of the cultural and historical patrimony of the various immigrant waves that settled in its territory . . . The retrieval of individual and collective memory, and its contribution to provincial identity, is the major axis for the work of this Area" (Chiaramonte et al. 1995: 1). But there had been attempts to preserve disappearing witnesses of the past, whether people or artifacts, before this official policy formulation. For example, in 1993 the ORT school had launched an audiovisual archive of interviews with pioneers;[3] in 2002 the province commissioned architects to select deteriorating housing heritage for preservation; in 2002 a documentary of the Jewish Colonization Association program, called *Legacy* (Legado), was produced locally and marketed abroad. Let us examine the local impact of the 1996 legislation in Villa Clara through two important institutions of heritage: the creation of a museum and rituals of origin commemorating the village's foundational date.

CASE 1: THE MUSEO HISTÓRICO REGIONAL DE VILLA CLARA: PROVIDING MEMORY TO THE VILLAGE

We might wonder why a museum would be relevant to constructing and disseminating a version of the past. Why does a particular museum incite us to imagine a specific past? Not all versions of history are remembered in a museum, of course. If a museum needs to remember origins, why are some remembered and others not? Are there museum versions of the past that distinguish "people with history" from "people without history," as Eric Wolf (1984) asks? We should explore the purpose of an institutional memory, the reasons for becoming involved in producing history through writings, performances, and artifacts. What do Clarenses consider "history" and not "legend"? What versions of the history of the previous hundred years of village life will visitors be urged to remember when they visit the museum? Naturally, the chosen version will need to correspond to the artifacts housed there. To what extent does that version correspond to the written and oral histories described here? Why is it important to remember? And who remembers what and whose memory is preserved?

Remembering the past is a political act, and one intended role of a museum is to legitimate what to remember. What is memorialized in the museum does not reflect the experiences remembered by the various social groups residing in Villa Clara in the present. The oral versions of the past differ by age and gender, social class, ethnic background, place of birth, place of current residence, and political affiliation. The versions of the past that tell a more heterogeneous view of regional social history contribute to understanding and legitimizing the present social structure. To explore the overt and covert roles of a museum, let us explore the history of the museum in Villa Clara and understand how its collections and organizational structure relate to the past and the present.

ORIGINS   Two contrasting versions of the history of the museum itself exist. Both are important to review in order to understand whether written versions of history have a higher chance of being remembered than the official one. In 1967 well-respected resident Miguel Muchinik was appointed vice-president of the Municipal Commission of Culture and charged with the so-called Museum Area. The son of a Jewish immigrant, he had already started to collect artifacts and archives for a future museum. In the 1970s, in collaboration with another pioneer, Ida Isuz de Schulman, Muchinik created the conceptual framework for the future museum. It was contained in an undated handwritten manuscript found in the personal library of a Villa Clara resident that contained personal memoirs interspersed with a chronological depiction of the village's institutional history and a description of the artifacts collected thus far. According to the Muchinik and Isuz de Schulman manuscript, the museum was planned and advocated as early as the 1960s. The manuscript contains notes on the role and functions of a museum: for example, "A museum keeps testimonies from the past of our village"; "A museum means submerging yourself into the past"; "A labyrinth lost in time"; "You cannot live with the past, but you cannot do away with it"; "Time has implacable installments of forgetfulness"; "When visiting a museum you evade your immediate reality"; "Those people who do not know their past will not know their future"; "In a museum silence and time rest"; "The people who do not conserve their patrimony mutilate themselves culturally." The commitment to the village's Jewish origins is visible:

> Clara was a small village with a large community of Jews that left its human greatness, bequeathing numerous institutions. Today we are a large village with a very small community of Jews that fortunately still palpitates [i.e., is still beating like a heart] and knows, even through difficulties, how to maintain its inheritance alive. (Muchinik and Isuz de Schulman n.d.a)

The manuscript alludes to difficulties in establishing the museum but clarifies that, although it originally had been a project of the Commission of Culture, many people had participated:

> This Museum is for everybody, and its cultural heritage is the people's . . . The plan is to open a museum that will have cultural and educational impact, and to preserve the past . . . *the contribution of this museum is to provide memory to the village.* (Muchinik and Isuz de Schulman n.d.a; emphasis added)

The official version of the origin of the museum, however, does not acknowledge this conceptualization of the museum as early as the 1960s. Rather, it centers on the implementation of the project in a physical site, which only occurred in the late 1990s. This version, disseminated through municipal publications, the press, and radio, maintains that a sixth- and seventh-grade schoolteacher and librarian at School No. 84 (Río Negro) trained her students in 1996,[4] to "go out in search of objects and documents to reconstruct the history of our village."[5] Her initiative gained the support of Mayor Baldoni, who authorized the use of the building previously owned by the first village physician (Dr. Wolcomich), then on loan to the Municipality, to house the artifacts. When the old house needed to close for repairs in 1997, Mayor Baldoni obtained the consent of the General Urquiza Railway to use the unused station free of charge and provided funding to restore and remodel the space and to transfer the collection.

The use of the village's foundational space to remember its foundational story (over which there was uniform consensus) for a museum was symbolic of the need to "provide memory to the village" in the 1990s—a concern of Muchinik and Isuz de Schulman in the 1960s. The collection moved to the railroad station in 1998 included hundreds of books and objects. The first museum coordinator aimed to "continue to preserve the memory of our ancestors so we can transmit it to future generations." But she was also conscious of the need to recover the

Railroad station built in 1902: current location of the Museo Histórico Regional de Villa Clara.

railroad station as a heritage site when she asked herself: "how to recover something that united and communicated us for so many years?" (Fink 1996).

NAME, HISTORICAL PERIOD, AND FUNDING SOURCE   In spite of showcasing the terms "historical" and "regional," the museum seems to be limited in both dimensions. The museum conveys primarily the history of the pioneer immigrants settled in Colonia Clara by the JCA, and the story told is limited to the initial period. This official history is endorsed by the Municipality, which owns the museum and provides the salaries for its staff. The museum, however, does not qualify as a "regional historic" museum, as it is named: few memorabilia concerning other immigrant populations are part of the permanent collection, although some have been placed on loan since the organization of the centennial. And yet we know from written and oral histories that the various immigrant groups would not have survived in complete isolation from one another or from *criollos*, who are relegated to a corner of the museum.

Two other museums on regional immigration are located in close proximity to Villa Clara. The closest one (about thirty minutes away on a bumpy dirt road, impassable on rainy days) is the Museo y Archivo Histórico Regional de la Colonias (Historic and Regional Museum and Archive of the *Colonias*). Founded in 1985 in Villa Domínguez to re-create the saga of the immigrants who started arriving in 1891 at the railroad station with the same name under the sponsorship of the JCA, the museum contains archival and material testimonies of daily life during the first years of their settlement, primarily in Colonia Clara. The other immigrant museum (about two hours from Villa Clara on a paved road) is the Museo Histórico Regional de la Colonia San José (Historical Regional Museum of the Colonia San José). It depicts the immigrant saga of the Swiss (Canton de Valais), French (Savoy region), and Italians (Piedmont region) (see Chapter 2). These immigrants were attracted to Argentina by General Urquiza, who settled them in the *colonia* named San José in his honor. While preparing for the centennial in 1957, the Comisión de Festejos in San José asked residents to donate their most cherished objects relevant to the epic in order to establish a museum. In both of these regional museums, the Municipality provides the funding and selects an Association of Friends of the Museum.

In telling the history of Villa Clara to outsiders, the museum reifies the persistence in the present of the foundational story: a distant past, a story about the origins of a particular population's settlement, and a homogeneous past. Visitors will not learn about diverse versions of village history that enliven the oral histories I collected from individuals. The visitors will be unable to imagine how all these different peoples interacted in the past or how versions of the past might relate to the current social structure. They will not understand how the past, when the majority of the population was Jewish, relates to the present, when the Jews are a minority. Thus the narrative presented by the museum creates a myth rather than a realistic account of the complexity of the region's social history.[6]

ARTIFACTS   The museum has operated in the railroad station since 1998. Housed in this symbol of progress for the village, donated items are used to transmit the process of immigrant assimilation. The following explanation is representative of those throughout the museum:

An antique samovar of Russian origin is the "artifact of the month" selected by the Department of Museum Extension [Departamento de Extensión Museográfica]. The bronze artifact, worked artistically, dates from 1870 and was brought to our province in 1891 by Mrs. Rosa Anapolsky de Costianoski, a member of a founding family of Villa Clara (Department of Villaguay) and a member of our admired "Jewish gauchos." The artifact shown, part of the Jewish heritage through acculturation, is a symbol of their presence in Entre Ríos. As with our *criollo* hearth [*fogón criollo*], the samovar had the power to rally family, friends, and strangers around it. Taking root in our land by gradually incorporating its habits and customs and assimilating in their own way the idiosyncrasies of rural people, the passengers of the *Pampa* gradually replaced their traditional tea with our *mate*.[7] However, the Argentine families of Jewish ancestry preserve the samovar of their ancestors as a relic. (Museo Histórico: Pieza del mes n.d.)

The Grandmother's Dining Room: one of the exhibited rooms in the Museo Histórico Regional in Villa Clara.

Such descriptions offer very little interpretation of the museum artifacts, following the museological assumptions of the schoolteacher and librarian who helped acquire its first physical site. According to her, "objects speak for themselves" (*Villa Clara, 100 años* 2002: 24).

Let us go on a tour of the Museo Histórico Regional de Villa Clara. It is 2002, and the village is bustling with activity in preparation for its centennial celebration. It is a hot summer day, and there is no ventilation inside the museum. As soon as we enter, we see two interesting, if contrasting, signs. One asks for donations, given that "the museum is past, present, and, above all, future." The other is a note stating that "245 families arriving on the ship *Pampa* in 1892 settled in groups in Domínguez, La Capilla, Eben Haroscha, Kiriath Arba, Rosh Pina, Baron Hirsch, Miguel, Rachel, Carmel; 50 families arrived in 1894 from Russia and settled in three groups, Bélez, Feinberg, Sonnenfeld; 150 families in Perliza and Desparramados; 40 families in Baron Guinzburg." This, in essence, describes the population of Colonia Clara, portrayed in this room through objects and photographs. Railroad paraphernalia are found throughout. In a corner, luggage pieces and a genealogical chart represent the immigration of the Swiss-French, Germans, and Belgians. These items are there temporarily, we are told, at the insistence of these collectivities as they prepared for the centennial.

The second room memorializes the beginning of institutional life in the village, which the labels tell us started after the opening of the railroad. Testimonies about the Caja Rural, Fondo Comunal, schools, Junta de Fomento, and Municipalidad are interspersed with railroad objects. The third room is dedicated to the practice of physicians, dentists, and pharmacists: objects, clothing, pictures, and photographs. A display case contains historical documents of the province, including a note on Colonia San Jorge. The fourth room contains a full-sized dining room more representative of a large village house built by successful middle-class *colonos* than the small model homes built by the JCA in the countryside. Many domestic artifacts are displayed, and all donations except one are from Jewish families. The fifth and last room contains objects "used by gauchos" and "Indians," appropriately labeled Gaucho Corner (Rincón Gauchesco).

In memorializing the history of the village through material culture, the museum portrays the first historical period (of Jewish immigration in both Colonia Clara and Villa Clara) and reifies the settlement's foundational history. But it pays secondary attention to the populations native to the area that the immigrants would settle: gauchos, poor *criollos*, and indigenous peoples. A similar brief treatment is accorded the descendants of non-Jewish immigrations (Swiss, French, Belgian, German) who arrived in the village later: they are allocated limited space—and only since the centennial celebration. It is interesting to note the importance accorded to the railroad, almost as if it were a social group.

FRIENDS OF THE MUSEUM COMMITTEE   In 2002 mayor César Den Dauw organized a Commission of Friends of the Museum and institutionalized its operation through an official document that declared it of municipal interest. He called on three "collectivities" to carry out cultural activities through the museum, as a unit of the Municipality. On extended fieldwork there at the time, I was invited to become a member as well and asked to do basic training of the staff, two women in the welfare program who had been assigned this role due to their extensive schooling (one of them, the only staff at present, had been a social worker at the Municipality before she left to live in Buenos Aires).

CASE 2: ANNIVERSARY CELEBRATIONS

Commemorating the establishment of the railroad station has become a central ritual in the village and increasingly noticed in the region. Starting in 1987, the newspaper *El Pueblo* (published in the closest city, Villaguay) started a special column to report news about the village. The Municipality hailed the appearance of the "Página de Villa Clara" (Page of Villa Clara):

> Conscious of the need to keep the residents of this village well informed and to transcend our own borders to aim at progress, we are optimistic about the birth of this journalistic page, a loyal reflection of the activity in Villa Clara. (*El Pueblo*, June 3, 1987)

The newspaper commemorated the ninetieth anniversary with several articles, because "making history is a task for everybody and remembering is the duty of many." But the excitement was unparalleled as the centennial drew near: Mayor Den Dauw exhorted the public through the Municipalidad's newsletter, *Gacetilla*, to associate the village's identity with their own. He noted the importance of commemorations and celebrations, as rituals and symbols of belonging to a community.

Several groups of village residents did not wait for the mayor: they had started organizing their participation about a year before the centennial. These groups shared an immigrant background and called themselves *colectividades* (collectivities): Israelite (for the Jews), German (for the Germans of the Volga), and Swiss-French (who decided to form one group because there were not too many descendants of each nationality). Insofar as only the Israelite collectivity had been operating since their arrival in 1892, this new development signaled an expression by other groups, who had arrived much later, that they were ready to sit at the table of the village's recognized elites. Descendants of other immigrant waves originating in Belgium, Italy, Spain, and other countries did not attempt to organize or ran out of time to do so. The mayor (of Belgian descent), for example, related how his cohort started organizing with the associations in Villaguay, where the largest number of Belgians had settled. He noted with frustration that these associations did not support their organizing efforts until it was too late. It was a combination of the size of the descendant group and organizational capacity that resulted in the creation of a *colectividad organizada* (organized collectivity).

The collectivities that started organizing began meeting in private homes and planning how they would stage their participation: for example, how they would dress to look like the original immigrants, or what they would bring to the parade. The Swiss-French consulted books and magazines to get an image of "traditional" clothing or the clothes worn at the time when their ancestors arrived in the country. Wary of imitations, the women took it upon themselves to sew the attire. As they rediscovered a collective past, they lobbied the Municipality for resources and recognition: in sum, for a larger role and louder voice in the celebration's preparations.

The Municipality centralized the planning of the event to make sure that outsiders would be attracted to the village's vibrant history. Marketing the event as a tourist attraction, rather than tapping the nostalgia of ex-Clarenses to stage a reunion, took courage and determination while coping with a major national political crisis that erupted near the close of 2001, only weeks before the celebration, which caused rampant inflation and the simultaneous circulation of three different currencies. Despite the turmoil, the mayor believed that hosting the celebration would foster solidarity and common purpose among the villagers. He reasoned that "in these difficult times, the Centennial is the most important event in Villa Clara, one that challenges us to find spaces to be together and share efforts for a better future" (*Gacetilla* no. 5, November 29, 2001).

Three primary stakeholders were involved in the organization of the centennial celebrations: the Municipality, the Centennial Commission (Comisión de Festejos), and the *colectividades organizadas*. Mayor Den Dauw had designated three national groups (German, Swiss-French, and Israelite) of *colectividades organizadas* in 2001, validating their transitioning from national to ethnic groups, and had rallied them as special interest groups. In fact, the mayor had full control over the planning for the event, since all positions in the organization of the centennial celebrations were appointed. It was predictable that the "official" history would be told: an uncomplicated, happy story of assimilated immigrants would encourage an outside public to spend money in the village, while well-known folk singer Soledad performed and the art of famous photographer Raota was displayed. But the Municipality also intended to have everyone in the village contribute to the celebration; for example, it funded schoolchildren to paint murals in the Centro with themes alluding to the history of Villa Clara.

In directing attention to the way in which Villa Clara was to be portrayed to outsiders and by whom, the Centennial mirrored the way in which ethnicity and social class served as mechanisms of inclusion and exclusion in defining social interactions. Among many, a *criollo* woman was bitter about what she believed was co-opting of the centennial celebration by Clarense elites; she particularly singled out the first immigrant group and its impact on her family:

You know what happens? I ask for an appointment at the museum and do you know what they say? "Here comes this *negra*[8] because she wants her father to be recognized. She is looking for trouble." Or you tell them your opinion . . . It's so much like this that when they were preparing the list to send invitations for the Centennial they asked for the addresses of those who had been born here and were living in Buenos Aires or other places. And who was asked for those addresses? The people living in the Centro and the Jewish people. Who came? Only Jews.

I have twin daughters, born here, who have a dance school in Villaguay;

Members of the Swiss-French collectivity in 2002.

they've won a ton of awards, perhaps you've heard of them. They were born here in Clara and they didn't invite them. Of course not. They are not Jews.

One day I say to my son, "What's wrong?" He says to me, "I'm against the Centennial, because the Centennial centers on one class of people, and here there isn't only one class of people, there are many classes of people, so I can't show up at a place that I'm opposed to." There was no way to make him go.

The centennial was an eight-day celebration. Public events included theater plays, essay and poetry readings, photo exhibits, sports competitions, music, film and dance shows, visits to cemeteries, and street parades orchestrated by the three organized collectivities. An Asociación Tradicionalista (Traditionalist Society), in which members of various ethnic backgrounds interested in gaucho culture participated, was asked to represent the *criollo* population with a parade of horse-riding gauchos, although they were not appointed to be organizers. Vendors of food, drink, and crafts were stationed at major thoroughfares where street events took place. Many informants, however, complained that those who had businesses away from this area or who lived in the La Clarita periphery were not able to profit from selling anything to the visitors. A carpenter of German descent who had stocked crafts for the event in his shop in the Centro, though five blocks away from the Municipality, still had them for sale in 2005.

Transnational Pasts, Ethnic Presents: Genealogical Links as Social Status

As they collaborated in organizing the centennial, making sure that their ethnic group represented their ancestors well, the organized collectivities turned memory into tradition. A manuscript that the German group shared with me provides a definition of a collectivity: it is "synonymous with sharing, cooperating, having the same feelings, dreams, searching for a goal. People gather as *pueblos*, as communities, because their roots are similar, their customs are similar, their language is similar, their religion derives from a common God."[9] Apparently banal pursuits, such as combining colors or choosing the distribution of fabrics in clothes that they imagined were used by their ancestors, created solidarity groupings among previously unconnected people. During organizing meetings, they perused European magazines to learn about the fashions at the time when their ancestors immigrated to Argentina. Dress, dance, music, and language were all used as visible confirmations of group distinctiveness. The collectivities were keen on staging public demonstrations of old lifeways, themselves "myths" or ideal forms reified for the occasion.

As they banded together to celebrate a common past, the Germans and Swiss-French, two *colectividades organizadas* that had arrived more recently in Villa Clara, imagined a common future: being inscribed in the history of the town. One important gain for the *colectividades* after the centennial was their recognition by the mayor in what he termed the role of "cultural ambassadors," whose activities benefited the village. Responding to the lobbying by the Israelite collectivity to form a Comisión de Amigos del Museo (Friends of the Museum Committee), the mayor issued a decree approving its constitution on July 2002 and invited the German and Swiss-French to join it, along with the Israelite collectivity.

Legitimizing the two new *colectividades* (the Swiss-French and the Germans) as important stakeholders in the village was accomplished through their association beyond the centennial. Their recent search for a deeper link to their countries of origin had stirred their curiosity and (unbeknown to them) created traditions that differentiated them even further from other social groups in Villa Clara.

The centennial of the arrival of the Germans of the Volga had been celebrated in 1978 in the localities where the first immigrants had settled.[10] Since then "a reevaluation has occurred, there has been a rethinking of the history of the descendants of Germans of the Volga that gave rise to a stage of maturity and social conscience that remembers the past with legitimate pride" (Honeker de Pascal and Jacob de Hoffmann n.d.: 288). By 1995 Santa Anita, the German *colonia* closest to Villa Clara and the origin of most German descendants in the village, was chosen as the site for the annual commemoration of the arrival of the Volga Germans in Argentina. The Germans in Villa Clara felt ready to participate as full members of civil society during the centennial celebrations, as they announced in a pamphlet:

> The German collectivity is present in the Centennial of Villa Clara.
>
> Present, because Germans have contributed to shape this beautiful village, together with their brothers in the struggle, the Jews, Swiss-French, Italians, Spaniards, and *criollos*.
>
> Here we are, with our music and song, traditional dress, with our children, youth, and elderly.
>
> Here we are, Villa Clara! The descendants of the Germans of the Volga say Happy Birthday to you today! Dear village, Happy One Hundred Years!

The collectivity announced its desire to share its worldview with others and explicitly affirmed its "hope [that] this Centennial serves as an incentive to communicate the values of the German people, their profound faith, their love of family and spirit of struggle at work and in everyday life." And it was also ready to boast its numerical superiority among the ethnic populations of Entre Ríos: "In spite of the penuries [they suffered], the Germans of the Volga fulfilled the biblical mandate to multiply and, at present, one in four Entrerrianos [persons born in Entre Ríos] carries German blood." To confirm their diffusion in the province, the centennial paraders brought paraphernalia from several locations, most specifically old tools and machinery, which they made functional for the occasion. The contingent opened with a horseman carrying a flag representing Argentina and Germany together, followed by walkers of all ages dressed in what they imagined the pioneers wore and carrying a German flag, the elected queen,[11] and three carts. The carts, called Russian carts and also used by Jewish agriculturalists, were elementary four-wheeled transports. Two of these carts were to stage a "traditional" wedding carrying the bride, bridegroom, and their families to church, to the sound of loud accordion music and accompanied by men drinking heavily. The third cart represented the move: German immigrants often needed to move shortly after their arrival in search of lands to purchase. This cart depicted a real scene on the day of the move, when the immigrants packed mattresses, luggage, furniture, and agricultural tools.

The German descendants' organization as a collectivity in Villa Clara was sustained well after its participation in the January centennial: in October of the centennial year the German collectivity organized its first Oktoberfest. Its president boasted:

> Now, after the centennial, Saturday is the Germans' party, Oktoberfest. It seems like we're more united. I don't know why the Belgians don't get together. Maybe because there aren't as many of them as Germans, because there are a lot of Germans! (1er Oktoberfest 2002)

Interestingly, in the brochure announcing the Oktoberfest program, we read: "Since they [the first immigrants] arrived, they practiced occupations they did not know, like agriculture and raising cows" (1er Oktoberfest 2002: 1). This contrasts with the written history on this immigration, which characterized them as being expert agriculturalists after having practiced that occupation in Russia for a century.

The endorsement by other stakeholders in Villa Clara's heritage (the Colectividad Israelita Clara-Bélez, the Colectividad Suizo-Francesa, and the Municipalidad) was clear in the Oktoberfest printed program, as was the presence of major businesses, who placed advertisements. A new radio program on "the music and history of the German collectivity" was inaugurated at that time on the local radio station. The Germans' status as the ethnic group with the most prominent organizational capacity in contemporary Villa Clara was assured.

CASE 2: THE SWISS-FRENCH COLLECTIVITY

During the centennial preparations, the Swiss-French collectivity contacted Entidades Valesanas Argentinas (EVA: Valaisan Argentine Organization), an ethnic organization whose goal to reunite Valaisans colonized in Argentina was inspired by the dictum "the past is our inheritance, the present urges us to maintain the links to the history of organized colonization, and the future will judge us severely" (Entidades Valesanas Argentinas 2003: 1). EVA was founded in 1993 to represent the Argentine contingent after a 1991 visit to Switzerland with the "Valaisans of the World" (descendants of immigrants from the Valais

Valley dispersed in Brazil, Canada, Argentina, and the United States). By 2003 EVA had accepted the request from the Colectividad Suizo-Francesa de Villa Clara for membership affiliation.[12] By becoming a part of a larger association, the descendants of the Swiss and the French in Villa Clara were able to establish connections with immigrants of similar origin and with the pioneer migration settled in San José.

On a trip to the museum in San José with this collectivity, I was intrigued by the members' interest in establishing possible genealogical connections with the pioneers and thus upgrading their ethnic status. Some members avidly asked the director about their origins. She proceeded to search in books written by historian Celia Vernaz, who, however, had limited her research to the French-speaking immigrants from the Valais. One member, for example, was surprised to find out that he and his dad "thought that we were of French origin, but when we visited the San José museum we found out that we were Swiss because we are from the other side of the Valais region." Another member, providing an example of how families dislocated by immigration were still searching for members, reported a recent visitor from France who was looking for family members in Villa Clara. Thus, valuing an immigrant past is very recent in the area.

Case 3: Circuito Histórico de las Colonias Judías del Centro de Entre Ríos

At the end of the nineteenth century, assimilation into a homogeneous Argentine nationality was believed to obliterate cultural diversity, but as in other nations with large immigrant stocks Argentine ethnic groups were incorporated into a larger multiethnic polity. Under a new ideology of immigrant assimilation, cultural pluralism asserts that a citizen can be Argentine and ethnic at the same time. Even if this cultural mélange was accepted in daily life, the Argentine state legitimized the belief in 2000, as it launched heritage tourism programs based on cultural diversity. A program entitled Mosaico de Identidades (Mosaic of Identities) sought to promote and preserve ethnic, cultural, and religious heritage. The first project in this program was entitled *Shalom Argentina: Huellas de la colonización judía* (Hello, Argentina: Tracing Jewish Settlement). The Jewish descendants of Colonia Clara started meeting immediately to assess how best to capitalize on the material and architectural culture still existing at the sites of past JCA settlements and implemented this program in the province with the name Circuito Histórico de las Colonias Judías del Centro de Entre Ríos (Historical Circuit of the Jewish Colonies of the Center of Entre Ríos). Villa Clara became one of four sites in a tour organized by the Israelite Associations of Basavilbaso, Villaguay, Clara-Bélez, and Villa Domínguez with the support of the Secretaría de Turismo Nacional and the Subsecretaría de Turismo of Entre Ríos and the technical assistance of the Instituto Superior de Turismo Santa Cecilia and a tourist agency, Mirst Travel, in Villaguay. The Israelite Associations of the four selected sites signed a Foundational Act that stated their goal of preserving their heritage and promoting cultural tourism for the benefit of all:

> After more than one hundred years have passed since this unique and unrepeatable epic, we, the descendants of those pioneers, commit ourselves to our elders, to recover and preserve their memory, leaving this rich cultural and historical patrimony as an inheritance to our children and to the Argentine people; to maintain, preserve, and protect natural and cultural resources; to improve the quality of life for the region's inhabitants; to make a joint effort among the four associations to achieve our proposed objectives; to create diverse ways to strengthen the regional economies with a new tourist product in the province; today we inaugurate the "Circuito Histórico de las Colonias Judías del Centro de Entre Ríos." (Circuito Histórico 2000)

Two explanatory signs in Villa Clara, one outside the Municipality and another at the entrance of the only functioning synagogue, announce the tourist program and specify the attractions selected for the site: synagogue, Hebrew school, museum, home of the first physician, Israelite cemetery, and Salón Barón Hirsch. Many other Circuito Histórico sites contain no or very few material remains of the memorialized patrimony.

It was in the context of another centennial (commemorating the Revolución de Mayo, which severed ties with Spain) that Gerchunoff wrote the book *The Jewish Gauchos* to legitimize the presence of Jews as full members of society in rural Argentina during a time when some opposed Jewish immigration on the ground that they could not possibly adapt to the Argentine countryside and other pretexts that concealed ethnic, religious, and racial prejudice.

Epilogue: The Jewish Gaucho Revisited

Integrating Argentine history and its social memory in a locality helps us understand the metaphor of the Jewish gaucho. Villa Clara as a case study of the construction of national identity can be broadened to stimulate research in three different fields of study: immigration, memory, and a historically grounded ethnography. None of the current theories of immigration processes seriously focuses on the referent when discussing assimilation or acculturation. What are the major characteristics of the society and culture of destination that would help isolate the factors promoting a successful integration? Two important cultural mechanisms are embedded in social memory in addition to generational transmission of identity: an inherited collective identity and an induced (that is, having external referents, politicized) identity. Because social memory must be grounded in the political economy of a locality, it has spatial and chronological frameworks. Finally, the combination of anthropology and history (including related fields of inquiry, such as cultural geography) is a fruitful way to understand the connections between the global and the local: a historically concerned ethnographic approach elicits social memory as well as individual memory. While historians mostly use written documents as memory, ethnographers rely on living raconteurs to understand not only what happened but how people perceive their past, present, and future.

I have apprehended past and present reality through written documents and spoken testimonies. Since both records are motivated selections that fulfill the need to invent a particular version of history, I have combined them in an effort to understand the impact of international, national, regional, and local events on a contemporary village's unraveling of the meaning of its past. During that exercise I found both consensus and discrepancy between written and oral sources of perceived reality. Sometimes both could be used to fill in or to augment the same reality, such as establishing a rationale for European immigration to Argentina in the nineteenth century. At other times, written documents and oral testimonies diverged, presenting conflicting versions of the representativeness of the population of Villa Clara in planning for its centennial. Many times there were also discrepancies within the data sets of the written documents and oral testimonies: two written documents existed on the origins of the museum in Villa Clara, and the people who talked to me held different opinions about the relationships between *criollo* and gringo. While the sources themselves competed for the more "authentic" version, my position was that they all enriched the social history of Villa Clara by providing a complex web of ideological rationales for identity formation along personal, ethnic, class, regional, national, and transnational axes.

There is a difference between construing the self (personal identity), identifying as a member of a cultural group (ethnic identity), and interpreting the way in which one's identity is constructed by other members of the nation (cultural representation of identity). As Clarenses started preparations for the centennial celebration in 2002, their discourse about the public representation of Villa Clara, including establishing differences between inside and outside audiences, entailed considerations about personal, ethnic, and national identity. Thinking about oneself with others from the same place (insiders) about how to represent oneself to outsiders opened up reflection about vital issues regarding the historic identity of the place. To what extent and in what circumstances would outsiders perceive Clarenses as individuals, as members of ethnic groups, as "organized collectivities," as residents of a village with an immigrant past, as Argentines? As stakeholders, Clarenses prepared for the centennial by answering an important question: "Who were we?" At this significant ritualized time, where the past reigned supreme, the questions "Who are we now?" and "Who might we become?" were put aside. Yet it is the political economy of a place at the time when memory is activated for presentation of the past that legitimizes the present.

The memorializing activities in Villa Clara have illustrated the dilemma of documenting a plurality of histories when the sources themselves are multiple (written and oral, archival documents and scholarly interpretations) and when life histories sometimes confirm and sometimes contest the other sources. In fact, a breach separates the "official" history—as it is told to the outside world, taught, or written—from alternative stories that people tell about their own lived or narrated experiences of interaction among ethnic and social class groupings. A history-minded ethnography contributes to understanding the meanings of ethnicity and social class in the construction of national identity.

The Jewish Gaucho as a Metaphor of Immigrant Incorporation

The historical production of symbols of national identity, their reemergence in heritage-based projects, and the demystification of official histories by testimonial records also contribute to understanding the metaphor of the Jewish gauchos. Originally coined by Gerchunoff in 1910 as the title for a book of vignettes on Jewish life in rural Argentina, the phrase was useful to express a sense of belonging to a nation-state. But it was motivated by the desire of a Jewish writer "to integrate in the nonthreatening peace of the liberal republic" (Leonardo Senkman, cited in Feierstein 2000: 7–8), at a time when nationalist xenophobes were contesting the urban Jews as true Argentines. Gerchunoff was a well-known writer for the prestigious daily newspaper *La Nación* and an activist in the Partido Demócrata Progresista (Progressive Democrat Party). His father had died at the hands of a drunken gaucho soon after his immigration from Russia.

Gerchunoff's phrase established similarities between two apparently different social types, Jews and *criollos*, as embodied in the gauchos of the time. To understand the meaning of the metaphor fully, however, it becomes important to examine the terms "Jewish" and "gaucho" and compare their meanings in two historical periods, before and after the end of the nineteenth century.

At the time of Argentine independence from Spain, the gaucho was a social type defined by his (the gaucho is mostly described as a male) nomadic horse-oriented lifestyle. He took fierce pride in freedom from the state and private property, and his unrestricted exploitation of the pampas for immediate gratification of his needs resulted in many violent confrontations with political authorities. Construing the gauchos as "barbaric" mestizos who represented backwardness, the ideologues of the new nation believed that their policies that promoted European immigration and agricultural settlement of Europeans on the pampas during the mid-nineteenth century would naturally supplant and efface the "wild" gauchos. In addition to promoting European immigration, between 1860 and 1880 the Argentine government embarked on what Federica Cavallo (2005: 144) called "the final solution" to get rid of the gauchos as the last obstacle to agrarian expansion. Thus, by time of the arrival of the first Jewish immigrants in 1889, nomadic gauchos were disappearing as a social type and were being transformed into laborers employed in temporary or permanent jobs in *estancias*. There the class differences became even more notorious.

Toward the end of the nineteenth century the earlier formulation of the gaucho as a free roamer of the pampas was recovered and reinstalled in the popular imagination, and the gaucho was assigned the role of authentic Argentine native. By then, in fact, this gaucho type, immortalized in José Hernández's Martín Fierro,[1] was no longer roaming the pampas. He had been subdued and evicted, much like the previous Indian populations.

At the beginning of the twentieth century the working class in Buenos Aires, preponderantly of European extraction, staged social movements protesting work conditions. This period of political turmoil (including strikes and unionization) incited the governing elites' repudiation of the foreigners as troublemakers and legitimized their repression in street protests. The foreigners, once seen as "civilized" but now seen as intruders, were considered outsiders in this newer formulation of Argentine cultural citizenship.

The phrase "Jewish gaucho" was applied to landed Jews as they were rooting themselves in the homeland of the *criollo* gauchos, whom they either employed or learned from through culture contact. Especially in the second generation, Jewish farmers acquired the explicit attributes of the native culture of the *criollo* gauchos (dress, language, music and dance, food, and work habits), becoming gauchos themselves in appearance. The essence of a Jewish gaucho lies in being a second-generation Jewish immigrant living in a rural area in a *colonia* established by the JCA. In particular it refers to a young male hungry to belong to the country where he had been born or had come at a very young age, as described below:

> Wide *bombachas* [riding pants], a wide leather belt adorned in its entirety with silver coins, armed with both a knife and a gun, mounted on a nice lively saddled *pingo* [horse] with a good leather lasso and a whip. (Hojman 1908: 2)

> [They] quickly adopt[ed] *criollo* customs: drinking *mate*, wearing gaucho clothing, enjoying an *asado*, and working the fields on a daily basis. (López de Borche 1987: 80–81)

> [They] learned little by little from the *criollos* to sit on cows' heads, old wooden boxes, piles of bags and wood and tree trunks, and even on the floor with legs dangling over a well. (Schallman, cited in Quiroga 1990: 12)

> The second generation, that of the *criollo* lads, was of gauchos who were no less Jewish. In typical attire, with guitars and drums, they beat out Argentine dance, music, and songs. They had an invisible link with the *criollos:* tradition and respect. (Zago 1988: 99)

> More than any material contribution, the immigrants' biggest legacy was their role in the creation of a new social paradigm, the *Jewish gaucho*, and a figure that synthesized the liberal, multicultural ideals prevalent in nineteenth-century and early-twentieth-century Argentina. The mystique surrounding the somewhat fictitious character—real *gauchos*, their only home their horse, were already extinct by then—grew out of the seamless way in which the immigrants preserved their Jewish traditions while assimilating the customs and language of their new neighbors. At the same time that they learned to herd cattle, drink bitter *mate* from a gourd, and strum melodic *zambas* on their Spanish guitars, the pioneers built synagogues, observed the Jewish Sabbath, and educated their children according to the precepts of their millennial faith. (Goodman 2002: 11–12)

Although they shared cultural elements, the Jewish gaucho was far from being a *criollo* gaucho: a landless, marginalized, poor employee of the new owners of the land. Rather, the Jewish gaucho (the term usually referred to a male, as noted) was a JCA settler who lived off farming on land he currently leased but aimed to own once financial obligations to the colonization company were met.

Moreover, the background of the Jewish gaucho was different from that of the *criollo* gaucho: his ancestors were non-Christian Europeans who lived off trade or business in sedentary settlements.

Similar yet different, the two versions of the gaucho cannot be understood by themselves but only within the context of political changes in the Argentina of the early twentieth century that altered the imagining of the other. Gerchunoff's *The Jewish Gauchos* was published in 1910, the first centennial commemoration of national independence, a period of optimism in the swift development of the country. Partly an homage to both Argentina and Baron de Hirsch for providing asylum and freedom to persecuted Jews, the book was hailed as proof that cultural pluralism was working. Since then, numerous authors in both popular and scholarly writings have appropriated, criticized, and evaluated the phrase. A new generation of writers (labeled "parricide on the pampa" by Aizenberg 2000) criticized Gerchunoff for having idealized the integration of the Jews, pointing out the many obstacles, some violent, that they encountered in their path.[2]

At one level, the metaphor is emblematic of a mode of immigrant incorporation, where assimilation is a survival strategy but does not entail complete acculturation. Although Jewish immigrants were diverse in terms of national origin, occupations, and social class backgrounds, they were forced by circumstances to accommodate to each other as a religious group in order to face their new life in Argentina. Despite major differences, they shared a common religion and a common lingua franca, Yiddish. They also shared a common urban background, and many were new to farming. Because they were fleeing persecution, they can be more fully understood as refugees as well as immigrants. They were uprooted but prized their new freedom. While Jewish gauchos as well as native gauchos valued both freedom and belonging, the native gaucho did not live from agriculture or own land. The Jewish gauchos' referent for Argentine culture was the only non-Jews nearby, the *criollos*, with whom they had daily interaction. The Jews adapted in terms of their dress, language, song and music, food, and occupation but not in their religion or moral precepts.

The metaphor also symbolizes ideological changes that are best understood chronologically. Looking at these changes in three stages illuminates the structures of opportunity open to Eastern European Jews as they became Argentine, regardless of their religious observance. The first stage covers the arrival of the JCA settlers, when survival was predicated upon learning from the environment. The JCA administrators had little expertise about the natural, social, or political environment; rather, as employees of the colonization company they understood their job as organizers of the settlements, distributing land and farming tools and advancing credit. Their poor understanding of the cultural diversity of the immigrants and the local culture left the new settlers on their own as they developed relationships with the *criollo* gauchos and with other immigrants in the area. Their contact with the gauchos, however, was confined to learning to work the land. Soon after their arrival, an asymmetry was established between the two interacting populations in terms of knowledge and class: the *criollo* gauchos were experts at horse-centered modes of production and, although elementary agriculturalists, had an intimate knowledge of the natural environment and ways to master it. They knew, for example, how to clear the woods, a task the new farmers had to complete before the planting began. The immigrants who hired the gauchos depended upon them to make the new agrarian life successful. But, unlike the *criollo*, the immigrant had access to land, a home, and a well. "The metaphor describes the integrationist, *mestiza*, and pluralist Argentina that received him" (Feierstein 2000: 15). But the metaphor also alludes to the structure of opportunity available to the newcomers and their lack of choices, since the "integration with the environment was more tragic than epic. The process of *agaucharse*, of becoming gauchos, was an alternative without choice imposed by the circumstances" (Chiaramonte et al. 1995: 203).

Within a decade after their arrival (as early as 1902 in the case of Villa Clara), many JCA settlers were ambivalent about their ability or desire to become agriculturalists and started to prefer living in villages, whether holding onto the land or selling it. In this preference, they demonstrated a greater comfort with their preimmigrant communal patterns in Europe. No longer needing to assimilate to a dying breed of lower-class, landless, and marginalized *criollo* gauchos, many JCA settlers moved permanently to the village, larger towns, or Buenos Aires. Their incipient urbanization included their desire for upward social mobility, as they moved out of agriculture and into trades or businesses. A descendant of the Jewish immigration recalled the impact that a young man from his village who had moved to a city made when he came back to the *colonia* for a visit, clad in a white linen suit, boasting of an easier life in the city.

When Gerchunoff's book appeared in 1910, the majority of the population of Buenos Aires was of foreign origin, with a large working class and the beginnings of efforts to unionize the workers. The image of the *criollo* gaucho as the legitimate, native Argentine served as an antidote to the concern about social conflict in Buenos Aires, since the concept of the Jewish gaucho demonstrated the adaptability of the Jewish immigrants. The gaucho, writes Cavallo (2005: 146), "becomes the archetype of Argentinean for the landholding oligarchy as self-legitimating and as an antidote to social conflict."

At present the only reference to Jewish gauchos is through heritage promotion and cultural tourism projects that attempt to preserve the memory of the past through written and material culture at the locations previously inhabited by the JCA settlers. This communication of the past is possible in an atmosphere that celebrates diversity and policies that communicate a pluralistic ideology of national identity. The early history of the Jewish immigrants in rural areas is told mostly through material remains of a living culture. This representation is strengthened by the immigrant museums in the province of Entre Ríos, whose collections attempt to resurrect the past as patrimony.

Another significant similarity among the immigrant museums in the province is their aim to educate the public—descendants, schoolchildren, visitors—about the importance of linking that past to the present, with two important objectives: better understanding the history of the nation and the region and framing their own connection with the diverse population streams during their process of identity formation.

Demystifying the Metaphor of the Jewish Gaucho

The Jewish gaucho can be taken as a metaphor for a type of immigrant incorporation in rural areas. There are several ways to understand the power of this metaphor to represent the Jewish immigrant experience. First, becoming gauchos was the most accessible assimilation strategy for the Jewish immigrants since there were no other populations nearby. Second, the phenomenon only lasted about one generation or until the children of the pioneer settlers left for urban centers. The cultural type was ephemeral because it was an artifact of social mobility. Third, the Jewish gauchos alluded to rural living, mostly in Entre Ríos: a 1942 census taken by the JCA shows that almost two-thirds of the Jewish population lived in rural areas of Entre Ríos and 43 percent were dedicated to agriculture. As compared to the number of farmers settled in the province in 1941, the proportion of Jews was approximately 6 percent. Thus one should not be surprised that "the legendary *Jewish Gauchos* immortalized by Alberto Gerchunoff's 1910 book could only have lived in Entre Ríos" (Senkman, in Chiaramonte et al. 1995: 12). That would change dramatically soon after the 1940s. Finally, Gerchunoff's seminal opus opened a third alternative for a national identity that incorporated the diversity of the nation: representing neither melting pot nor cultural pluralism, the Jewish gaucho is an icon of a hybrid identity: rather than being pure types, each is open to transformation into the other. Instead of an opposition of "civilized" versus "barbarian," there is the pairing of a helpful gaucho and a foreigner eager to learn. Neither contradicts the notion of the nation-state; indeed, together they strengthen it. But this speaks to a possible, not real, world.

Appendix I: Methodological Notes

Understanding the uses of memory for the creation and preservation of Villa Clara's cultural patrimony entailed a process that spanned several years: from 2001, when the field site was selected, to 2006, when fieldwork seemed completed, at least for the purposes of this book. Every ethnographer knows that it is easier to mark the beginning of research than the end of it. Like others, I continue to nurture relationships with—and thus learn from—the people of Villa Clara through e-mail, telephone calls, and personal visits. As I write this appendix in 2008, I am planning my next visit—some of my informants have died, others are sick (and one has requested a copy of his interview), and younger ones have married or had children. The village is engaged in supporting the *ruralistas*, the rural producers who are contesting tax raises by government. In addition to socializing, I will discuss the next phase of the oral history archive with the museum coordinator, review the funding raised by the sale of my 2005 book *Memorias de Villa Clara* when meeting with the Comisión de Amigos del Museo Histórico Regional de Villa Clara, and review the boarding arrangements for my upcoming visit with students from the United States next January. The presentation of this book will surely come up, and I will probably pursue questions that readers of the manuscript and I have pondered about. While in the region, I will travel to neighboring Villa Domínguez and visit with Osvaldo Quiroga, director of the local museum, so that I can obtain a copy of the video he recently produced on the history of the region and discuss our common interests.

Like any commodity, memory is produced and disseminated for use. This appendix provides a chronological account of the methods I used to understand the biographical and social context of recollection as well as the impact of my staged dissemination of collective memory. Bridging the past and the present is significant to both historians who freeze the past in printed text and Clarenses who enliven it through words, rendering their own version of what should be remembered. To understand how collective cultural patrimony was preserved, I analyzed the material culture displayed in the local museum and representations of identity in performances, such as festivals and anniversaries.

It goes without saying that participant observation is the alter ego that follows me when in Villa Clara whether I am there either in person or in thought, although the persona changes. It was one thing to be a tourist of the Circuito Turístico in 2001, when the regional story was told by a guide or by her selected hosts at designated stops. It was another thing to travel to Villa Clara to evaluate where to settle for a semester of fieldwork in early 2002. I played other roles as resident for four months during the fall of 2002, when I needed to buy goods in Argentine pesos but pay rent in U.S. dollars (given rampant inflation) or followed the local advice to make an illicit arrangement to share a telephone line with a neighbor since the length of my stay would not assure getting my own. I shared food and gossip with my landlady, went on morning walks with the widow of the ex-mayor, or shared *mate* with *torta frita* with neighbors on rainy days.

Although collectively the village seemed receptive to my interest in writing about its history, some individual residents were suspicious of my motives. Why would someone from so far away be interested in the history of a small village? As an Argentine-born working for U.S. employers, to whom was I providing information? As I was observed in public taking notes on street signs and my student from the University of Maryland was seen drawing a map of a block, a rumor started and quickly spread that we were there as agents of the Central Intelligence Agency. This initially surprised me, since I had talked about my research interests on the local radio and expanded on my motives during conversations with all kinds of people. The rumor prompted my decision to turn participant observation to participatory action research earlier than anticipated: what the residents thought of me, my students, and my motives was as relevant to ethnographic research as what I would learn in due course about the local culture and social organization. I reasoned that short-term empirical research might be understood, while a resident fieldworker might be suspect. Asking for help, I felt, would help demystify anthropological fieldwork and would assure from the start that my stay not only would be to my professional benefit but also would be of service in aiding the village to plan programs to provide services and preserve its rich past. Perhaps, I reasoned, the lack of communication and understanding between program planners and anthropologists might result from a concentration on the numerator alone (the selected informants) while paying insufficient attention to the population denominator (the object of program design).

The first step I took to transform my role of participant observer from an individual to a public persona was to invite villagers publicly to collaborate with me in figuring out how to tell the history of Villa Clara. The invitation, supported by the mayor, who facilitated the dissemination of the event at the local auditorium, drew about a hundred persons but reached the whole village through radio announcements, flyers, and verbal invitations. I structured the public event to include both a presentation and a call for collaboration. I began by presenting my interests:

> You recently celebrated the one-hundredth birthday of the village. I ask you to imagine Villa Clara as a very old person who has gone through different stages in her life and has a lot to remember. Mrs. or Mr. Villa Clara, that elderly lady or gentleman, is here among us and is sitting in one of these chairs. Help me recognize her or him here with a round of applause. What does this person have to say? If we were to talk about Villa Clara to somebody who is not from here, what would we tell her or him? How would we describe Villa Clara? Where would we start the story? How would we tell the story? Orally or using written text or using videos? Where should this story be told? At your homes, or the municipality, or the schools? When should we tell the story? Shall we start today, or wait until we get resources, or wait until the next centennial?

After some discussion, I asked the audience to group themselves into three focus groups divided by age (one to twenty-five, twenty-six to forty-nine, and over fifty). Two students from Argentine universities who were training with me coordinated the youngest groups, and I worked with the older group. We all elicited comments, spurred discussion, and wrote down suggestions from our respective groups. A representative of each focus group shared its suggestions, and then we held a general discussion. This exercise provided the first shared model of what was important in telling the history of Villa Clara: the relevance of the railroad to economic development, the role of immigration, the existence of religious tolerance. These themes were accorded diverse meanings by the different age groups. At the end of the session I announced that we would be knocking at their doors to conduct a survey.

Property Register of Villa Clara

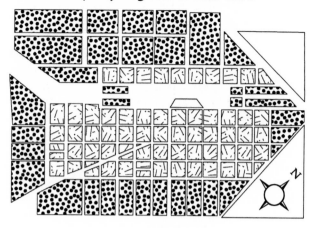

▨ Original blocks ▨ Quintas

Ethnographic Map of Villa Clara

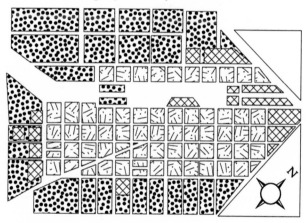

▨ Inhabitated areas not documented in property registry
▨ Original blocks ▨ Quintas

Property register of Villa Clara and ethnographic map of Villa Clara.

I explained that we wanted to understand their recollection of their own biography and asked for collaboration.

If the goal of the study was to reconstruct village history through the collective memory of its inhabitants, it was imperative to talk to all inhabitants at least once, both to obtain information and to provide news on my team's activities. To give the ethnographic research validity and representativeness, I needed to add additional steps to traditional ethnographic research. The traditional sequence requires participant observation, informant selection, ethnographic interviews of key informants, and data analysis, in that order. I added a household survey based on the existing map and produced an ethnographic map to enrich participant observation and the informant selection process.

The map (Plan Catastral) provided by the Municipality was taken as evidence of the local government's understanding of the population it served. This map served two purposes at this stage of research: as a visual description of the distribution of occupied and open space in the village and as a tool to identify households for the survey. The household survey had three objectives: (1) to assure that everyone in the village was represented, (2) to assess generational memory in the village, and (3) to establish a sampling frame for selecting informants for ethnographic interviews. An interview instrument designed to operationalize the goal of the study elicited the following information from the head of household (or, if unavailable, the oldest person at the residence at the time of our visit): name, address, sex, age, birth date of four generations (two ascending and one descending generation—self, spouse, children, parents, paternal and maternal grandparents), and present residence of two generations (the respondent's and her or his children's). The survey helped provide a social face for the municipal map.

Three findings were relevant to the research. The first was methodological and demonstrated the power of ethnographic fieldwork to generate maps that visually rendered social structure in space. As we collected information on individuals and households rather than only on the built environment, we were able to overlay social content on the descriptive map provided by the government. A second finding had implications for service provision: the map provided by the Municipality divided space into two categories: the urban center, subdivided into *manzanas* (blocks) and *quintas* (areas considered sparsely inhabited). Contrary to this information, we found that many of the *quintas* were actually densely settled, with makeshift housing unrecorded in the official map, and exhibited the highest household density due to both high fertility and overcrowding. Despite the Municipality's description, the *quintas* had an informal system of urbanization, with open paths to connect homes and systems of shared electricity and water, their collective response to the lack of formal services.

Although all inhabited space in principle had the right to services, the informal discourse of the Municipality was one of duty toward the urban center and of philanthropic aid to the poor living in the periphery or *quintas*. In fact, many well-meaning women from the center organized philanthropic drives to aid the people in the *quintas* to help themselves through projects such as providing education on how to start vegetable gardens in backyards (*huertas*), organizing used clothing fairs (*roperos*) or informal exchange systems of produce and cooked goods (*trueque*), and cooking free meals at the church on Sundays (*comedores*). By not labeling the *quintas* as *manzanas*, the Municipality was omitting the spaces inhabited by the poor from service planning. Another finding was substantive: generational memory was stronger among households with higher socioeconomic status who resided in the center of the village.

The process of constructing the ethnographic map aided in additional participant and nonparticipant observation; for example, we could note the distance of households from commercial establishments, the Municipality, health centers, schools, recreational and open spaces, and informal services such as the *roperos* and *trueque*. The ethnographic data obtained from the household survey were overlaid on the municipal map to allow for a comparison with the municipal distribution of the population and to provide a spatial correlate for memory. Thus space became a social referent that permitted us to ascertain that the center had higher socioeconomic indicators, older populations, and higher frequencies of people with considerably longer periods of continuous living in the village.

To sum up, the ethnographic map provided a more accurate mapping of used places and a better understanding of social space. While the household survey resulted in a temporal description of the population (their recollection of their and their ancestors' length of stay in the village), the ethnographic map allowed for their placement in social space (the center being closer to the Municipality in both distance and service provision than the periphery). There are two orders of discrepancy between the ethnographic and the municipal map: they describe used space differently and they provide alternate types of knowledge. While the municipal map provides basic information on the urban landscape (street names, north-south orientation, determination of the urban and suburban space), the ethnographic map updates institutional information on the population. The municipal map alone is submitted to the provincial and federal authorities to obtain services on the basis of population characteristics; only extreme cases of indigence become the province of social workers.

The survey was administered to 526 households representing 70.3 percent of the village population (consisting of 748 housing units documented through nonparticipant observation, some of which did not fit the study design criteria of being at home or having an adult respond to our knock on the door). After discounting errors, the original 526 turned into 510 households. As soon as the survey was completed, and simultaneously with the elaboration of the ethnographic map, a data set was compiled to systematize the information collected and provide the basis for selecting a representative sample. The data set could provide information on individuals as individuals, as members of households, and as residents of a block identified in the ethnographic map. The population surveyed was skewed to the very young and very old: only 18 percent were thirty to forty years old, while another 19 percent were forty to fifty. About half of the population had lived all or most of their lives in the village: while 22 percent had lived there for twenty to thirty years, another 19 percent had lived there for thirty to forty years. The final data set grouped individuals by age, sex, length of residence in the village, and generational memory for the birthplace of two ascendant generations (67 percent of those surveyed remembered the birthplace of two generations and 8 percent did not remember either one).

The findings of the household survey were coded and entered into an Excel spreadsheet designed to systematize the information collected and provide a sampling framework for the ethnographic interviews. To address the study goal, a sample was obtained through the combination of two variables: chronological age and generational memory (the assigned values were 0 for lack of memory of the birthplace of parents or grandparents, 1 for memory of parents' birthplace only, and 2 for memory of birthplace of the two ascending generations).

The selection of the ethnographic sample was based on the following variables: highest chronological age and memory of the birthplace of up to two ascending generations. Using the variables discussed, sixty individuals (12 percent) were selected for in-depth interviews, distributed in fifty-three *manzanas* and six *quintas*. One informant per block was selected (covering both the center and the periphery) who exhibited two variables—longest time of residence in Villa Clara and oldest chronological age—to have the necessary assurance that the informant would remember the lifeways of the two ascending generations. Because some rapport had already been established through the household census, we did not experience any rejection when we went back to the selected households to arrange the timing of an ethnographic interview. The purpose of these interviews was to elicit memories using life history techniques that repeatedly prompted the recall of stages in the life-course. All interviews were conducted in the informant's home and taped. The interviews were transcribed and coded using Atlas Ti for thematic analysis. They provided individual versions of village history, which might differ from those of others or from the officially accepted history.

At the end of this exercise, it was possible to produce a visual rendition of the population in three dimensions: (1) Spatial Dimension: Ego and her or his family in the social structure, taking the household or space occupied for housing as an indicator of social class; (2) Temporal Dimension: Ego and her family in time (their time, meaning their personal biography in relation to three generations); and (3) Social Dimension: Ego's placement in the history of the locality where she or he carries out daily life. This richer context allowed an understanding of the individual in the context of society well before selecting a statistical sample for ethnographic interviews of individuals. Unlike selecting informants for in-depth ethnographic interviews solely on the basis of participant observation—the traditional method—this staged procedure allowed me to select informants based on two conditions: representativeness of the general population and of a population profile mirroring both the study goals and population characteristics. This methodology obviated the need to classify data separately as quantitative or qualitative and referred to a population profile that could be understood by policy makers and/or planners, thus assuring effective communication between researcher and decision maker.

In conclusion, this ethnographic method demystified traditional ethnography and contributed to systematic and rigorous ethnographic practices. To the extent that ethnographers can become methodologically more transparent, they can produce results that contribute to decision-making in democratic societies and more specifically to distributing services equitably: in this case, both those in the urban center and those in more marginal areas, inevitably left behind by both administrators and historians. The method devised for this research could be applied to the study of other small-scale social groupings (such as villages or neighborhoods) and contribute to an anthropological practice actively committed to democratic governance through sharing relevant findings with public administrators and devising a common language to structure collaboration.

As I disseminated my research and engaged in collaboration, its utility became better understood. I was assured that the people knew that the initial rumors had no substance, and I started to behave as a member of the village: I donated a tree to the central plaza, offered free English classes to children, and collaborated in writing a banner that the Swiss-French collectivity paraded in the nearby city of Concordia during the celebrations of the Day of the Immigrant. I was approached by the mayor to train a coordinator for the local museum so that it could remain open all week and to become a member of the newly formed Comisión de Amigos del Museo (Friends of the Museum Committee). It was during meetings of this committee that I became aware of its funding needs and proposed to write a book for that purpose. *Memorias de Villa Clara* (published in 2005) funded the purchase of a computer, printer, and tape recorders and helped pay the coordinator's salary.

Throughout the process of fieldwork, I was attentive to every possible lead concerning archives and documents that could help piece together the history of the village. That search yielded written documents in Villa Clara, including history books in the local library, minutes of meetings of founding institutions such as the Junta de Fomento and the Caja Rural in the museum's library, and unpublished manuscripts on the daily history of the village as well as a variety of materials borrowed from the homes of informants whose libraries I was allowed to browse. I learned much from using the library of the Museo de las Colonias Judías located in Villa Domínguez and from conversations with its director and collected tourist information on the province, the Circuito Histórico, and the municipality, particularly the information produced on the centennial celebration.

Having committed myself to write a book in Spanish geared to the general public and to donate its proceeds to the museum, I returned to Villa Clara in 2003 for two weeks of fieldwork with the purpose of collecting information on material culture contained in artifacts and photos. I had announced the motives of this visit by radio and flyers and through the informants. After arrival, I set up office in the museum to scan documents and photograph the artifacts and called the villagers again to a "community consultation" with the purpose of having them comment on the first draft of *Memorias* as they came to share their personal documents and photos. To elicit their comments, I produced a poster as a visual prompt to entice villagers to provide feedback on the book's contents. The poster, based on the analysis of the three focus groups the previous year, presented a summary of major themes associated with the history of the village: railroad and immigration:

Book on the Museum of Villa Clara

Here are selected pages from the book that tells the history of Villa Clara. On one page you can see the railroad station that operates at the time as a museum. These were some of the things said last year at the meeting in the Municipal Room:

The first page showed the railroad station, now housing the museum.
The children said: "It is a village with a small population, with a plaza, a hospital, a school, a police station, a bank, running water, a museum, one rail, a library, a radio."

Older people said: "It is a village that lost much of its economic and social life due to the lack of a railroad."

They also said: "We went to see the train on Sundays to have fun."

The second page showed the synagogue and the parade of the Swiss-French collectivity.

The children said: "There were *criollos*—who are from the countryside—and immigrants, who are Turkish, Polish, Russian, German, Italian, Spanish, Jews, Swiss, French, . . . and some are still here."

Older people said: "We are like a big family, there is much goodwill" and "Jews go to Catholic celebrations and vice versa."

To contextualize the material culture, I asked for the collaboration of informants while photographing artifacts and scanning photos and documents. As I photographed the artifacts contained in the museum collections, I asked the coordinator to describe their history and meaning. I had the self-selected villagers describe the photos and documents that they brought. As they understood the project better, some informants donated photos or documents to the museum.

In 2004 I returned for one week to submit final drafts of *Memorias* and engage the villagers in feedback and discussion. I selected four different locations to ensure greater and more representative participation. Overall, the response was positive. I finalized the manuscript and returned in 2005 to give formal presentations of the book and publicly donate the books to the museum.

Appendix II: Chronology of
Relevant Events in Villa Clara

1892: The Jewish Colonization Association establishes Colonia Clara. Seventy families are settled in Bélez, close to the contemporary Villa Clara.

1902: Railroad Station Clara is inaugurated.

1905: The cooperative Fondo Comunal with headquarters in Villa Domínguez opens a branch in Villa Clara.

1905: The first synagogue, the Artisans' Synagogue (Sinagoga de los Artesanos), opens.

1911: The first school, School No. 37, opens.

1912–1917: The second synagogue, Beith Jacob, is built.

1917: The Caja de Ahorro y Préstamos (Savings and Loan Association) opens to provide banking services and financial advice to small business owners and artisans.

1918: The first physician, Dr. Wolcomich, and his wife, Olga, arrive in the village.

1920: Villa Clara reaches 1,500 inhabitants.

1921: The Junta de Fomento, the first governing body, holds its first meeting.

1921: The first flour mill opens.

1922: Ferias Francas begin, to lower the cost of basic goods during a difficult economic crisis.

1922: The first police station opens.

1922: The Caja Rural moves to its own building and begins providing services to the village and other *colonias*.

1924: The village gets electrical lighting.

1927: The first municipal cemetery is established on a lot donated by the Jewish Colonization Association.

1928: The first public provision of electricity begins.

1936: The first Catholic chapel, Cristo Rey, is constructed.

1938: The Union of Workers in Diverse Services (Sindicato de Obreros de Oficios Varios) is founded.

1940: The Jewish Colonization Association estimates 1,000 Jews in the village.

1941: The Fondo Comunal reaches 467 members.

1943: Villa Clara achieves the status of second-class municipality (*municipio de segunda categoría*).

1943: Fifth grade and sixth grade are offered at Complementary School No. 60.

1945: Construction of the Casa Social Barón Hirsch starts. It will open in 1947.

1952: A professional school for women (ORT) opens.

1965: Cristo Rey Parish is inaugurated.

1970: Low-cost housing projects are built to replace the mud houses (*ranchos*) on land donated by the Jewish Colonization Association.

1970–1980: Public services are improved and expanded.

1971: The Caja Rural sells its assets to a regional bank.

1972:   The first high school, Instituto Delio Panizza, opens.

1974:   The Jewish Colonization Association donates 95 additional lots to the Municipality.

1977:   Villa Clara celebrates its first seventy-five years.

1991:   Villa Clara reaches 2,358 inhabitants, according to the National Census.

1996:   The local museum (Museo Histórico Regional de Villa Clara) opens.

2001:   The National Census registers 2,794 inhabitants in Villa Clara.

2002:   The village celebrates its first centennial.

NOTES

Preface

1. Historical Circuit of the Jewish Colonies of the Center of Entre Ríos (see Chapter 7).

2. *Zeide* is the Yiddish term for grandfather; *bobe* is the Yiddish term for grandmother.

Chapter 1

1. Maurice Halbwachs (1992) is credited with contesting the notion that memory is a private activity and with generating the theoretical dialogue on the collective nature of memory (Armstrong 2000; Schneider 2000; Shackel 2001).

2. A *municipio* (municipality) is the smallest administrative unit in a *provincia* (state). Villa Clara was given this status in 1920. Because of its small population, Villa Clara is considered a *municipio de segunda categoría* (a second-level administrative unit); Villaguay, capital of the department, is a *municipio de primera categoría* (first-level administrative unit). As I initiated fieldwork in 2002, I was told by the Municipality that the population of Villa Clara was 2,794, an increase from the population of 2,358 in 1991.

3. Buenos Aires, the last province to ratify the 1853 Constitution, did not do so until 1860.

4. Alicia Bernasconi (personal communication, 2007).

5. Hides, salted beef, and tallow exports doubled between 1837 and 1852 (Rock 1985).

6. Moisesville, a *colonia* in the province of Santa Fé, is the first organized settlement of Jewish immigrants to Argentina. See Chapter 2 for details of its history.

Chapter 2

1. Montiel is a wooded area in the center of the province. Legend had it that many gauchos had hidden there to escape military draft or other impositions of the new government.

2. The Greek word for "between the rivers" is "Mesopotamia." The provinces located in the northeast of Argentina (Misiones, Corrientes, and Entre Ríos) are often referred to as the Argentine Mesopotamia, given their geographical location and the fertility of their soil.

3. The institutions that distributed indigenous labor to the Spaniards were *encomiendas* and *reducciones*.

4. Archaeologists and ethnologists categorize these indigenous people according to tribe: Yaros, Mbohanes, Chanaes, Guaycurúes, Timbúes, Chandules, Manchados, Martidanes, Mocoretáes, Zemaes, Zelvaiscos, Golqueraros, Tocagües, Mepenes, Curumíes, Caletenes, Guenoas, and Mbeguaes. Some analysts argue that Minuanes, Yaros, Mbohanes, and Chanaes are all Charrúas (*Enciclopedia* 1977). Ethnographers distinguish two ethnic groups on the province's mainland: the Chaná-Timbús (Mocoretáes, Caletenes, Timbúes, Begúaes) on the margins of the Paraná River and the Charrúas (Guenoas, Bohanes) on the margins of the Uruguay River. The largest indigenous populations in the center of the

province were the Minuanes and Charrúas. A third group (the Guaraníes) was concentrated on the province's southern islands (Bosch: 1978).

5. *Enciclopedia* 1977; Pérez Colman 1937.

6. Some of these attacks were reportedly instigated by political authorities in Santa Fé, as a way to counteract the growing influence of the well-off Jesuits. The Portuguese settled in Uruguay, originally inhabited by the Charrúas, were also said to be the instigators of indigenous attacks, in support of their continued conflict with the Spanish (Pérez Colman 1937).

7. The Jesuits were powerful political stakeholders in Argentina until their 1767 expulsion from the American possessions of the Spanish Crown.

8. Large land properties for raising sheep and cows emerged as early as 1777 (Ciapuscio 1973).

9. A *montaraz* is a person (usually a man) who lives in isolation on mountain terrain and is uncivilized.

10. A *paisano* is a native of the same country, a fellow countryman/countrywoman.

11. The slave traffic was abolished in 1853.

12. The supporters of federalism in Argentina were known as *federales*, in opposition to the *unitarios*, who advocated a centralized government of Buenos Aires Province, with no participation of the other provinces in the custom tax benefits of the Buenos Aires port.

13. This event, known as Pronunciamiento or Pronouncement, took place in the central plaza of Concepción del Uruguay, Entre Ríos, in 1851. Urquiza had a long political career: he was governor of the province for three periods between 1842 and 1854 and president of the Confederación Argentina (Argentine Confederation) between 1854 and 1860. As the nation organized as a federal republic in 1860, Urquiza continued to rule the destiny of Entre Ríos, whether as governor (1860–1864 and elected for the term 1868–1870) or by exerting a major influence on elected officials. His assassination in 1870 triggered a federal intervention in the province to counteract the anarchy spread by a myriad of new caudillos roaming the land. The caudillo operating closest to contemporary Villa Clara was Polonio Velásquez.

14. The second national census of 1895 registered 291,324 inhabitants in the province, of whom 228,356 were Argentine and 62,989 were foreign born.

15. Devoto (2003) observes that private individuals or organizations were the ones actually handling the process of implementation of state legislation regarding colonization policies.

16. Alicia Bernasconi (personal communication, 2007) believes the limitations might relate to the fact that notions of nationality, nation, and national citizenship were ambiguous at the end of the nineteenth century.

17. The immigrants entering Argentina during that conflicted period were registered in Buenos Aires upon arrival but not in Entre Ríos.

18. But the opposite could have occurred as well. Bernasconi (personal communication, 2007) notes that Italians arriving from Brazil with their children registered the whole family as Italian.

19. Immigrants arriving in Argentina from the neighboring country of Uruguay were often registered if they arrived in Buenos Aires across the Río de la Plata but were not registered if they crossed the Uruguay River to arrive directly in Entre Ríos.

20. Urquiza's grandfather had arrived from the Basque region of Spain in 1774.

21. A *quintero* is a farmer who works a *quinta* (parcel of land where fruits and vegetables are grown).

22. The term "Swiss-French collectivity" is used by the current descendants of this immigration in Villa Clara to designate immigration originating in the Alpine region of Europe before contemporary nation-states drew political boundaries.

23. Agencies headquartered in Geneva traversed the valleys instigating emigration, through the combined effects of the printed media and household visits. By 1860 there were 235 emigration agents in France alone (Vernaz 1986). Many were not considered reputable.

24. The agency Beck & Herzog had contracted with the governor of the province of Corrientes on behalf of the immigrants. When the contract was canceled after the contingent had already sailed, Urquiza helped them settle, implementing his plan to use colonization as a strategy for agricultural development.

25. This is the village with the largest bibliography about the history of Swiss immigration to the area.

26. Peyret was appointed *inspector general de tierras y colonias* (general inspector of lands and colonies) in 1889, a position he held until 1899.

27. The majority of the Swiss-French came from the Canton de Valais, which at the time of emigration had a high proportion of French and German speakers.

28. Immigration from the Piedmont region took place before the establishment of the Italian Kingdom, at a time when regional affiliation overrode national affiliation. The descendants of this immigration probably mention their regional ancestry to differentiate them from the massive southern (and poorer) Italian immigration that arrived in Argentina later, settling primarily in Buenos Aires.

29. Until Colón harbor was built, products were taken in carts (pulled first by oxen and later by horses) to the closest urban center, Concepción del Uruguay, thirty-five kilometers away. Colón, in contrast, was only eight kilometers from San José.

30. La Rioja is a province located in northwestern Argentina.

31. The name "Tres de Febrero" commemorates February 3, the date when Urquiza defeated Rosas.

32. The legislation planned the size, distribution, and layout of these *colonias*, which were replicated throughout the colonization period.

33. Landowners who settled *colonos* in their property and then sold them plots to be paid for in installments benefited from the 1876 Law of Colonization, which exempted them from paying taxes on their property for ten years.

34. The term "British" was used to refer to the largest foreign investors in Argentina, though in reality the term includes Irish, Scottish, and English investors.

35. Impoverished by wars, about thirty thousand people (primarily from Germany but also from Holland, Poland, Sweden, Yugoslavia, Switzerland, and France) accepted German-born Catherine II of Russia's 1763 offer: if they moved to Russia, they would be given free land upon arrival and allowed to purchase more should they wish to become agriculturalists, be exempted from paying taxes and serving in the armed forces, and hold autonomy over the so-called Republic of the Volga, including education, governance, and religion. Since Germans, the most affected by the wars, had predominated in this eastward migration, the other nationals soon became Germanized. Despite Catherine's promises, these newcomers were

not free to choose an occupation or a place to live upon arrival: once in Russian territory, they were directed to the banks of the Volga and instructed to become agriculturalists, even though many had no knowledge of farming. In fact, the newcomers soon understood that their sedentary settlements fulfilled Catherine's mission to defend Russian sovereignty by repelling nomadic invasions. The first German colony was established in 1764. The number of colonies had reached 103 "mother colonies" and 91 "daughter colonies" by the time of emigration to America. They continued to flourish until 1861, although the advantages offered to Germans in Russia had been canceled in 1872. After that date they were forbidden to acquire new lands for their growing families, making their holdings unproductive after inheritance distributions. This situation became intolerable with the additional pressures to convert to the Russian Orthodox Church and submit to the compulsory military draft.

36. Russian Germans came directly from Russia or from Brazil, where a previous contingent had settled but had not found lands that they considered adequate for wheat production.

37. Immigrants were sold land at insignificant prices, to be paid in thirteen years.

38. Although most of the new Volga contingents had originated in Russia, some eight hundred arrived from Brazil, where they had initially settled.

39. Settlers in Colonia Crespo are said to have paid the highest price, made payable in three years.

40. A *tropero* is a worker who is hired to lead a large number of cattle from one destination to another in rural areas. A *puestero* is a permanent worker hired to oversee a section of an *estancia*.

41. The Hotel de Inmigrantes was the first stop for many of the millions of Europeans who arrived in Argentina between 1880 and 1930.

42. Many refer to Villa Clara as Clara for short.

43. The Alliance Israélite Universelle, headquartered in Paris, funded education on site and supported a self-organized Jewish migration to Argentina.

44. The prince of Bavaria gave the title of baron to his grandfather in 1820.

45. Clara was the daughter of senator Rafael Bischoffsheim, owner of an international banking firm in Brussels with branches in Paris and London.

46. The JCA established agricultural settlements in Canada, the United States, Brazil, and Argentina, which received the largest contingents.

47. To obtain the authorization of the Russian government for the emigration of future colonists, the baron enlisted the help of a well-known British negotiator, Arnold White.

48. "I contend most decidedly against the old system of alms-giving, which only makes so many more beggars; and I consider it the greatest problem in philanthropy to make human beings who are capable of work out of individuals who otherwise must become paupers, and in this way create useful members of society" (Hirsch 1935: 275).

49. Prominent Jewish businessmen invested in the JCA. Among the best known were Baron Horace Guinzburg and David Feinberg. Also cited are Julian Goldschmit, Ernesto José Kassel, D. Makata, S. G. Goldschmit, Salomon Reinaj, and Benjamin Kohen (*Nuestra Clara* 1, no. 2 [March 1953]: 8–10).

50. The JCA purchased land mostly in Argentina, though it also established agricultural settlements in the United States and Brazil.

51. The Baron de Hirsch Fund, created in 1890, had as its first goal to improve the living conditions of people in low-income urban enclaves, such as the Lower East Side in New York City. After 1894, with more favorable reception of immigration to the United States, it also promoted and often funded the relocation of Russian, Polish, and Rumanian Jews. When the fund became linked with the Jewish Colonization Association after the baron's death, it expanded operations within the United States and in Canada and focused on agriculture. Unlike traditional charity organizations, the fund focused on acculturating immigrants to U.S. society, including training people in occupations in demand in the labor market or funding small entrepreneurs and home industries, especially in the textile and clothing industries. The Jewish Colonization Association established settlements during the 1880s in the United States in New Jersey, New York, Connecticut, Oregon, Kansas, Minnesota, Michigan, New England, Colorado, and the Dakotas. One of the best known was Woodbine (or Hirschville), founded in 1891 in New Jersey and settled with immigrants from southern Russia, who were believed to have some agricultural background.

52. Cited in Senkman 1984: 41.

53. The granting of legal philanthropic status was reiterated in 1940, during the presidency of Ramón Castillo.

54. Hojman (1964: 209) provides the foundation and size of the *colonias* in the five provinces. Entre Ríos: Colonias Clara (1892), Lucienville (1894), and San Antonio (purchased in 1892 and 1894): 231,367, Barón de Hirsch (1905), López y Berro (1907), Curbelo Moss (1908), Santa Isabel (1908), Palmar Yatay (1912), Louis Oungre (1925), Leonardo Cohen (1937), and Avigdor (1936); Buenos Aires: Colonias Mauricio (1892) and Barón de Hirsch: 154,351 (1905); Santa Fé: Colonias Moisesville (first purchased 1891) and Montefiore (purchased 1902): 147,494; La Pampa: Colonia Narcise Leven (purchased 1908): 81,466; Santiago del Estero: Colonia Dora (purchased 1910): 2,980.

55. The baron purchased 43,485 hectares in the province of Santa Fé from landowners Palacios and Monigotes. Moisesville was settled with the Podolian contingent and Monigotes with a smaller group from Bessarabia.

56. Moisesville grew to be an important center of Jewish cultural life, received Jewish immigration until the period after World War II, and had 2,572 inhabitants in 2001 (*Censo de Entre Ríos* 2001). The original name of Moisesville was Kiryat Moshe (Town of Moses) to honor the baron, whose Hebrew name was Moses and who was considered, like the prophet, a redeeming figure by these early immigrants.

57. Bernasconi (personal communication, 2007) suggests that "exodus as a sign of success rather than failure is common to other immigrants. In the case of Italians, for example, their return to Italy could have been considered a failure by Argentine authorities but a success for those who were able to return to their place of origin with savings. Sending children to study in the city signaled economic capacity for all immigrant groups (peasants in Italy or Spain were not able to do that)."

Chapter 3

1. A *boleadora* is a lariat with balls on one end that is thrown at an animal's legs to entangle them.

2. *Bombachas* are loose trousers fastened at the bottom.

3. A *chambergo* is a soft hat.

4. A census carried out by the JCA in 1942 showed that about two-thirds of the Jewish population of the country (about 35,000 families) lived in rural areas of the province (Guionet 2001).

5. President Roca had granted legal status and recognized the philanthropic nature of the JCA in 1892.

6. Since the JCA had bought the land before the arrival of the immigrants, they escaped the fate of the first immigrants, who came independently from Russia.

7. Some stayed in the area. At the time of the founding of Colonia Clara, there were farms worked by descendants of Dutch, Belgian, and German immigrants (*Cincuenta años* 1939: 176).

8. A *chacra* was an assigned lot of land containing a house, a well, and an orchard.

9. A *grupo* (group) was the name given to a series of houses, usually five or more, built next to one another. As a settlement pattern, a group had its origins in Russia, where people lived close together both to promote sociability and to erect a line of defense against pogroms. The Freidenberg family, for example, lived in Group 2 of Las Moscas, also known as Rosh Pinah.

10. *La ganadería y la agricultura en 1908* (1909).

11. Residents in Villa Clara that I term "local historians" are Miguel Muchinik and Abraham Schejter (both deceased) and Ida Isuz de Schulman.

12. *Mishpuje* is the Yiddish word for family.

13. *Paraísos* and *álamos* are species of Argentine trees.

14. The members of this family returned to Paris and were taken to concentration camps during the German occupation.

15. *Felser* is the Yiddish word for curer.

16. *Mikveh* is the Yiddish term for a communal bathtub used for purification purposes after polluting events (such as menstruation or delivery) or in preparation for ritually sanctioned events such as weddings. According to the Jewish religion, body immersion in a ritual bath confirms inclusion in the community.

17. Engineer Miguel Sajaroff was the most famous promoter of the cooperativist movement in the region.

18. Cooperativa Fondo Comunal (Communal Fund Cooperative) was an agricultural cooperative founded in 1904 in Villa Domínguez with funding from the JCA colonists to promote their interests, particularly obtaining good seeds and other items to be repaid after the harvests; marketing agricultural and cattle-rising products; dealing with the administrators in regard to contracts, loans, and evictions; and providing and sharing information through meetings and a newspaper, *El Colono Cooperador* (The Cooperative Colonist).

19. The Historical Circuit is a heritage tourism organization established in 2000 to promote visits to the Jewish settlements.

20. The parallels are striking. The similarities in the experiences of the agricultural colonization of Eastern European Jews in the Colonia Clara in Argentina and Woodbine in New Jersey include problematic beginnings of agricultural production and/or failing of agricultural colonization programs; revolt of colonists against administrators (only two out of sixty

colonists signed the original contracts as drawn by the JCA in Woodbine); dispossession or eviction of defaulting farmers; establishment of cooperatives; abandonment of agriculture by the second generation; founding of newspapers by colonists to share news and struggles to improve living conditions (the *Jewish Farmer* in the United States and *El Colono Cooperador* in Colonia Clara); administrators inexpert at agriculture who placed excessive demands on the farmers; and unpredictability of harvests and thus difficulty in compliance with meeting payment plans. The major difference between any group in Colonia Clara and Woodbine was the zeal of the U.S. operation in acculturating the newcomers to the new country: the Hirsch Fund created vocational schools to instruct children of immigrants in crafts and trades, opened or supported factories in the vicinity of the agricultural fields to provide sources of employment other than agriculture, and provided the new families with free instruction in the English language and their civic rights and duties. In both Clara and Woodbine the conflict-ridden relationship between administrators and colonists and the administrators' frequent reconsiderations of Jews' aptitude for farming did not taint the image of the baron, whose idealism permeated his undeterred confidence in the feasibility of a "return" to farming as the major occupation in biblical times and who was always honored and revered as a savior by the displaced Jews.

21. Exceptions were accounts of assassinations and vandalism, which were attributed to limited police protection in the area.

22. Although the agricultural colonization programs in Argentina and the United States either were doomed to failure or fell short of expectations, there was a difference in the occupational background of the recruits in Eastern Europe, according to Ellen Aizenberg (1994). She notes that the provenance of the New Jersey farmers in 1880 was the south of the Zone of Residence (Podolia, Bessarabia, Kherson, and Ekaterinoslav), a region with a tradition of Jewish farming. In 1898 the JCA surveyed about 150,000 people working part-time or full-time in agriculture in Russia. To face the mounting restrictions on accessing land, these farmers might have taken other occupations to make a living, but they were sought by the JCA because of their past agricultural experience. The north of the region (Lithuania) was more urban and contained a larger proportion of people involved in crafts and trades. According to Aizenberg (1994), Colonia Clara received a mix of groups from the north and the south, though later organized migration as well as independent arrivals might primarily have originated in the north. Aizenberg notes that the proportion of agriculturalists recruited by the JCA was actually very large, given that only 2.3 percent of Jews practiced agriculture in Russia.

23. Most of the descendants of the JCA settlers interviewed maintained that their ancestors were forbidden to practice agriculture due to restrictions on land ownership. Others said that there was some limited ownership. For example, Yoine Paikovsky said that his father owned some land and animals, though he was very poor.

24. Alicia Bernasconi (personal communication, 2007) points out that the rural areas also had a need for artisans: "The quick growth of the Argentine population . . . generated a demand for craftsmen, a semi-skilled and an unskilled workforce in rural areas as well, since as settlements appeared it was necessary to manufacture bricks, build houses and carts, place horseshoes, etc., in addition to staffing small manufacturing plants of liquor and baking goods, and providing services to meet local needs."

25. Naúm Wainer (personal communication, 2006).

26. Though I am referring here to Argentina, the same outcome was described for the United States, particularly Woodbine (Joseph 1935).

Chapter 4

1. Compulsory military service also facilitated assimilation to a shared homeland, though it was restricted to males.

2. The Jewish immigrants, however, did not usually intermarry.

3. The second national census (1895) registered 291,342 inhabitants in the province, of whom 228,356 were Argentine and 62,986 were foreign-born.

4. The largest landowner, Urquiza, was the grandchild of Basque immigrants. The British acquired large properties when investing on railroads. Other landowners were descendants of the Spanish expeditions.

5. The best-known case is Colonia San José, founded by Urquiza on his own land.

6. *Joda* and *chupa* are slang terms that mean "hanging around" and "binge drinking."

7. *Querencia* refers to the home and also implies nostalgia for one's place of origin.

8. Stang and Britos 2000.

9. Bunge & Born and Dreyfus were later augmented with immigrant-owned firms (for example, the Belgian firm Van Vanvaren, the German Graus Mahn & Co., and the Jewish-owned Kaplan company).

10. Weyne 1986: 199.

11. Most of the Jewish arrivals at Colonia Clara were people from southern Russia (particularly Bessarabia), who had practiced agriculture and taught it to the arrivals from northern Russia, particularly those from Lithuania.

12. Dupey (personal communication, 2005).

Chapter 5

1. Now that Colonia Clara no longer exists, informants often refer to Villa Clara as Clara for short, and to themselves as Clarenses.

2. A *caserío* is a small cluster of dispersed houses (a hamlet).

3. Though not much is known about the Africans, some informants referred to them (probably descendants of slaves escaping from Brazil or Uruguay) and took me to a small cemetery that, according to them, confirmed the presence of Africans in the area. This story was confirmed in an interview with a descendant living in La Capilla, who reported that seven African-descended families lived in Corralón de los Negros (Black Hamlet), where they were known as *manecos* or Brazilian blacks (Chiaramonte et al. 1995: 116–117).

4. An *estanciero* is the owner of an *estancia* (large rural estate).

5. Although I cannot provide evidence to support this hypothesis, I suggest that Hirsch's decision to register his company in England, the foreign country with the largest investments in Argentina at the time, might conceivably have helped the economic viability of the JCA, philanthropic considerations aside.

6. Kosher refers to a ritual method of killing the animal in compliance with the regulations of the Jewish faith.

7. Currently there is a small supermarket at this site bearing the same name, Fondo Comunal, though it is not a cooperative.

8. *Asado con cuero* refers to beef grilled with the skin on.

9. The number of cars must have increased, since one of the first decisions of the Junta de Fomento was to establish a maximum speed of 12 km/hour (Muchinik and Isuz de Schulman n.d.a: 22).

10. "I remember having seen him, covered by a black cloak and with his photographic box mounted on a tripod, on the roof of the Fondo Comunal to obtain a photo of the parade organized to celebrate the Balfour Declaration in 1917" (Muchinik and Isuz de Schulman n.d.a: 22).

11. In fact, some *colonos* did well and were able to extend the original land obtained through the JCA to quite extensive landholdings, by Villa Clara's standards. These are among the contemporary wealthy landowners in the village.

Chapter 6

1. *Tapera* is the name given in the countryside to what is left of an abandoned house, the ruins of a once inhabited place.

2. There are many remembrances of Villa Clara of the 1930s and 1940s. *El Pueblo* (February 1, 1992) mentions Leopoldino Francia, head of the First Aid Clinic; Hernany Nery, a music teacher who founded a municipal band; police commissioner José Kistianovsky; Sigutkin, owner of a carpentry store; blacksmith Abraham Fuksman, who was also very involved in civic organizations; Mauricio Budeisky and his service station; Vostovoy's soda shop; the general stores of Kaplan and Elinger, Kleiman, León Golonsky, Marcos Koham, and Rafael Glimbeg; Abraham Burislovsky's shoe store; the "Negro" Santa Cruz's mechanic workshop; Juan Baldoni's agricultural machine repair shop; Abraham Bortnik's Teatro Opera; Don Pardo, the man in charge of Plaza General Urquiza, "very strict with the children who were always after its flowers"; Jaime Ulfhon's press; Aronson's sawmill; "Petiso" Godman and Borovinsky's bakery; La Obrera, owned by the Sindicato de Obreros de Oficios Varios, founded by "Manco" Valsechi; and Don Florentino Reynoso, the well-known chauffer for Dr. Jorge Wolcomich.

3. Marta Muchinik (personal communication, 2007).

4. *Cosecha fina* refers to the type of crops and their cultivating cycle. These crops, which include wheat, flax, rye, and oats, are planted between May and July and harvested between November and December.

5. *Forraje para animales* refers to crops used to feed cattle because of their fattening qualities.

6. A junta is a small number of military leaders who take over the government of a country through a coup d'état.

7. This is an important change: a *parroquia* (parish) has regional jurisdiction.

8. There were cases of anti-Jewish vandalism in the late 1970s. One was the defilement of Jewish tombs, shot with pressurized air slingshots. The Colectividad Israelita Clara-Bélez denounced the attack. The president told me that a police investigation took place only because many of the tombs belonged to families who had moved to Buenos Aires, who prompted the press to document the event. The police determined that the attack had been carried out by minors, but there was no punishment.

Chapter 7

1. The siesta (a nap taken after lunch) is a traditional custom in Villa Clara, where stores are closed from 12:00 to 4:00 daily for that purpose. *Mate* is a traditional green herbal infusion that is sipped through a metal straw from a gourd; it is used for refreshment and socializing in Argentina, Paraguay, Uruguay, and southern Brazil. *Asado* is Argentine barbecue.

2. There is, in fact, one rail used by cargo trains. The other rail has been dismantled.

3. "ORT" is the abbreviation for the Russian name of the Society to Promote Crafts, founded in Russia in 1880 to instruct Jews in technical professions, including agriculture. ORT was founded in 1936 in Argentina and opened branches in Villa Domínguez and Villa Clara during the 1950s.

4. Stimulating the schoolchildren planted the seeds for their long-term commitment to the project: during a few months in 2002 when the museum closed for lack of staff, these children—now high school graduates—volunteered to keep it open.

5. Quiroga de Fink n.d.; *Villa Clara, 100 años de historia* 2002; Danses de Fink 1996.

6. Alicia Bernasconi (personal communication, 2007) notes that "it is possible that the museum legitimizes the most disseminated of the myths since the individual memories, especially of the successive generations to the initial immigrant generation, are full of myths incorporated to the narratives received directly from the protagonists."

7. *Pampa* was the name of the ship bringing the first contingent of JCA immigrants.

8. The use of *negra* is contemptuous here and refers to skin color (*criollos* tend to be darker-skinned than immigrants).

9. Muchinik and Isuz de Schulman n.d.b: 1.

10. Alicia Bernasconi (personal communication, 2007) notes that the German collectivity in Argentina does not consider the Germans of the Volga true Germans, since they had not lived in Germany since the eighteenth century. In Villa Clara, however, they represent themselves as Germans. There was no mention of Oktoberfest among their celebrations since their arrival in Argentina until recently.

11. The Colectividad Alemana de Argentina, with headquarters in Crespo, Entre Ríos, published the regulations for the position of queen. Among other requirements, the participant had to demonstrate that she was a direct descendant of Germans and be able to dress in a "typical German dress." The details of the dress were attached to the application form (Application Form for Queen, Octoberfest 2000).

12. The Board of Directors for the Swiss-French Collectivity of Villa Clara at the time was headed by president Bibiano Lyardet.

Epilogue

1. Martín Fierro is an idealized literary figure of a type that was also on the verge of extinction as Hernández's book was published (Alicia Bernasconi, personal communication, 2007).

2. Examples include the pogrom-like week of violent repression of workers in Buenos Aires known as the Semana Trágica (Tragic Week) in 1919 and the bombing of the Asociación Mutual Israelita Argentina (AMIA) in 1994.

GLOSSARY OF TERMS

Barrio: literally, a neighborhood. In Villa Clara, the term was reserved for localities where poor people lived, usually in government-sponsored housing.

Caserío: a small cluster of dispersed houses.

Caudillo: a political boss exerting power in a local, usually rural, area.

Centro: literally, center. In Villa Clara, the term was used for the older area of the village, where the best-built houses were located in close proximity to the administrative center (Municipalidad).

Chacra: a small farm with a house and a well.

Clarense: "from Villa Clara," a name given by residents in Villa Clara to themselves.

Colonia: a rural settlement of immigrants dedicated primarily to agricultural production.

Colono: a resident of a *colonia* defined by a relationship to the land as a farmer and by dependency on the colonizing agency.

Criollo: any person born in Argentina. There are important differences among *criollos* by wealth, ancestry, and identity. Upper-class *criollos* are usually white and of Spanish or other European descent, while lower-class *criollos* are mestizos, of mixed descent.

Gaucho: a native of the Pampas born in Argentina, Uruguay, or Rio Grande do Sul (Brazil) during the eighteenth and nineteenth centuries. Gauchos developed excellent skills in working with horses (equivalent of a cowboy in the United States). They are usually lower-class *criollos*.

Hectare: the metric unit equivalent to 2.471 acres.

Immigrant: a person born outside of Argentina who establishes residence in that country. The slang term "gringo" is also used, often pejoratively.

Indian: a descendant of indigenous populations resident in Argentina at the time of the Spanish conquest (thus a true native of Argentina).

Jewish gaucho: an immigrant of the Jewish faith who adopts the lifeway of the gaucho and whose children born in Argentina are *criollos*.

Mestizo: a descendant of more than one ethnic group, of mixed ancestry. The term is mostly used to designate the mix of indigenous and Spanish parentage but could also include African origin. In Entre Ríos most mestizos are descended from Spaniards and Minuane and Charrúa indigenous groups. During the early years of nation-building, the combination of *criollo* and mestizo was sometimes considered an ethnic advance over the indigenous type but was sometimes taken as an evolutionary backward leap.

Pampa: the fertile lowlands that include the Argentine provinces of Buenos Aires, La Pampa, Santa Fé, and Córdoba.

Patagonia: the geographic region containing the southernmost portion of South America. Located mostly in Argentina and partly in Chile, it includes the Andes Mountains to the west and south and plateau and low plains to the east.

Peón: a rural employee, usually *criollo*.

Pogrom: an organized massacre, originally and especially of Jews in Russia.

Puestero: a permanent worker hired to oversee a section of an *estancia*.

Sulky: an open horse-drawn cart.

Tapera: a house in disrepair, often without a roof.

Tropero: a worker who is hired to lead a large number of cattle from one destination to another in rural areas.

Yevich: a distortion of the name of the Jewish Colonization Association by the settled immigrants.

BIBLIOGRAPHY

Brochures and Pamphlets

1er Oktoberfest. 2002. Colectividad Alemana de Villa Clara, October 12.

Application Form for Queen, Oktoberfest. 2000.

Nuestros abuelos los pioneros: Colonos europeos en la costa del Río Uruguay. 1999. San José, Entre Ríos: Museo Histórico Regional de la Colonia San José.

Villa Clara, 100 años de historia: Un pueblo con una corta historia tiene tanto para contar, para aprender, para recordar. 2002. Villa Clara: Municipalidad de Villa Clara.

Weinstein, A. E., and M. Salomón. 1991. Las causas del olvido. In *Colonia Mauricio, 100 años,* 134–141. Publicación oficial de la comisión centenario colonización judía en Colonia Mauricio (Carlos Casares).

Ephemera and Archives

Alberdi, J. B. 1852. *Bases, puntos de partida para la organización política de la República Argentina.* N.p.

Atlas des colonies et domaines de la Jewish Colonization Association en République Argentine et au Brésil. 1914. Paris: Jewish Colonization Association.

Beaurain Barreto, J. 2001. *De Flandes a Montiel: Así llegaron los colonos belgas a Villaguay.* Villaguay, Argentina: Author's edition.

Casa Social Barón Hirsch. 1947. Estatutos. Villa Clara, Argentina.

Centro de Documentación e Información sobre Judaísmo Argentino Mark Turkow. Archivo de la Palabra (oral histories). Asociación Mutual Israelita Argentina (AMIA), Buenos Aires, Argentina.

Cincuenta años de colonización judía en la Argentina. 1939. Delegación de Asociaciones Israelitas Argentinas (DAIA), Buenos Aires, Argentina.

De Paoli de Bellman Eguiguren, G., and A. Oyenden. 1993. *Nuestra memoria: Historia de Entre Ríos.* Paraná: Ediciones del Ateneo de Paraná.

Devetter, E. 2000. *Que fue de ellos: Hechos protagonizados por inmigrantes belgas llegados a Villaguay a partir de 1882.* Villaguay, Argentina: Author's edition.

Enciclopedia de Entre Ríos. 1977. Paraná: Arozena Editores.

Estatuto: Fondo Comunal Cooperativa Agrícola Limitada. 1983. Villa Domínguez, Entre Ríos.

Fondo Comunal: Cincuenta años de su vida (1904–1954). 1965. Villa Domínguez, Entre Ríos: Fondo Comunal Cooperativa Agrícola Limitada.

Gerchunoff, A. 1910. *Los gauchos judíos.* La Plata: Joaquín Sesé.

———. 1973. *Entre Ríos, mi país* [1950]. Buenos Aires: Plus Ultra.

Guionet, H. 2001. *Inmigrantes, La Colonia San José: Memorias, Entre Ríos, e imágenes, 1857–2000.* Concepción del Uruguay, Argentina: Artes Gráficas Yusty.

Hernández, J. 2004. *El gaucho Martín Fierro y La vuelta de Martín Fierro* (originally published 1872 and 1879, respectively). Buenos Aires: Tientos Editora.

Hirsch, Baron de. 1935. My Views on Philanthropy. In *Samuel Joseph: History of the Baron de Hirsch Fund: The Americanization of the Jewish Immigrant*, Appendix A, 275–277. New York: Jewish Publication Society.

Hojman, B. 1909. *Materiales y memorias de la colonización judía en la Argentina*. Buenos Aires: Talleres Gráficos Julio Kaufman.

———. 1964. *Memorias y materiales de la colonización judía en la Argentina*. Buenos Aires: published by the children of the author.

Jewish Colonization Association. 1891 and 1900. *Memorandum and Articles of Association*. London: Waterlow and Sons Printers.

———. n.d. *Su obra en la República Argentina: 1891–1941*. Buenos Aires, Argentina: Jewish Colonization Association.

Kreimer, J. 1984. Aportes de la colectividad judía al cooperativismo nacional: Exposición efectuada el 12 de julio de 1984 en el Centro Cultural Israelita de Rosario. Rosario, Adhesión del Centro Cultural Israelita al Día del Inmigrante.

Leibovich, A. 1965. Anotaciones íntimas 1870–1946. In *Fondo Comunal: Cincuenta años de su vida (1904–1954)*, 52. N.p.

Shalom Argentina: Huellas de la colonización judía. 2001. Buenos Aires: Ministerio de Turismo, Cultura y Deporte.

YIVO Institute for Jewish Research. Jewish Colonization Association. Correspondence Records, 1898–1913.

Government Publications and Archives

NATIONAL

Archivos Generales de la Nación Argentina.

Censo general de educación, Tomo II: Estadística escolar. 1910. Buenos Aires: Talleres de Publicaciones de la Oficina Meteorológica Argentina.

Cuarto censo general de la nación, Tomo I: Censo de población. 1947. Buenos Aires: Dirección Nacional del Servicio Estadístico.

La ganadería y la agricultura en 1908. 1909. *Censo agropecuario nacional, Tomo I: Ganadería, Tomo II: Agricultura*. Buenos Aires: Talleres de Publicaciones de la Oficina Meteorológica Argentina.

Primer censo de la República Argentina (1869). 1872. Buenos Aires: Imprenta del Porvenir.

Registro de inmigrantes (1895 to present). n.d. Buenos Aires: n.p.

Segundo censo nacional (1895). n.d. Buenos Aires: n.p.

Situación demográfica de la Provincia de Entre Ríos. 1998. Buenos Aires: Instituto Nacional de Estadística y Censos.

Tercer censo nacional de 1914, Tomo II: Población. 1916. Buenos Aires: Talleres Gráficos de L. J. Rosso.

PROVINCIAL

Censo de Entre Ríos. 2001. Paraná: Dirección de Estadística y Censos.

Los municipios de la Provincia de Entre Ríos: Estadísticas básicas. 1991. Instituto Nacional de Estadística y Censos. Paraná: Ministerio de Economía y Obras y Servicios Públicos.

MUNICIPAL

Boletín Informativo Mensual. Municipalidad de Villa Clara.

Gacetilla. Municipalidad de Villa Clara.

Gacetilla Evocativa del Septuagésimo Quinto Aniversario de Su Fundación, 1902–1917. Municipalidad de Villa Clara.

Museo y Archivo Histórico Regional de las Colonias Judías. Villa Domínguez, Entre Ríos.

Periodicals

SCHOLARLY JOURNALS

Aizenberg, E. 1994. La influencia del lugar de origen de los integrantes de las colonias judías de Entre Ríos, Argentina, 1890–1910. *Estudios Migratorios Latinoamericanos* 27 (9): 401–411.

Armstrong, K. 2000. Ambiguity and Remembrance: Individual Collected Memory in Finland. *American Ethnologist* 27 (3): 591–608.

Bargman, D. 1992. Un ámbito para las relaciones interétnicas: Las colonias agrícolas judías en Argentina. *Revista de Antropología* 7 (11): 50–58.

Cavallo, F. 2005. *Los gauchos judíos:* Geografie identitarie degli Ebrei d'Argentina. *Geostorie* (13): 139–169.

Elkin, J. 1978. Goodnight, Sweet Gaucho: A Revisionist View of the Jewish Agricultural Experiments in Argentina. *American Jewish Historical Quarterly* 67 (3): 208–223.

Epstein, D. 2006. Judíos de Marruecos en Argentina: La inmigración política (1955–1970). *Estudios Migratorios Latinoamericanos* 20 (59): 69–98.

Ford, A. G. 1971. British Investment in Argentina and Long Swings, 1880–1914. *Journal of Economic History* 31 (3) (Sept.): 650–663.

Levin, Y. 2007. Labor and Land at the Start of the Jewish Settlement in Argentina. *Jewish History* 21: 341–359.

Magnani, I. 2006. Proyectos identitarios en la construcción del Museo Nacional de la Inmigración de Buenos Aires. *Estudios Migratorios Latinoamericanos* 59 (20): 139–154.

Shackel, P. 2001. Public Memory and the Search for Power in American Historical Archaeology. *American Anthropologist* 103 (3): 655–670.

MAGAZINES

Armony, P. 1998. La historia de los pampistas. *Toldot* 8 (Nov.): 15–18.

Aronson, J. 1953. Añoranzas de un pasado. *Nuestra Clara* 25 (4): 25–26.

Chajchir, M. 1998. Viaje al país de la esperanza: Relato de un viajero del Pampa, Mauricio Chajchir. *Toldot* 8 (Nov.): 19–21.

Entidades Valesanas Argentinas (EVA). *Xo aniversario de EVA, 1993–8 de mayo 2003.* 2003. Special issue: *Boletín* 22 (10).

Friedlander, B. Sijanovich de. 1953. ¡A tí, Colonia Bélez! *Asociación de Ex Residentes de Villa Clara y Sus Alrededores* 1 (4): 13–17.

Goodman, J. 2002. Return to a Promised Land on the Pampas. *Americas* 54 (11) (Feb.): 6–15.

Lemelson, J. 1953. Carta al director, Dr. Víctor Givré. *Nuestra Clara* 1 (4): 18–19.

Museo Histórico: Pieza del mes. n.d. *Boletín Informativo*. Dirección de Información Pública, Gobierno de Entre Ríos.

Palomar, J. 2001. Tras las huellas de los gauchos judíos. *La Nación*, Oct. 21, 19–29.

Smuckler, S. 1953. Villa Clara y sus colonias. *Nuestra Clara* 1 (4): 27–29.

Valenzuela, D. 2008. Viaje al corazón de los gauchos judíos. Supplement to ADN *Cultura* (*La Nación*), Apr. 26, 24–25.

Villa Clara y sus colonias. 1953. *Nuestra Clara* 1 (4): 27–28.

NEWSPAPERS

Korin, M. 2005. Vida del Barón Maurice de Hirsch antes de la creación de la J.C.A. *Mundo Israelita*, Mar. 18, 11.

Los 90 años de Villa Clara. 1992. *El Pueblo*, Jan. 23.

Schejter, A. 1996. Jalones de historia de Villa Clara: Especial para el diario en su 60 Aniversario. *El Pueblo*, Feb. 11.

Books

Aizenberg, E. 2000. *Parricide on the Pampa?: A New Study and Translation of Alberto Gerchunoff's "Los Gauchos Judíos."* Madrid: Iberoamericana.

Anderson, B. 1991. *Imagined Communities: Reflections on the Origin and Spread of Nationalism.* London: Verso.

Avni, H. 2005. *Argentina y las migraciones judías: De la inquisición al holocausto y después.* Buenos Aires: Editorial Milá.

Bernasconi, A., and C. Frid (editors). 2006. *De Europa a las Américas: Dirigentes y liderazgos (1880–1960).* Buenos Aires: Editorial Biblos.

Bosch, B. 1978. *Historia de Entre Ríos, 1520–1969.* Buenos Aires: Edición Plus Ultra.

Chambers, E. 2006. *Heritage Matters: Heritage, Culture, History, and Chesapeake Bay.* Chesapeake Perspectives: A Maryland Sea Grant Publication. College Park: University of Maryland Sea Grant College.

Chiaramonte, S., E. Finvarb, N. Fistein, and G. Rotman. 1995. *Tierra de promesas: 100 años de colonización judía en Entre Ríos—Colonia Clara, San Antonio y Lucienville.* Buenos Aires: Ediciones Nuestra Memoria.

Climo, J., and M. Cattell (editors). 2002. *Social Memory and History: Anthropological Perspectives.* Walnut Creek, Calif.: AltaMira.

De Grave, G. 1966. *La colonización belga en Villaguay.* Concepción del Uruguay, Argentina: Escuela Normal Superior de Profesores.

Devoto, F. 2003. *Historia de la inmigración en la Argentina.* Buenos Aires: Editorial Sudamericana.

Enciclopedia de Entre Ríos. 1977. Paraná: Arozena Editores.

Feierstein, R. 1999. *Historia de los judíos argentinos.* Buenos Aires: Ameghino Editores.

——— (editor) 2000. *Alberto Gerchunoff, judío argentino: Viaje temático desde "Los Gauchos Judíos" (1910) hasta sus últimos textos (1950) y visión crítica.* Buenos Aires: Editorial Dila.

Freidenberg, J. 2005. *Memorias de Villa Clara.* Buenos Aires: Antropofagia.

Frischer, D. 2002. *Le Moïse des Amériques: Vies et oeuvres du munificent Baron de Hirsch.* Paris: Bernard Grasset.

Gutkowski, Hélène. 1991. *Vidas en las colonias: Rescate de la herencia cultural.* Buenos Aires: Editorial Contexto.

Halbwachs, M. 1992. *On Collective Memory.* Edited, translated, and with an introduction by L. A. Coser. Chicago: University of Chicago Press.

Hobsbawm, E., and T. Ranger (editors). 1983. *The Invention of Tradition.* New York: Cambridge University Press.

Honeker de Pascal, O. E., and M. de los A. Jacob de Hoffmann. n.d. *Santa Anita: Nuestras raíces, una historia apasionante.* Santa Anita: Editorial de los Autores.

Joseph, S. 1935. *History of the Baron de Hirsch Fund: The Americanization of the Jewish Immigrant.* New York: Printed for the Baron de Hirsch Fund by the Jewish Publication Society.

Llanos, M. 2002. *Privatization and Democracy in Argentina.* New York: Palgrave.

López de Borche, C. G. 1987. *Cooperativismo y cultura: Historia de Villa Domínguez, 1890–1940.* Paraná: Editorial de Entre Ríos.

MacCann, W. 1969. *Viaje a caballo por las provincias argentinas (1847–1850).* Buenos Aires: Solar-Hachette.

Macchi, M. 1977. *Formación y desarrollo de una colonia argentina, Caseros, en Entre Ríos 1874.* Palacio San José, Museo y Monumento Nacional Justo José de Urquiza: Ediciones Del Palacio San José. Paraná: Impr. Oficial de la Provincia.

Martínez Estrada, E. 1942. *Radiografía de la Pampa.* 2 vols. Buenos Aires: Losada.

Massoni, O. de. n.d. *Gualeguay 1765–1900: El aporte migratorio.* Santa Fé: Ediciones Colmegna.

Napp, R. 1888. La República Argentina. In *La Provincia de Entre Ríos bajo sus diversos aspectos,* edited by C. Ripoll, 230–231. Paraná: Editorial La Opinión.

Pérez Colman, C. 1937. *Historia de Entre Ríos.* Paraná: Imprenta de la Provincia.

Peyret, A. 1889. *Una visita a las colonias de la República Argentina.* Buenos Aires: Impr. "Tribuna Nacional."

Popp, V., and N. Dening (editors). 1977. *Los Alemanes del Volga: Tras largo peregrinar por Europa hallaron patria definitiva en América.* Buenos Aires: Biblioteca Cemla.

Quiroga, O. C. 1990. Villa Domínguez . . . 100 años de historia, 1890–23 de septiembre 1990. Comisión Pro-Festejos del Centenario de Villa Domínguez, Provincia de Entre Ríos.

Rock, D. 1985. *Argentina, 1516–1982: From Spanish Colonization to the Falklands War.* Berkeley: University of California Press.

Schallman, Lázaro. 1971. *Historia de los "Pampistas."* Biblioteca Popular Judía 47. Buenos Aires: Congreso Judío Latinoamericano.

Schneider, A. 2000. *Futures Lost: Nostalgia and Identity among Italian Immigrants in Argentina.* Oxford: Peter Lang.

Senkman, Leonardo. 1984. *La colonización judía: Gente y sociedad.* Buenos Aires: Centro Editor de América Latina.

Shumway, N. 1993. *The Invention of Argentina.* Berkeley: University of California Press.

Solberg, C. 1970. *Immigration and Nationalism: Argentina and Chile, 1890–1914.* Austin: University of Texas Press.

Stang, G. M., and O. Britos. 2000. *Alemanes del Volga, ayer . . . Argentinos, hoy.* Crespo, Argentina: Authors' edition.

Vernaz, C. 1986. *Colonia San José y la inmigración europea.* San José: Ediciones Colmegna.

———. 1992. *La Colonia San José: Escritos.* Entre Ríos: Ediciones Colmegna.

Weyne, O. 1986. *El último puerto, del Rhin al Volga y del Volga al Plata.* Buenos Aires: Instituto Torcuato di Tella, Editorial Tesis.

Wolf, E. 1984. *Europe and the People without History.* Berkeley: University of California Press.

Wright, Winthrop. 1974. *British-Owned Railways in Argentina: Their Effect on Economic Nationalism, 1854–1948.* Latin American Monographs 34. Austin: University of Texas Press for the Institute of Latin American Studies.

Zago, Manrique. 1988. *Judíos & argentinos: Judíos argentinos.* Buenos Aires: Manrique Zago Ediciones.

Unpublished Manuscripts

Ciapuscio, P. 1973. Villaguay en la Memoria de un Periodista.

Circuito Histórico de las Colonias Judías del Centro de Entre Ríos. 2000. Acta fundacional, Dec. 17.

———. n.d. Instituto Superior de Turismo Santa Cecilia, Villaguay.

Danses de Fink, Z. 1996. La escuela hacia la comunidad: Construimos juntos el Museo Histórico Regional. Project presented to the Municipality of Villa Clara.

Hojman, B. 1908. Domínguez, una metrópoli. In Memorias y materiales de las colonias israelitas en la Argentina.

Isuz de Schulman, I. n.d. Manuscritos para la historia de Villa Clara.

Muchinik, M., and I. Isuz de Schulman. n.d.a. Apuntes manuscritos sobre la historia institucional para aportar a un futuro museo.

———. n.d.b. Desgranando recuerdos: Notes for the Establishment of a Museum in Villa Clara.

Nuestra historia. 2005. Museo Histórico Regional de Villa Clara.

Quiroga de Fink, F. n.d. El Museo Histórico de Villa Clara cobra nueva vida a través de nueva organización y equipamiento.

Reynoso de Fleitas, L. n.d. Dedicado a la memoria de Leopoldo Baldoni (1942–1999), intendente de Villa Clara, Entre Ríos.

Schejter, A. 1986. Pueblito, mi pueblo. Villa Clara, Argentina.

———. 2001. Villa Clara: Jalón de progreso y confluencia (1902–2002). Villa Clara, Entre Ríos.

———. n.d.a. De donde vengo: Raíces de mi origen. Villa Clara, Entre Ríos.

———. n.d.b. Se lo merecen: Mi homenaje a los inmigrantes. Villa Clara, Entre Ríos.

Szmurmuk, M. n.d. Home in the Pampas. Alberto Gerschunoff's Jewish Gauchos.

Tepper, G. 1990. Narrativa. Haifa, Israel.

INDEX

Note: Page numbers in italics refer to illustrations.

acculturation, 1, 6, 11, 54, 60, 71, 75, 76, 131, 143, 147, 165n51
Africans, 15–17, 83, 84, 168n3
agriculture, xvi, 1, 5, 6, 7, 8–9, 12, 14, 17–21, 24–26, 29, 31, 34, 40, 42, 45, 48, 53, 58–59, 63–64, 108, 110–111, 124, 139, 149, 163, 170n3; abandonment of, 61, 88, 99, 108, 114; and *colonias*, 11, 18, 22, 37, 40, 42, 122, 163n24, 164nn46,50, 165n20, 166n18; 167n22; diversity in, 5, 24, 25, 28, 31, 34, 42, 45, 109, 124; immigrants' experience in, 12, 26, 48, 58, 59, 61, 72, 74, 139, 147, 148, 165n51, 167n22, 168n11; promotion of, 85, 120, 145
Alliance Israélite Universelle, 36, 37, 164n43
anti-Semitism, 61, 117, 169n8, 170n2. *See also* pogroms
Aramburu, Pedro Eugenio, 112
archival sources, ix, 61, 65–66, 83, 128, 130, 144
Argentina, ix, x, xi, xii, xvi, 6, 7, 10, 12, 14, 18–20, 24, 34, 36, 42, 68, 71, 79, 107, 112, 137, 138, 143, 145, 147, 148, 162nn12,13,17, 163nn28,30, 164nn41,46,50, 167n22, 170n1; and economic potential, 103–104; and 1880 economic crisis, 26; and 1810 Revolution against Spain, 16, 17; and foreign investment, 8, 85, 163n34, 168n5; and immigration, 1, 4, 9, 26, 40, 131, 143; and military junta of 1976, 114–115; and modernization, 104; and the Proceso de Reorganización Nacional, 115; and promotion of European immigration, xv, 5, 8, 35, 145; and the railroad, 85, 104, 125
artifacts, 6, 127–129, 131–133, 149, 157–158
assimilation, xi, 7–8, 10–12, 49–51, 66–68, 70–71, 79, 110, 131, 143, 147, 149, 168n1; and cultural pluralism, 12, 140, 147; of Russian Germans, 29, 30, 66
Avellaneda, Nicolás, 9, 28, 67

Baldoni, Leopoldo, 115–116, 129
Baron de Hirsch Fund, 165n51, 166–167n20
Basques, 13, 22, 162n20, 168n4
Bélez, 43, 46, 48–53, 60, 91, 94, 98–99, 110–112, 132, 159; decline of, 105; education in, 91, 93; incorporation of, in Villa Clara, 105–109; and religion, 116
Belgians, 2, 12, 22, 23, 30–32, 42, 45–46, 66, 69, 72–73, 103, 113, 132–134, 166n7
Bessarabia, 35, 74, 165n55, 167n22, 168n11

Brazil, 24, 34, 38, 140, 162n18, 163nn36,38, 168n3; and JCA, 164nn46,50
British, 2, 8, 16, 17, 26, 85–87, 104, 163n34, 164n47, 168n4
Buenos Aires (city), xiii, xvi, 9–10, 16, 19, 33, 43, 59, 62, 122, 145, 148; anti-Semitism in, 169n8, 170n2; and the Hotel de Inmigrantes, 10, 31, 43, 164n41; immigration to, xvi, 22, 43, 104, 106, 108, 133, 148, 162nn17,19; 163n28; as JCA headquarters, 12, 54–55, 57, 61, 74; migration to, xvi, 62, 106, 108, 120, 133, 148, 169n8; population of, 9, 12, 67, 148; and the railroad, 5, 87; and reverse migration, 120; social conflicts in, 11, 148, 170n2
Buenos Aires (province), 2, 7, 9, 12, 14–17, 20, 22, 31, 33, 38, 39, 106, 161n3, 162n12, 165n54

Caja Rural de Villa Clara, Cooperativa de Crédito, 91, 94–95, 114, 133, 157, 159, 160
Canada, 24, 26, 38, 140, 164n46, 166n51
Casa Social Barón Hirsch, 105, 159
Castillo, Ramón, 112, 165n53
Catherine II, 35, 163n35
cattle industry, 5, 8, 15–17, 20, 26, 28, 42, 45, 63, 109, 112, 120, 124, 139, 162n8, 169n5
centennial celebration of Villa Clara, xv, xvi, 123, 127, 132–138, 143, 144; and *colectividades organizadas*, 135; and the Municipality, 135
El Centro, 102, 114–122, 124, 126, 135; employment in, 124
Charrúas, 15, 17, 161n4, 162n6
children, x, 61–62, 77, 102; and education, 34–35, 59, 70, 91–92, 106, 107–108, 110, 141, 165n57, 166n20; and inheritance, 111, 113; and maintaining the land, 102, 106; and rural desertion, 11, 102, 107, 149
Circuito Histórico de las Colonias Judías del Centro de Entre Ríos, xi, xii, xiii, 53, 86, 140–141, 151, 157, 161n1, 166n19
Colectividad Alemana de Argentina, 170n11
colectividades organizadas, 134–135, 137. *See also* collectivities
Colectividad Israelita Clara-Bélez, 139, 169n8
collectivities (*colectividades*), 123, 133–140, 137
Colonia Clara, xvi, 1, 38, 41, 43–44, 46, 55, 59, 62, 74, 83, 110, 113, 130, 132–133, 140, 165n54, 166n20; abandonment of, 60–61, 168n1; and agriculture, 42, 45, 63; and cattle raising, 28, 42, 45, 63; and cooperativism, 63, 72–74

founding of, 42, 159, 166n7; and the JCA, 43, 54; population in, 74, 132, 167n22, 168n11

colonias, xiii, 9, 14, 18–20, 22, 23, 26, 28, 30, 33, 37–38, 39, 41, 44–45, 50, 51–54, 55–56, 67–68, 71, 72, 74–75, 92–94, 99, 101, 103, 109, 113, 122, 146, 148, 159, 163nn26,32, 165n54; abandonment of, 58, 60–62, 103, 108–109; ethnic diversity in, 110; Jewish, 71–72, 94, 103

colonos, 28–29, 31–32, 33, 45, 49, 50, 53, 61, 63, 66, 71–72, 74, 88, 89, 95, 101, 108, 111, 113, 133, 163n33; and abandonment of *colonias*, 58, 60–62, 107, 108, 112–113; and agricultural practices, 48, 58–59, 89, 108, 110; as artisans, 88, 89, 94, 99, 110; in commerce, 71, 88, 110; as craftsmen, 58, 63, 99, 167n24; and education, 17, 28, 34, 37, 52, 54, 62, 66, 67, 68, 70, 91, 107, 118; hardships of, 66, 93–94, 111; and the JCA, 54–57, 69, 74–75, 88, 94, 112, 169n11; and land, x, 8, 9, 12, 18, 19, 20, 24–27, 29, 34, 37, 38, 42, 45, 56, 58–61, 66, 68–70, 73, 99, 102, 106, 107–109, 110–111, 112, 139, 148, 164n37, 167n23, 169n11; and natural environment, 55–56, 57, 93–94, 99, 107, 112; and social stratification, 59–60; and trades, 54, 59, 63, 167n24

Comisión de Amigos del Museo (Friends of the Museum Committee), 137, 157

commemoration, x, 67, 105, 121, 123, 127, 131–139; centennial of arrival of the Germans of the Volga, 138; centennial of San José, 131; and Comisión de Festejos, 131; Day of the Immigrant, 157; eightieth anniversary of Villa Clara, 121–122; and ethnic contributions, xvi, 90, 133–139; International Day of Cooperation, 120; 1910 centennial celebration of Argentine independence, xi, xii, 11, 51, 90, 125; ninetieth anniversary of Villa Clara, 95, 134; Oktoberfest, 139, 170n10; Revolución de Mayo, 141; seventy-fifth anniversary of Villa Clara, 121, 160

Comunidad Israelita Clara-Bélez, 98

Comunidad Israelita de Villa Clara, 109

Confederación Argentina, 20, 162n13

Constitution of 1853, 7–8, 12, 17, 19, 22, 85, 161n3

Cooperativa Fondo Comunal, 52–53, 63, 72–73, 133, 166n18

cooperativism, xi, 53, 57, 63, 72–74, 82, 89–90, 91, 94–95, 99, 109, 114, 120, 166nn17,20; and Ferias Francas, 96–97; and the Instituto Movilizador de Fondos Cooperativos, 89

Corrientes, 14, 15, 85 161n2, 163n24

criollos (Creoles), ix–x, xi, 2, 8, 10–11, 13, 15, 25, 31–32, 41, 53, 66, 68–69, 74, 76, 103, 170n8; and centennial celebration of Villa Clara, 135;

definition of, xv–xvi; dislocation of, 113; employment of, 28, 29, 69, 71, 74–75, 99, 107, 113; exploitation of, 72; as gauchos, 146–148; as gaucho Jews, 76; Germanization of, 28; and gringos, 69, 74, 76, 143, 145; and Jewish gauchos, 62, 145–147; and Jews, 6, 68–69, 74–79, 113, 143; and home ownership, 114; and intermarriage, 66–67; landless, 68, 113, 146; landowning, 68, 70, 78; marginalization of, 42, 70; and migration, 111; nomadic life of, 83–84; obliteration of, 8; perception of, 70, 76; and poverty, ix, 70, 84, 113, 114, 126, 146, 148; and rural desertion, 113; wealthy, 11, 68, 69–70, 74. *See also* gauchos

cultural pluralism, x, 11–12, 140, 147–149. *See also* assimilation

dairy industry, 42, 45, 73, 105

Dauw, César Den, 133–136

de Schulman, Ida Isuz, 43, 128, 129, 166n11

Dutch, 42, 163n35, 166n7

Eastern European immigrants, xiii, xvi, 1, 2, 56, 166n6, 167n22, 168n11; and experience in agriculture, 36, 167n23

Eastern European Jews, ix, xiii, xvi, 1, 2, 20, 22, 34, 35, 36, 37, 38, 56, 57, 58, 66, 93, 101, 134, 145, 147, 165n51, 166n20, 167n22, 168n2; diversity of, 48–50; and retention of culture, 51

education, 35–36, 43, 50, 54, 62, 66, 91–92, 93, 106, 107, 114, 154, 159, 166n20, 170n3; and children, 34–35, 59, 70, 91–92, 106–108, 110, 141; and gauchos, 70; universal, 66–67

1876 Colonization Law, 19, 163n33

1876 Law No. 817, 9, 22, 27

Entre Ríos, xvi, 2, 5–6, 10–11, 14–16, 19–20, 54, 61, 65, 81–82, 138, 149, 161n2, 162nn13,17,29, 165n54, 170n11; and agriculture, 19–21, 34, 54; and Area de Comunidades, 127; becoming Argentine in, 66–79; and *colonias*, 9, 12, 19, 33, 41–42; and Constitution of 1860, 19; and co-operativism, 72–74, 89; cultural assimilation in, 67–74; decline of, 122; diversity in, 13, 21; and establishment of political administration, 17; and European immigration, xii, xiii, 12, 13, 20–26, 69; and the First Census of 1869, 20; geography of, 18, 65; and Jewish immigrants, 1, 5, 34, 41, 69; and nation-building, 14, 16–17, 69; and the railroad, 24, 26, 34, 85, 87, 125; and the Second Census of Population in 1895, 20; social interaction in, 67–74; and spontaneous integration, 18

Estación Clara, 43, 82–84, 87–88, 91, 94, 159

ethnic substitution, 109–114

European immigration, x, xvi, 1–2, 4–6, 10, 14, 17–19, 48, 67–69, 74, 97, 103, 118, 164n41; assimilation of, 7; and becoming Argentine, 66; decrease in, 103; influence of, on native populations, 8–9; and national identity, ix, xv, 9; promotion of, 7–9, 14, 18–22, 85, 145; reasons for, 14, 19, 22, 35, 143; and social mobility, 19

Ferias Francas, 96–97, 159

Fierro, Martín, xi, 145, 170n1

Fondo Comunal, 56, 72, 73, 90–91, 98, 100, 101, 114, 120, 133, 159, 179n9

Fondo Comunal Cooperativa Agrícola, 52–53, 89–90, 95, 97, 100, 101, 114, 120, 166n18

Fondo Comunal: Sociedad Cooperativa, Agrícola, Limitada, 63

French, ix, 2, 12, 17, 19, 20, 23, 24, 25, 42, 87, 103, 125, 158, 163n35; depiction of, in museums, 131–133; descendants of, 17; and intermarriage, 66. See also Swiss-French

gaucho Jews, 76, 79

gauchos, x, xi, 6–9, 11, 16, 75, 133, 148, 161n1; appearance of, 145–146, 166nn2,3; and Asociación Tradicionalista, 77, 136; displacement of, 70; and education, 70; emergence of, 17; emulation of, 11; and fences, 26, 68–69, 77; and "the final solution," 145; and Jewish gauchos, 145–146; and Jews, ix, 12, 50, 75, 147–148, 149; landless, 1, 7, 147; and landowners, 77; marginalization of, 8, 11, 15, 16, 20, 68; as national character, 9, 11, 145, 148; and natural environment, 77, 148; perception of, 9–10, 11, 16–17, 70, 75, 148, 168n6; physical description of, 145, 166nn2,3; society of, x; subduing of, 145

Gerchunoff, Alberto, 10–14, 34, 141, 144–145, 147–149

German collectivity, 134, 135, 137, 138–139, 170n10

German organized collectivity, 137

Germans, 2, 20, 24, 26, 32, 69, 73–74, 87, 103, 125, 130–133, 138, 163n35, 166n7; and assimilation, 71; exploitation of, 72. See also Germans of the Volga

Germans of the Volga (Russian Germans), 12, 20, 22, 26–28, 31, 42, 71, 122, 134, 138–139, 178, 163n35, 164nn36,38, 170n10; and assimilation, 29, 30, 66–67; descendants of, 109, 122, 138; and "double migration," 26; and intermarriage, 29; persecution of, 36; and retention of culture, 26, 30; work ethic of, 29–30

gringos, 26, 32, 41, 68–70; and criollos, 69, 74, 76, 143

Guaraní, 161n4

heritage, ix, x, xii, xvii, 3, 11, 67, 120–121, 123, 127, 129, 130, 140, 144; and Area de Comunidades, 127; dissemination of, 123; and the Foundational Act, 141; and Israelita Clara-Bélez, 98, 139; material, xv, 148–149; and Mosaic of Identities, 12, 140; and national identity, 144; oral, ix, x, xv; private, 123, 125; production of, 123; promotion of, 148; public, 123, 125; religious, 140; and Shalom Argentina, 12, 140; of Villa Clara, xv, xvi, 121, 139

heritage tourism, x, 126, 135, 140–141, 148, 166n19

Hirsch, Baron Maurice de, x–xi, 8, 35–36, 38, 40, 42, 44, 54, 56, 60, 61–62, 104, 108, 147, 164nn44,47, 165nn55,56, 166n20, 168n5

history, ix, 65, 83, 128, 143–144; absence of, of non-Jewish populations, 6, 135–136; and archival sources, ix, 4, 61, 65–66, 83, 115, 127, 130, 144; and artifacts, 6, 128, 131, 157; dissemination of, xv, xvii, 2, 11, 127, 129, 151, 152, 170n6; institutional, 128; as legend, 123, 127, 128, 131; material, 5, 126; official, xvi, xvii, 5, 66, 126–127, 135, 144; oral, xvii, 5, 6, 65, 117, 126, 128, 143, 144; popular, 4–5, 126–127; production of, 128; social, 4–5; sources of, 4–5, 144; "true," 126; written, 5, 126, 128, 143, 144, 148

identity, 2, 149; collective, 143; cultural, 144; ethnic, 2, 144; generational transmission of, 143; historic, 144; hybrid, 149; national, xv, 3, 9, 143–144, 148–149; personal, 144; politicized, 143

Immigration and Colonization Law (No. 817), 9, 22, 27, 67

indigenous people, ix, x, xi, 13, 15, 17, 68, 74, 83, 84, 161nn3,4, 162n6; and Campaign of the Desert, 9; defeat of, 85; extermination of, 16; and interaction with immigrants, 14, 75; and railroad, 85; subduing of, 14–17, 145

intermarriage, 30, 32, 126, 168n2; and assimilation, 30, 66–67, 109

Israelite Collectivity (Colectividad Israelita), 105, 134, 137, 139, 169n8

Italians, 2, 12–13, 17, 22–25, 32, 42, 45–46, 72–73, 101, 103, 125, 131, 162n18, 163n28, 165n57; descendants of, 17, 23, 45, 134; and intermarriage, 66; and railroad construction, 23, 88

Jesuits (Compañia de Jesús), 15, 162nn6,7

Jewish Colonization Association (JCA), ix, x, xi,

xiii, xvi, 1, 8, 37–38, 39, 42–43, 48, 54–57, 60, 61, 63, 64, 69, 83–84, 88, 89, 94–95, 98–99, 105, 107, 120, 146–147, 164nn46,50, 165n51, 166n5; administration of, xi, 54–59, 61, 63, 74, 94, 98, 147, 166n20; and Baron de Hirsch Fund, 165n51; and education, 51, 91; founding of, 37; and health care, 52; and heritage, 127; and Jacobo Spangenberg, 38, 42; and Junta de Fomento, 96; mission of, 58; and railroad, 85; and Sociedad Anónima La Argentina, 42. See also *colonias*; *colonos*; Yevich

Jewish gauchos, x, xi, xiii, xvi, 1, 10–12, 14, 34, 41, 62, 63, 75–79, 88, 121, 145–146; acculturation of, 5, 75–79, 131; and *agaucharse*, 148; and agriculture, 149; and assimilation, 77, 146, 149; and *criollos*, 62, 75–79, 145–147; displacement of, xiv; diversity of, 99; as icon of hybrid identity, 1, 79, 149; landowning, 145; as metaphor of immigrant incorporation, 5, 6, 10, 11, 12, 143, 144–149; and social mobility, 149

Jewish immigrants, 5–6, 11, 13, 75, 83–84, 88, 125; adaptability of, 34, 75, 81, 148; as artisans, 88, 89; and assimilation, 49–50; and becoming Argentine, 62–63, 147; in commerce, 71, 88, 110, 148; and *criollos*, 68–69, 74–79, 113, 143, 145; diversity of, 48–49, 147; as founders of Villa Clara, 81; and intermarriage, 168n2; and relationship to land, 107–109; and retention of culture, 51

Junta de Fomento, 94, 95–96, 98, 101, 133, 157, 159, 169n9

La Clarita, 113–122, 124, 137

landowners, 12, 15, 20, 26, 38, 42, 44, 68, 74, 75, 112, 113, 114, 124, 168n4, 169n11; and colonization programs, 110; and *colonos*, 163n33; and *criollos*, 68, 70, 78; and exploitation of *criollos*, 69; and gauchos, 79; private, 19, 25, 77; and promotion of immigrant settlements, 69

libraries, 53, 62, 91, 94, 97, 124, 128

life histories, ix, 66, 81, 144, 156; and historical documents, 5, 81

Lithuanians, 35, 36, 58, 168n11

material culture, ix, 65, 83, 151, 157

meat-curing industry, 17

memory, ix, xii, xvii, 2–4, 65, 83, 126–127, 141; and archival records, 65–66, 83; collective/social, x, xi, 3, 127, 134, 143, 151, 154, 161n1; dissemination of, 151; generational, 154, 155; global, xii; individual, 127, 143; institutional, 121, 128; and "larger histories," 66; local, xii; and nostalgia, 51, 104, 112–113, 120–121, 168n7; oral, xv, 65–66,

81; and the present, 82; preservation of, 141; private and public, 125; and producing history, 128; regional, xii; selective, 3, 78, 127; and "smaller histories," 66; social construction of, 3, 78; written, xv, 65–66, 81, 83

Menem, Carlos Saúl, 104, 125

mestizos, 15, 31, 145

Mitre, Bartolomé, 85

Moisesville, 10, 39, 40, 68–69, 161n6, 165nn54–56

Mosaico de Identidades (Mosaic of Identities), 12, 140

Muchinik, Miguel, 43, 53, 128, 129, 166n11

Municipalidad (Municipality), 91, 94, 101, 114–116, 117, 121, 126, 130–131, 134–135, 154, 155; and centennial celebration, xi, 133, 134–135, 139, 157; and employment, 124; and JCA land, 120, 160; and Museo Histórico Regional de Villa Clara, 129

Museo de las Colonias Judías, 157

Museo Histórico Regional de la Colonia San José, 131, 140

Museo Histórico Regional de Villa Clara, 5, 127–133; and Rincón Gauchesco, 6

Museo y Archivo Histórico Regional de las Colonias (Historic and Regional Museum and Archive of the *Colonias*), 130

museums, ix, xi, 127, 130, 143, 149; and archives, 128, 130; and artifacts, 6, 128, 130–133; and Association of Friends of the Museum, 131; and Commission of Culture, 129; and cultural activities, 133; and memorabilia, 130; and paraphernalia, 132; purpose of, 127–128, 149

natural environment, 44, 55, 56, 57–58, 65, 66, 93, 94, 99, 111, 147; adaptation to, ix; and becoming Argentine, 65, 75, 77; and *criollo* gauchos, ix, 77, 148; and economy, 101; and rural desertion, 112

nostalgia, 23, 51, 88, 104, 112–113, 120–121, 135, 168n7

Onganía, Juan Carlos, 112

"other," the, 4, 6, 16, 147

Pale of Settlement, 35–36, 42

Palestine, 37–38

pampas, xi, 38, 43, 85; exploitation of, 145; farmers in, 19; and indigenous people, ix, x, 9; and Jews, 10

Paraguay, 15, 24, 170n1

Paraná River, 14, 16, 161n4

past, the, 5, 148; and the future, 132, 144; and the present, 3, 82, 121, 126, 131, 143–144, 149; ritualizing of, 121; romanticizing of, 5; versions of, 2–3, 123, 128. *See also* history; memory

Patagonia, 9

patrimony, 27, 141, 151; cultural, 151; memorialized, 127–137, 149. *See also* heritage

Perón, Juan Domingo, xi, 102, 103, 104, 107, 112

Peyret, Alejo, 24–25, 29, 163n26

pig raising, 31

Podolia, 35, 165n55, 167n22

pogroms, ix, x, 35, 36, 38, 44, 46, 166n9, 170n2

Polish, 23, 35, 42, 58, 69, 88, 125, 158, 163n35, 165n51

Portuguese, 100, 162n6

poultry farming, 26, 31, 42, 45, 124

Proceso de Reorganización Nacional, 115, 169n6

railroads, ix, xi, xvi, 5, 23, 34, 44, 52, 84–85, 124–125, 129, 131; arrival of, 61, 85, 87, 89, 133; and British, xi, xvi, 8, 26, 85–87, 104, 111–112, 168n4; closing of, xi, 5, 85, 125; and the Constitution of 1853, 85; and education, 91–92; as heritage site, 130; history of, 85, 88, 104; and indigenous people, 85; and JCA farmers, 89, 108; nationalization of, xi, xvi, 85, 104, 125; and national unification, 84–85, 87–88; privatization of, xi, 85, 104, 125

religion, x, xi, 13, 14, 24, 28, 30, 34, 45, 50–51, 53, 70–71, 96, 99–100, 105, 116–117, 120, 121, 125, 141, 146, 147, 151, 158; and confrontation, 24; freedom of, 34; and kosher practices, 77, 90, 168n6

Roca, Julio A., 9, 27, 30, 38, 166n5

Romania, x, 35, 38, 165n51

Rosas, Juan Manuel de, 17, 26, 163n31

rural desertion, 11, 60–61, 71, 99, 103–104, 113–114, 122, 166n20; and cattle raising, 109; causes of, 106–109, 120; and industrialization, 110; as success, 62, 165n57

Russia, 35, 163n35, 164n36

Russians, 35, 57, 58, 88, 125, 132, 158, 165n51, 166n6, 168n11

Sajaroff, Miguel, 52, 166n17

San Martín, José de, 121

Santa Fé, 10, 14, 15, 38, 162n6, 165nn54,55

Sarmiento, Domingo Faustino, 7, 26

Schejter, Abraham, 75, 88, 92, 101, 121, 166n11

Sephardic Jews, xi, 57, 91

Shalom Argentina: Huellas de la colonización judía (Hello Argentina: Tracing Jewish Settlement), 12, 140

sharecropping, 20, 29, 61, 111, 112, 113

sheep raising, 162n8

social class, xvii, 2–4, 49, 67–68, 104, 114, 118, 128,

135, 144–145, 147; in El Centro and La Clarita, 114–122; and ethnicity, 4, 12, 126, 135, 144; and Jewish immigrants, 49–50, 74, 147; and oral history, 117, 128; and social interaction, 68, 135; and spatial dimension, 156

social construction, 3, 4, 78

social history, xvii, 4, 14, 22, 34, 64, 83

social interaction, 28, 67–70, 98

social mobility, 19, 59, 126, 148, 149

social movements, 69, 95, 124, 145, 148

social stratification, 59–60, 117–118, 126

Spanish, 2, 12, 13, 22, 23, 25, 42, 125, 158, 162n6; descendants of, 17, 134, 162n20; and intermarriage, 66

Swedes, 56, 163n35

Swiss, 2, 19, 20, 22, 23, 24, 25, 46, 53, 69, 87, 125, 158, 163nn25,35; depiction of, in museums, 131, 132–133; descendants of, 24, 53, 101; and intermarriage, 66. *See also* Swiss-French

Swiss-French, 22, 24, 25, 30, 32, 132–134, 135, 137, 163n27. *See also* French; Swiss

Swiss-French collectivity (Colectividad Suizo-Francesa), 24, 134, 135, 136, 137, 157, 163n22, 170n12; and Entidades Valesanas Argentinas, 139–140

Swiss-French organized collectivity, 137

Synagogue of the Artisans in Colonia Bélez, 99, 116, 159

Turkey, 8, 36, 37, 38

Turkish, 38, 125, 158

Ukrainians, 35, 38

United States, x, 12, 17, 24, 26, 38, 42, 54, 94, 140–141, 167n22, 168n26; immigration to, 165n51; and JCA, 164nn46,50, 165n51

Urquiza, Justo José de, 17, 19, 22, 24, 25, 27, 31–32, 41, 45, 53, 69, 94, 101, 131, 162nn13,20, 163nn24,31, 168nn4,5

Uruguay, 22, 24, 32, 34, 68, 162nn6,19, 168n3

Uruguay River, 14, 16, 24, 32–33, 161n4, 162n19

Velázquez, Polonio, 31–32, 162n13

Villa Clara, 20, 46, 53, 64, 74, 79, 82, 93, 103, 117, 122; celebrations of, 5, 95, 121–122, 131–139, 160; diversity in, 103, 112, 114–115, 118, 124–125, 126; and ethnicity, 121–122; founding of, 34–35, 81; health care in, 92, 97, 105; and heritage, x, xv, xvi, 125; and industrialization, 104; as melting pot, 103; as memory site, 123; and national identity, 143; population increase in, 59; poverty in, 154, 155; as producer of heritage, x, 123; public service in, 93, 101–102,

114–115, 117, 154, 159; and the railroad, 82, 104, 124, 125, 152; as reflection of Argentine history, xv, 5, 87, 114; social history of, 14, 22, 34, 65, 83, 123, 143; social stratification in, 117–118; and social structure, 117, 123; writing the history of, 124, 157

Villaguay, 2, 5, 20, 23, 30–33, 42, 88, 119, 135, 161n2; and Belgian immigrants, 113, 134; Israelite Association of, 140

Western European immigrants, xvi, 2, 6, 42; descendants of, 110, 120; representation of, in museums, 6

Wolcomich, Jorge, 45, 52, 91–92, 97–98, 159,

169n2; and Fondo Comunal, 97; and Junta de Fomento, 97; and Museo Histórico Regional de Villa Clara, 129

women, x, 30, 52, 71, 76, 77, 99; and chicken farming, 31; and education, 159; employment of, 74; roles of, 28–29, 30, 48, 99

Woodbine, New Jersey, 54, 165n51, 166n20, 168n26

Workers' Union of Diverse Trades, 95

Yevich, 56, 58, 59, 60, 91. *See also* Jewish Colonization Association

Yrigoyen, Hipólito, 97

Yugoslavians, 88, 163n35

CPSIA information can be obtained at www.ICGtesting.com
Printed in the USA
BVOW071531020112

279578BV00001B/32/P